BASEBALL RESEARCH JOURNAL

Volume 52, Number 2
Fall 2023

Published by the Society for American Baseball Research

BASEBALL RESEARCH JOURNAL, Volume 52, Number 2

Editor: Cecilia M. Tan
Interior design and production: Lisa Hochstein
Assistant editors: King Kaufman, Davy Andrews
Proofreader: Keith DeCandido
Fact checker: Clifford Blau

Front cover art by Gary Cieradkowski / Studio Gary C

Published by:
Society for American Baseball Research, Inc.
Cronkite School at ASU
555 N. Central Ave. #406C
Phoenix, AZ 85004

Phone: (602) 496–1460
Web: www.sabr.org
Twitter: @sabr
Facebook: Society for American Baseball Research

Contents

From the Editor .... Cecilia M. Tan 4

CLASSICS

Norman Rockwell's *The Three Umpires* .... Ron Backer 5

Tyrus
A Study and Commentary on the Name .... William R. Cobb, PhD 12

MISFORTUNES

Softball and Swastikas
The Riot at Toronto's Christie Pits .... Stephen Dame 22

Alex Johnson and Tony Conigliaro
The California Angels' Star-Crossed Teammates .. Paul Hensler 31

Dick Such's Hard-Luck Season
Going 0–16 for the York (PA) White Roses .... Barry Sparks 38

HISTORICAL ANALYSIS

Erasing Moments and Memories
Iconic Games Reconsidered with the Automatic Runner .. Francis Kinlaw 42

The 1945 Pennant Races .... Douglas Jordan, PhD 47

Going Downtown with a Golden Sombrero
Combining Baseball's Best and Worst True Outcomes .. Herm Krabbenhoft 55

MAJORS AND MINORS

Henry Chadwick and the National League's Performance vs. "Outsiders"
1876–81 .... Woody Eckard, PhD 67

The History of the Manchester Yankees .... Christopher Chavis 77

Examining Dusty Baker's Hope
Is Help on the Way? .... David C. Ogden, PhD 86

ANALYTICAL ASSESSMENTS

Keith Hernandez and Cooperstown
A Data Synthesis and Visualization Project ... Stephen D. Dertinger, Phd 97

Balancing Starter and Bullpen Workloads in a
Seven-Game Postseason Series .... David J. Gordon, MD, PhD 105

More Relief Pitchers Belong in the Hall of Fame: Which Ones? .. Elaina and John Pakutka 113

Baseball's 4-Dimensional Players .... George W. Towers 124

Contributors 135

From the Editor

By the time you read this, SABR members, the 2023 season will be over and some team will have been left standing triumphant on the field after the last out of the World Series. But as I write this in advance of the *Journal* being printed, manufactured, and shipped, I don't yet know which team it will be.

I do know—without using any sabermetrics at all—that the winning team will not be the Boston Red Sox, nor the New York Yankees. No, at the moment the only question is whether either (or both) might manage to stay above .500 this season. As of today, FanGraphs projects them both to limp to 81–81 finishes and tie for last place in the AL East. Which raises the question, what's less precedented, the combination of New York and Boston losing 162 games, or a division with not a single losing record?

Season	Combined Losses
2014	169
1992	175
1991	169
1990	169
1989	166
1966	179
1965	185
1930	170
1926	170
1925	190
1913	165
1908	182
1907	168
1906	166

From the perspective of Yankees and Red Sox fans, the 2023 season has been a disaster. Every night pundits come up with new measures of how long its been since the Yankees (or Sox) "tanked" this hard. Truly it's a measure of just how spoiled rotten we are along the Northeast Corridor that a .500 season is considered disastrous, but out of curiosity I decided to look up how often it happens that Boston and New York combine for more than 162 losses.

Turns out, it doesn't happen very often, only 14 times over the 121 seasons these two teams have faced each other. While some in Red Sox Nation and the Evil Empire might say that only proves how bad this season is, I suppose I am more of a win-column-half-full type of person than a win-column-half-empty type.

And maybe 2023 never had a chance to be a memorable season for me. Living up to 2022's Aaron-Judge-fueled pursuit of history was always going to be difficult. Then there's the fact that this is the year I lost my Dad, and I got COVID-19. The last baseball game Dad and I watched together was the finale of the World Baseball Classic. Despite his dementia, Dad still knew about Mike Trout and Shohei Ohtani, and he still loved watching sports. He'd lost the ability to remember the score shortly after the game was over, but during the games, whether it was baseball, or tennis, or one of his other favorites (golf, figure skating, Olympic anything) he lived totally in the moment. In those moments he experienced so much joy, and wonder, and excitement. And if there was the disappointment of a loss, he quickly forgot it.

I decided to try that out as a philosophy, to care less about who won or lost, and to just enjoy the moments, however fleeting. This works fine while I'm at the ballpark, especially when the weather is nice and the company is good. But ultimately I can't live entirely in the moment. When the future looks bleak—or like .500—I take my solace in the past. There are plenty of memorable seasons and performances to be found in baseball history.

Hence, this *Journal*.

Congratulations to whomever won. Bask in the afterglow! To the rest, enjoy your offseason reading.

— Cecilia M. Tan

Norman Rockwell's *The Three Umpires*

Ron Backer

It may be the most famous baseball painting of all time. Created by Norman Rockwell, it goes by many different names, including *The Three Umpires*, *Game Called Because of Rain*, *Tough Call*, and *Bottom of the Sixth*. It depicts a baseball game between the Pittsburgh Pirates and the Brooklyn Dodgers at Ebbets Field in Brooklyn. According to the scoreboard, the game is in the bottom of the sixth inning, with Pittsburgh leading, 1–0. The Pirates scored their only run in the top of the second inning. The three umpires of the title are standing together, looking at the skies. The home plate umpire is in the center of the trio, with his hand out to determine how hard it is raining, trying to decide whether or not to call the game. If the umpires call the game, Pittsburgh will win, since the game became official with the completion of the fifth inning and Pittsburgh is still leading. To the right and behind the umpires, the managers from each team are in a heated argument, although it is not clear what the dispute is about. In the distance, three Pirates fielders are shown.[1]

The original painting is in the collection of the National Baseball Hall of Fame and Museum in Cooperstown, New York, where it is a favorite attraction for visitors.[2] *The Three Umpires* is so famous, it has become a part of pop culture, and has been printed on a variety of commercial products, including whiskey bottles, ties, watches, and clothing.[3] In 1982 it even appeared on a postage stamp of the Turks and Caicos Islands, a British overseas territory.[4] Numerous prints of the painting are still being sold to this day.

This is the story of *The Three Umpires*, a painting which has intrigued baseball fans and others since its first publication on the cover of the *Saturday Evening Post* over 70 years ago.

NORMAN ROCKWELL

Painter and illustrator Norman Rockwell was born in New York City on February 3, 1894. Rockwell displayed a natural ability for drawing as a youngster and after attending several art schools to hone his craft, embarked on a professional career while still a teenager.

He completed his first commissioned works before he was 16 (four Christmas cards for a client), illustrated his first book when he was 17, became art director of *Boy's Life* magazine when he was 19, and produced a cover for the *Saturday Evening Post* when he was just 22.[5] The latter is most significant because, despite numerous drawings and paintings for calendars, advertisements, commercial products, collectibles, and story illustrations, Rockwell is most famous today for his magazine covers. His works appeared on the front of virtually every major magazine, including *Life*, *Look*, *Literary Digest*, and *McCall's*.[6] But none rival the *Saturday Evening Post*, where Rockwell produced 323 covers over 47 years.[7]

Rockwell's works usually depict aspects of Americana, often renderings of his real or imagined views of bygone eras, but sometimes contemporary subjects such as *Rosie the Riveter* (*Saturday Evening Post*, May 29, 1943), a painting about a female industrial worker on the job during World War II, and *The Problem We All Live With* (*Look*, January 14, 1964), a civil rights painting about a young African American girl integrating a Southern school. Rockwell drew numerous works about baseball, from illustrations for advertisements and short stories to paintings for magazine covers, the latter primarily for the *Saturday Evening Post*. Among his most famous *Post* baseball covers are *The Dugout* (September 4, 1948), showing an upset Cubs' dugout presumably during a losing game being jeered at by the fans in the stands above, *The Rookie* (*Red Sox Locker Room*) (March 2, 1957) about a new player in a hat and suit, holding a suitcase and a bat in his hands, arriving in the Red Sox locker room and looking very out-of-place, and *Knothole Baseball* (August 30, 1958), depicting the view of an amateur or low-level professional game through a small hole in a fence.

By the mid-1930s, Rockwell usually painted his magazine covers from black and white photographs, first making a rough pencil sketch of the proposed work and then after obtaining preliminary approval from a publication, finding models he could pose in the positions he needed for the painting.[8] (The models were often his friends or neighbors.) He then created several preliminary drawings of the painting, known as studies, including a detailed, full-size charcoal sketch of the work and then a small color sketch, before proceeding to the final work, which was oil on canvas.[9]

Norman Rockwell died on November 8, 1978, at the age of 84, in Stockbridge, Massachusetts—the future location of the Norman Rockwell Museum. In a career that lasted more than 60 years, he produced over 4,000 original works of art.[10]

THE CREATION OF *THE THREE UMPIRES*

On September 14, 1948, before the first game of a doubleheader between the Pittsburgh Pirates and the Brooklyn Dodgers, Norman Rockwell brought a professional photographer to Ebbets Field in Brooklyn for the purpose of taking reference photos of umpires, managers, coaches, and players to aid in the painting of *The Three Umpires*. Rockwell chose the individuals to be depicted in the painting and posed them as he expected them to appear in his work. He also had reference photos taken of the Ebbets Field scoreboard. There are numerous reference photos from that day in the archives of the Norman Rockwell Museum, twelve of which are available for viewing on the museum's website.[11]

Despite the three umpires being grouped in the painting and the managers being face-to-face, reference photos were taken of each those models separately. Rockwell had such a strong image of the painting in his mind that even though not one bit of paint had yet been applied to canvas, he seamlessly blended the individuals into groups in the painting.

Because of the availability of the reference photos, the detail in the painting, and a blurb in the *Saturday Evening Post*, the five prominent individuals in *The Three Umpires* are easily identifiable.

The home plate umpire extending his hand is John "Beans" Reardon. Reardon umpired in the National League from 1926 to 1949—including five World Series and three All-Star games—before leaving the profession at age 52 to manage a beer business. He is one of the most memorable umpires in the history of the game, both for his tendency to swear at the players when he argued with them and for the great stories he told even after he left the game. Reardon also had a unique look, wearing a distinctive blue and white polka-dot bowtie (instead of the usual necktie used in the National League at the time), although there is little detail of it in *The Three Umpires*. Prominent in

the painting is the inflated, American League chest protector then worn by Reardon even though Reardon was a National League umpire, and he was supposed to wear a smaller chest protector underneath his coat.[12] To the left of Reardon is base umpire Larry Goetz. Goetz umpired in the National League from 1936 to 1956, appearing in three World Series and two All-Star games. To the right of Reardon is base umpire Lou Jorda, who umpired in the National League from 1927 to 1931 and again from 1940 to 1952. He worked in two All-Star Games and two World Series. Jorda is wearing the traditional necktie in the painting.

The Pirates manager is Billy Meyer. Meyer managed the Pirates for five seasons (1948–52), with his teams finishing in the first division in only one year and finishing in last place in two seasons. His Pirates team in 1952 lost 112 games, still the seventh worst finish by average (.273) in the combined history of the American and National Leagues from 1901 to 2022. Clyde Sukeforth, a Dodgers coach, is the person arguing with Meyer. As a scout, Sukeforth was instrumental in bringing Jackie Robinson to the Dodgers and Roberto Clemente to the Pirates. As an interim manager for the Dodgers in 1947, he managed Jackie Robinson in his first two games in the big leagues.[13] (The identities of the three Pirates players in the painting will be discussed below.) Even though Rockwell had already visualized the painting before arriving at Ebbets Field, he was not wedded to his original

The three umpires, Lou Jorda (above left), John "Beans" Reardon (above right), and Larry Goetz (below right) were individually photographed at the direction of Rockwell to use as references for the painting.

conception. For example, there are no reference photos of the two outfielders in right field taken on September 14, 1948 at Ebbets Field, and as will be discussed later, it seems likely that Rockwell decided to add the outfielders to his painting sometime after September 14, 1948. The two outfielders enhance the picture, keeping right field from being empty and boring, and balancing the second baseman to the left of the umpires.

Rockwell also changed the portrayal of Clyde Sukeforth. In the available reference photos, he is holding his cap in the hand above his head and his lower hand is empty, perhaps stretched out to feel the rain. In the final painting, the cap is in his lower hand and his upper hand has a finger pointing to the sky. It is unknown why Rockwell made these changes.

Norman Rockwell took the reference photographs to California, where he and his family spent the winter, and completed the painting there. Ralph Kiner, the Pirates slugging outfielder, also wintered in California. During that offseason, Rockwell called Kiner and asked him if he happened to have his Pirates uniform with him. Kiner did, because he had played in an exhibition-game tour after the regular season. Rockwell visited Kiner to look at the unform, as a reference for Billy Meyer's uniform. Rockwell later gave one of his original drawings to Kiner, for his help on the painting.[14]

The Three Umpires appeared as the cover of the April 23, 1949, issue of the *Saturday Evening Post*. As with most of Rockwell's covers for the magazine, the painting is unrelated to any story in the issue.

When Rockwell first viewed the published cover, he was quite surprised. The *Saturday Evening Post* had made changes to his painting without consulting him. One of the changes, the alteration of the "GEM" (razor blade) advertising on the outfield wall to the generic "SCM" is understandable (although Rockwell should have been consulted), because the *Post* hardly wanted to give free advertising on its cover to a consumer product, and there could have been trademark or copyright issues. The other changes were much more problematic. The *Post* changed Rockwell's dark gray clouds along the entire top of the painting into a blue sky with lightened gray and white clouds on the top right of the painting. It also darkened the Pirates' uniforms.

An upset Rockwell wrote to Ken Stuart, the art editor of the *Post* who had authorized the changes, disputing his decisions and telling him that the sky "was better as I conceived and painted it."[15] Because this was the fourth time the *Post* had altered one of Rockwell's paintings without his approval, "completely unethical" conduct according to Rockwell, the painter wrote, "I cannot go on painting with any strength or conviction with the threat of such changes to my work constantly hanging over my head."[16] The *Post* thereafter changed its protocols, at least with regard to Rockwell's work, requiring additional editors to approve any changes to his paintings and to consult with Rockwell before any changes were actually made.

ANOMALIES, CONTROVERSIES, AND INTERESTING FACTS
The Umpires

One of the apparent anomalies in *The Three Umpires* is that, in accordance with the title, there are only three umpires depicted, instead of the usual four. This was not, however, an error on Rockwell's part. Although four umpires were used in the World Series as early as 1909, a four-man crew was not officially instituted for all regular season games until 1952.[17] And, in fact, there were only three umpires officiating the Pirates-Dodgers doubleheader on September 14, 1948, the day the reference photographs were taken. This was a bit of luck on Rockwell's part. With only three umpires in the painting, the two base umpires provide a balance to the much larger home plate umpire in the middle. With four umpires, the picture would have been unbalanced and the home plate umpire would not have been the center of attention, as he is supposed to be.

Of course, baseball was played with more than three players on the field in 1948, but Rockwell chose to include only three in his painting. This falls into the category of artistic license. If there were nine players on the field, the painting would have been cluttered and the viewer's eye would have drifted away from the focus of the work—the three umpires and the tough call to be made. Similarly, while many people have commented that the scoreboard in the painting does not match any of the action in either game of the doubleheader that was played on September 14, 1948, Rockwell was not chronicling any specific game in his work. He used the real players, umpires, and coaches who were on the field that day only as a reference for a drawing which sprang entirely from his imagination.

Burt Shotton

In September 1948, the Dodgers manager was Burt Shotton, but it is coach Clyde Sukeforth who is shown arguing with Pirates manager Billy Meyer just behind the trio of umpires. This anomaly is easily explained. Burt Shotton was one of the last of the big-league managers who did not wear a uniform during the game. While in the dugout, Shotton usually wore a suit, although on some occasions, he wore a warm-up jacket or windbreaker with "Dodgers" across the front and a team cap. On warmer, sunnier days, he sometimes wore slacks, a sports shirt, and a wide-brimmed hat.[18] Thus, Shotton could hardly be used as the model for the Dodgers manager in Rockwell's painting, since a man in street clothes would have seemed out of place. Although there is no specific major league rule that requires a manager to be in uniform, Shotton was apparently not allowed on the field because he did not wear a uniform. During games, Shotton used two of his coaches, either Clyde Sukeforth or Ray Blades, to argue calls with an umpire or replace a pitcher.[19] Sukeforth, the better-known of the two, was the obvious individual to substitute for Shotton in the painting.

The Sprinkle Painting

Sandra Sprinkle, the granddaughter of Beans Reardon, passed away in 2015. Years before, she had placed what she thought was a signed print of *The Three Umpires* above the fireplace mantle of her home in Dallas, Texas. Sandra had obtained the artwork through inheritance. After Sandra's death, her husband, Gene Sprinkle, moved to a retirement community. In the process of downsizing, Gene's nephew emailed photos of Reardon memorabilia in Gene's possession, such as National League season passes, original photos, signed baseballs, and the Rockwell print, to an auction house. Since the print was signed by Rockwell, they believed it had, at least, a little value.[20] During this process, the nephew took a closer look at the Rockwell artwork and noticed brushstrokes. Could the print actually be an original painting by Rockwell? The auction house, along with some experts, thoroughly examined the piece and agreed—this was no print. It was an original, unknown painting by Rockwell.[21] On August 19, 2017, the painting, previously thought to have little value, sold at auction for $1.68 million.[22]

Sprinkle's painting was actually the Rockwell color study of *The Three Umpires*. The study is oil on paper, 16 x 15 inches.[23] (The final painting, which is oil on canvas, is much larger, 43 x 41 inches.[24]) The study is incomplete, with the scoreboard essentially just a blue rectangle, the skies blue and cloudless, and the two outfielders missing.[25] The newly found work is signed and inscribed in the lower right as follows: "My best wishes to 'Beans' Reardon, the greatest umpire ever lived, Sincerely, Norman Rockwell."[26]

The Three Pirates Players

As noted before, the umpires, the Dodgers coach, and the Pirates manager are easily identifiable in the Rockwell painting. The three Pirates players are not. Their figures are so small that their faces are unrecognizable.

It seems logical that the two Pirates on the back right of the painting are the Pirates' right fielder and center fielder, talking to each other during a break in the action. The playing position of the third fielder is more difficult to determine. Given his small size and what appears to be his proximity to the outfield wall, many have concluded that he is the left fielder. In fact, he is the second baseman, standing some distance from the outfield wall. In the painting, the third player appears to be taller than the two outfielders in right field, meaning that the player is standing closer to home plate than an outfielder would. From the perspective of the viewer, the third player is standing in line with the left side of the Ebbets Field scoreboard, which was located in right field of the stadium. Only the second baseman would logically be standing in the position shown in the painting.

Given the conclusion that the players depicted are the right fielder, center fielder, and second baseman, historian Larry Gerlach, in his seminal article on Norman Rockwell's baseball paintings, "Norman Rockwell and Baseball Images of the National Pastime," wrote that the players in the painting are Pirates right fielder Dixie Walker, center fielder Johnny Hopp, and second baseman Danny Murtaugh.[27] While there is logic to that conclusion, there are no independent facts to support the contention that Walker, Hopp, and Murtaugh were the models for those players, partly because there are no available reference photos of the two outfielders taken at Ebbets Field on September 14, 1948.[28] There are two reference photos for the infielder which were taken at Ebbets Field on that day. One shows a side view of the player and in the other, the player's eyes are obscured by the shadows caused by his cap. It is therefore difficult to determine who the player is, but he does not appear to be Danny Murtaugh. In particular, the nose and chin of the player in those two reference photos are dissimilar to Murtaugh's. Based upon the side view of the fielder in one of those reference photos, Rockwell may have originally intended to paint a shortstop or a third baseman to the left of the umpires, a further indication that the model was not Murtaugh.

After review of all of the reference photographs in the files of the Norman Rockwell Museum, it is clear that one person served as the model for the infielder and both outfielders. The files contain three reference photos of an unknown ballplayer in a Pirates uniform, taken not at Ebbets Field, but in a location in which the player is standing in front of a tree and a car.

In one of those three reference photos, the player is standing at the exact angle and in the exact pose as the second baseman in *The Three Umpires*, although he does not have a glove in his hand. In another, he is shot from a side view, in almost the exact pose of the right fielder in the painting, again without a glove. In the third photo, the player is posed just like the center fielder, this time with a glove in his hand. These are undoubtedly the reference photos that Rockwell used to paint all of the fielders in *The Three Umpires*, not the two photos that were taken at Ebbets Field.

It is plausible to conclude that Rockwell was unhappy with the two reference photos of the infielder taken at Ebbets Field, perhaps because the infielder's face in the photos was partially obscured from view. Around the same time, Rockwell must have decided to add the two outfielders to the painting. He therefore needed additional reference photos, which required a new model and a Pirates uniform. Since it was too late to go back to Ebbets Field and use multiple models, Rockwell must have decided to use only one model for all three fielders in the painting.

Who was the model for the new reference photos? It could be a different Pirates player, appearing in photos taken when the team returned to Brooklyn just a week after the original reference photos were taken. While the timeline fits, it is difficult to match the face of the model with any of the players on the 1948 Pittsburgh Pirates roster. A more likely possibility is that the three new reference photos were taken some time later in California, where Rockwell completed the painting, with a model who may or may not have been a ballplayer, wearing a Pirates uniform borrowed from Ralph Kiner.[29] There appear to be palm trees in the background of the photos, a likely indicator of California. Without any available documentation addressing the issue, all of this is conjecture. The identity of the model for the Pirates fielders used in *The Three Umpires* may never be known. It is clear, however, that Dixie Walker, Johnny Hopp, and Danny Murtaugh were not the models for those players.

The Scoreboard

There are no Brooklyn players depicted in *The Three Umpires*. However, the batting order on the scoreboard indicates that No. 35 is playing left field, and No. 42 is playing second base. Those are the uniform numbers of left fielder Marv Rackley and second baseman Jackie Robinson, respectively. The reference photos and the painting indicate that Rackley led off that day and Robinson batted second, and that was, in fact, the batting order for both games of the doubleheader. There was also a place on the Ebbets Field scoreboard for the insertion of the number of the player who was then batting, but since the reference photos were taken

Rockwell didn't complete the painting until months after taking numerous reference photos at Ebbets Field, supplementing those reference photos with additional pictures of a model wearing a Pirates uniform borrowed from Ralph Kiner, taken in California during the offseason.

before the games started on September 14, 1948, that space has a "0" in it in the photos. However, in the painting, Rockwell inserted No. 20 into that slot.

Three different players wore No. 20 for the Dodgers that year, including pitcher Elmer Sexauer, who was on the roster in September. However, Sexauer, who only pitched in two innings for the Dodgers that year, did not play in either game of the doubleheader on September 14, 1948.[30] It is unlikely that Rockwell was familiar with Sexauer and so, in this instance, Rockwell apparently randomly chose a uniform number for the "at bat" slot on the scoreboard, one which did not accurately reflect any ballplayer in the lineups that day for Brooklyn.

Rockwell made one mistake in his painting of *The Three Umpires*. On the real scoreboard, there are two lines at the bottom for the insertion of the batting orders of both teams. When the reference photos of the scoreboard were taken before the games on September 14, 1948, only the Dodgers lineup was on the board.[31] Rockwell re-created a part of that line in his painting by including the numbers of Marv Rackley and Jackie Robinson in the correct order in the Brooklyn lineup, as shown in the reference photos. The Pittsburgh lineup was not shown in the reference photos, probably because they had not yet been provided to the scoreboard operator. However, by the bottom of the sixth inning, the Pirates lineup would have been displayed on the scoreboard, and Rockwell should have included at least a part of the lineup in his painting, which he neglected to do.

The Controversy

The primary controversy about *The Three Umpires* is that Clyde Sukeforth, the Brooklyn coach, is smiling, while Billy Meyer, the Pirates manager, is frowning. Yet, if the game is called because of rain, the Pirates will win the game. Shouldn't their demeanors be reversed?

This incongruity was so worrying to the editors of the *Saturday Evening Post* that they addressed it on page 3 of the same issue in which *The Three Umpires* was published. In a paragraph titled "This Week's Cover," they first acknowledged that if the arbiters call the game, Pittsburgh will win. They then stated that this "irks the Brooklynites, who dislike having other teams win." They then opined that Clyde Sukeforth could well be saying, "You may be all wet, but it ain't raining a drop!" Bill Meyer is doubtless retorting, "For the love of Abner Doubleday, how can we play ball in this cloudburst?"[32] Whether that imagined conversation justifies the expressions of Sukeforth and Meyer in the painting is for others to decide.

Another theory, suggested by Gerlach, is that since the score in any half inning was not inserted into the scoreboard at Ebbets Field until the inning was over, even if runs had been scored in the inning, there is a possibility that Brooklyn had already scored two runs in the bottom of the sixth inning, but the scoreboard had not yet been updated to reflect that fact. In that case, Brooklyn would win the game if the umpires called it because of rain.[33] This contention seems to be too much "inside baseball" to be convincing, as it is hardly likely that Rockwell would have been cognizant of this practice in Brooklyn, or that Rockwell thought about it weeks later when he was painting the picture in California. In any event, if Rockwell had intended that Brooklyn was winning the game at the time of the tough call, why not simply make the scoreboard read 2–1 in favor of Brooklyn?

Among the other theories is one suggested by art critic Christopher Finch, who has argued that Clyde Sukeforth is happy because the rain is about to stop and the game will continue, giving Brooklyn a chance to win.[34] While an intriguing interpretation, it is unlikely that the three Pirates fielders would have remained on the field during a rainstorm, and it is more likely that the rain has just started. Also, since Rockwell's final version of his painting showed dark clouds in the sky, before the editors of the *Saturday Evening Post* modified it without Rockwell's consent, it seems clear that at least from Rockwell's perspective, the rain is not about to end any time soon.

Others have argued that Sukeforth and Meyer are merely acting out their differing positions concerning the rain. Sukeforth, with a maniacal expression on his face, has his cap off and is pointing to the skies, demonstrating to Meyer that it is not raining. The hunched-over Meyer, hands to his chest, seems to be showing Sukeforth that he is cold and wet, requiring the calling of the game for the health of everyone involved.

All of these explanations are possibilities. Rockwell often left ambiguities in his paintings, which made them subject to multiple interpretations, but also made them much more interesting. The interpretation of the expressions of Billy Meyer and Clyde Sukeforth in *The Three Umpires* is in the eye of the beholder.

OBSERVATIONS AND CONCLUSION

By painting the umpires from below, Rockwell made the arbiters into giants. They tower over the other people in the painting and even over the scoreboard and outfield fence. This makes the umpires the most important people on the field both symbolically and actually, because they are the ones who will make the tough call. The fact that Beans Reardon wore a balloon chest protector on the outside of his coat was fortunate for Rockwell. The insertion of the large protector in the most prominent spot in the painting adds interest to the already interesting tableau of umpires, stern and imposing, giving the viewer's eye a place of focus once the faces of the trio of arbiters and the outstretched hand of Reardon are observed and studied. The oversized chest protector, the largest prop in the painting, also adds to the effect that Rockwell was trying to evoke—the umpires as giants among men.

Norman Rockwell's baseball paintings are often fascinating because of some unusual aspects of them. Except for his earliest story illustrations, Rockwell seldom showed a batter batting, a fielder fielding, or a runner running. Rockwell was interested in the ancillary aspects of the game, such as the locker room, the dugout, the view of a game through a knothole in a fence, and in the subject piece, the decision by the umpires as to whether or not to call the game because of rain. Is there any other artwork about this particular circumstance in baseball, a circumstance which is unique to the sport? Only Norman Rockwell was able to envision the interest this situation could engender.

Although Rockwell painted portraits, he never painted landscapes or still lifes, being more interested in telling a story than catching a moment in time.[35] He once said, "I love to tell stories in pictures. For me, the story is the first thing and the last thing."[36] In *The Three Umpires*, by providing details about the status of the game on the scoreboard, the tough call by the umpires has become tougher, since if they call the game, Pittsburgh will automatically win, and if they let the game go on, Brooklyn has a good chance of winning, down only one run, with a chance to bat in four more innings.

No wonder the managers are in such a heated argument. There is a lot at stake in the umpires' decision. What will happen? The viewer of the painting has to decide, because although Rockwell is telling a story, it is the viewer who must provide the ending.

Thus, *The Three Umpires* has fascinated, perplexed, and interested baseball fans and others ever since the painting was first published on the cover of the *Saturday Evening Post* more than 70 years ago. And there is little doubt that more than 70 years from now, baseball fans and others will still be arguing about the tough call of the three umpires and whether or not the game should be called because of rain. ■

Acknowledgments

My thanks to Larry Gerlach, professor emeritus of history at the University of Utah and past national president of SABR, for answering my questions about *The Three Umpires* and reading an earlier draft of this article, and to Stephanie Plunkett, Deputy Director/Chief Curator, and Maria Tucker, Curatorial Assistant, of the Norman Rockwell Museum, for their kindness in assisting me in the review of the Museum's files about *The Three Umpires*.

Notes

1. The painting may be viewed on the Internet, by searching for "*The Three Umpires*" or "*Game Called Because of Rain.*"

2. "*The Three Umpires (Game Called Because of Rain/Tough Call)*," Norman Rockwell Museum Custom Prints website, https://prints.nrm.org/detail/261004/rockwell-the-three-umpires-game-called-because-of-rain-toughcall-1949.

3. Larry Gerlach, "Norman Rockwell and Baseball Images of the National Pastime," *Nine: A Journal of Baseball History and Culture* (Lincoln, Nebraska: University of Nebraska Press, Fall, 2014), 49.

4. Dominic Sama, "Tributes to baseball from the world over," *Philadelphia Inquirer*, March 23, 1986, 236.

5. Thomas S. Buechner, *Norman Rockwell: A Sixty Year Retrospective* (New York: Harry N. Abrams, Inc., 1972), 42.

6. Thomas S. Buechner, *Norman Rockwell: Artist and Illustrator* (New York: Harry N. Abrams, Inc., 1970), 19.

7. "Norman Rockwell's 323 *Saturday Evening Post* covers," https://www.nrm.org/2009/10/normanrockwells-323-saturday-evening-post-covers/. Other sources give slightly different figures for the number of the *Saturday Evening Post* covers by Norman Rockwell. See, e.g., Maureen Hart Hennessey and Anne Classen Knutson, *Norman Rockwell: Pictures for American People* (New York: Harry N. Abrams, Inc., 1999), 187, n. 16.

8. Ron Shick, *Norman Rockwell: behind the camera* (New York: Little, Brown and Company, 2009),16, 23. Rockwell used professional photographers to take the pictures.

9. Norman Rockwell, *How I Make a Picture* (New York: Watson-Guptil Publications, 1979), 24–27.

10. *Encyclopedia of Art*, "Norman Rockwell," accessed May, 2023: http://www.visual-arts-cork.com/famousartists/norman-rockwell.htm.

11. Norman Rockwell Museum website, accessed May, 2023: http://collection.nrm.org/#details=ecatalogue.55821.

12. Bob LeMoine, "Beans Reardon," SABR BioProject, accessed May, 2023: https://sabr.org/bioproj/person/beans-reardon/. Beans Reardon, Retrosheet, https://www.retrosheet.org/boxesetc/R/Prearb901.htm.

13. James Lincoln Ray, "Clyde Sukeforth," SABR BioProject, accessed May, 2023: https://13 sabr.org/bioproj/person/clyde-sukeforth/.

14. Stan Isaacs, "Kiner-isms liven dull moments," *Asbury Park Press*, June 29, 1985, 25. There is a slightly different version of that story, printed in the *Pittsburgh Press* the same week that *The Three Umpires*

was published on the cover of the *SEP*. In the *Press* article, baseball writer Les Biederman wrote, presumably on information received from Kiner, that "Rockwell borrowed a Pirate uniform from Kiner to make it [the painting] more authentic." Lester Biederman, "The Scorecard," *Pittsburgh Press*, April 22, 1949, 41.

15. Norman Rockwell Museum Website, accessed May, 2023: http://collection.nrm.org/#details=ecatalogue.55821.

16. Norman Rockwell Museum Website, accessed May, 2023: http://collection.nrm.org/#details=ecatalogue.55821.

17. "Umpiring Timeline," MLB Website, accessed May, 2023: https://www.mlb.com/official-information/umpires/timeline.

18. Rob Edelman, "Burt Shotton," SABR BioProject, accessed May, 2023: https://sabr.org/bioproj/person/burtshotton/.

19. Steven Booth, "The Story of kindly old Burt Shotton," *The Hardball Times*, February 4, 2011, accessed May, 2023: https://tht.fangraphs.com/the-story-of-kindly-old-burt-shotton/.

20. David Seideman, "Newly Discovered Version of Norman Rockwell's 'Tough Call' Up To $360K in Auction," *Forbes*, August 16, 2017, accessed May, 2023: https://www.forbes.com/sites/davidseideman/2017/08/16/family-discovers-norman-rockwell-baseball-print-is-an-original-painting-worth-up-to-1-million/?sh=bdedd2637124.

21. A copy of the newly discovered painting can be seen on the website of Heritage Auctions, accessed May, 2023: https://sports.ha.com/itm/baseball/1948-original-study-for-tough-call-by-norman-rockwell-gifted-tolegendary-umpire-beans-reardon/a/7195-80067.s?ic4=OtherResults-SampleItem-071515.

22. Bob D'Angelo, "Famous Norman Rockwell study drawing of umpires fetches 1.68M at auction," *Atlantic-Journal Constitution*, August 21, 2017, accessed May, 2023: https://www.ajc.com/entertainment/famous-normanrockwell-study-drawing-umpires-fetches-68m-auction/tSEFdANWqq0ipmg4Q2DPZN/. "Norman Rockwell baseball rendering sells for 1.6M," *Atlanta Constitution*, August 22, 2017, A2.

23. Heritage Auctions website, accessed May, 2023: https://sports.ha.com/itm/baseball/1948-original-studyfor-tough-call-by-norman-rockwell-gifted-to-legendary-umpire-beans-reardon/a/7195-80067.s?ic4=OtherResults-SampleItem-071515.

24. Norman Rockwell Museum website, accessed May, 2023: http://collection.nrm.org/#details=ecatalogue.55821.

25. According to Rockwell, his color sketches were not intended to be the equivalent of a completed work. Rockwell tried not to carry his color sketches so far that there would be no fun left in completing the final paintings. Norman Rockwell, *How I Make a Picture* (New York, NY, Watson-Guptil Publications, 1979), 156.

26. Rockwell wrote, "Some of my color sketches are, I am sorry to say, better than the finished paintings and I often sell them or give them to friends." Norman Rockwell, *How I Make a Picture* (New York, NY, Watson-Guptil Publications, 1979), 153.

27. Gerlach, 49.

28. Hopp, wearing No. 12, does appear in the outfield in one reference photo of the scoreboard, but since he is not standing in the same pose as the center fielder in the painting, that photo is not a reference photo for the center fielder but only for the scoreboard.

29. See note 14, above.

30. "Elmer Sexauer," Baseball Reference, https://www.baseball-reference.com/players/s/sexaue01.shtml, accessed August, 2023.

31. It is actually the starting lineup from the previous day's game, September 13, 1948. The only change in the starting lineup between the previous day's games and the first game of the doubleheader was the pitcher's spot.

32. *Saturday Evening Post*, April 23, 1949, 3.

33. Gerlach, 51.

34. Christopher Finch, *Norman Rockwell 332 Magazine Covers*, New York, NY, Abbeville Press/Random House 1979), 365.

35. Gerlach, 43.

36. Stephanie Haboush Plunkett, Deputy Director, Chief Curator, Norman Rockwell Museum, from her introduction to Ron Shick, *Norman Rockwell: behind the camera*, (New York, NY, Little, Brown and Company, 2009), 9.

Tyrus

A Study and Commentary on the Name

William R. Cobb, PhD

In 1904 when Tyrus Raymond Cobb arrived on the professional baseball scene, his first name was not at all well known. In fact, most fans had never even heard of anyone with that particular name—Ty himself apparently among them. That was to change in short order, however, as Tyrus Cobb's fame spread nationally within a few short seasons. As Ty's fame grew, so did the population with the name Tyrus, as many admiring fans gave that name to their newborns in honor of the rising star.

Today, every modern-day baseball fan knows the name. But many, if not most, fans believe the name to have been unique to Ty Cobb. Most Cobb biographers have felt the need to explain where this unique name came from—a testament to its uniqueness. Baseball fans, they reason, would want to know why Ty's parents gave him such an uncommon name and how they arrived at their choice. But over the course of Ty's much-documented life and career, multiple conflicting stories about his name have been told and retold. By examining the writings of Ty's biographers and of Ty himself, and reviewing relevant ancient and modern historical sources, this paper will delve into these myths, debunk some—or perhaps all—and propose a heretofore unexamined explanation.

WHO'S ON FIRST?

The earliest mention of the source of his name is a quotation from Ty himself in a 1956 biography by John McCallum.[1]

> Ty was always addressed as Tyrus in those days. Not until he climbed into the majors did Damon Runyon and Ring Lardner or one of the New York writers shorten it to "Ty." *Ty says he thinks he was the first "Tyrus" in the United States*, though folks have named their youngsters after him. (*Emphasis added.*)

To make such a statement, Ty must have believed that his first name was not only uncommon but also unique, and he must never have met anyone with that name before.

NAMED FOR A GOD?

Ty Cobb's 1961 autobiography, published just months after his death in July 1961, quotes Ty's own explanation of the source of his name.[2] This book was ghost-written by Al Stump, who would—sadly and with great detrimental effect—produce additional writings after Ty's death. In numerous magazine articles and books after Cobb's death, Stump proudly exercised his bent for besotted and perverted fantasies, sensational truth-twisting exaggerations, and out-and-out lies.[3] Stump would later assert that the content of the 1961 autobiography was under editorial control of Ty himself, which makes almost everything in the book believable. It reads:

> How my father came to pick my name, I am not entirely sure, but the story that it stems from Týr, the Norse god of war, is untrue. Father was an avid reader of ancient history. And the Tyrians of Tyre, an ancient Phoenician seaport, appealed to him....Tyrus, a Tyrian leader, resisted the Roman invasion, before Alexander slaughtered the population, and from him comes my name.

That a story had previously circulated about Ty being named for the Norse god of war was news to me. I did a thorough search and found no mention of this story in any of the newspapers available on Newspapers.com. Having no knowledge of Norse religion or mythology, I did not know if the name carried negative implications, but Ty seemed to think it did, and wanted to quash the story as a result.

I set out to study enough Norse mythology to learn who Týr actually was, and to get a feel whether Ty's well-educated father, Professor William H. Cobb, might have conceivably considered naming him after this mythical god. Týr is not only the Norse god of war, but also the god of law and honor, and I learned he is deemed extremely intelligent, clever, wise, and cunning—able to create puzzles unsolvable by human minds. Týr's superhuman powers and abilities allow him to excel in all forms of combat, both armed and unarmed, but he is also a natural pacifist and diplomat who uses his powers to seek peace for his people. All in all, pretty admirable and maybe not such a bad namesake as Ty seemed to believe. In fact, some of Týr's attributes sound much like attributes that Ty himself would grow up to possess.

Although, Týr is pronounced like "tier" in English, the Latinized name is "Tius," which is not so far removed from Tyrus. At that point in my investigation, it seemed no more a stretch to reach Tyrus from Týr or Tius, than from the name of an ancient city called Tyre.

WHO NAMES THEIR CHILD AFTER A CITY?

No one I ever knew named their first-born child after a city, ancient or modern. I have no friends or acquaintances named New York, Chicago, Atlanta, or even London, Rome, or Moscow. Certainly not Babylon, Memphis, Nineveh, Thebes, or Carthage. Who would do that?[4] Yet that definitely seems to be the consensus among biographers as to the source of the name Tyrus. Not even Ty himself asserted that he was named for the city of Tyre, but rather for a leader of that city by the name of Tyrus. Let's take a look at some of the assertions of Cobb biographers and their explanations.

In 1975, John McCallum wrote another, more in-depth biography of Ty Cobb. By that time, Ty's 1961 autobiography had been published, so McCallum updated this 1956 assertion with this statement:

> Professor Cobb, an avid reader of ancient history, had always liked Tyrus of Tyre, who had led his people in resistance to Rome before Alexander slaughtered the population of the ancient Phoenician seaport. So he named his son Tyrus Raymond.[5]

After extensive research I have not been able to find any reference to a person named "Tyrus of Tyre." So, I believe McCallum errs, as does Ty himself, in stating that Tyrus is the namesake of a person named Tyrus of Tyre. McCallum also errs by stating that Alexander slaughtered the population of Tyre. Actually, the army of Tyre was slaughtered, while the non-combatants were taken as slaves.

In 1984, Charles C. Alexander, a respected historian and university professor with no stated relation to Alexander the Great, wrote a scholarly, well referenced biography also titled *Ty Cobb*. Echoing Ty's own statement from 1956, Alexander attributes the name Tyrus to W.H. Cobb's knowledge of ancient history, expanding the story to include specific mention of Alexander the Great, but avoiding the attribution of Tyrus to a

Family portrait of a young Ty.

AUTHOR'S COLLECTION

person. Alexander states only that Ty's father "hit on" the name Tyrus when recalling the city of Tyre.

> W.H. Cobb had read about the stubborn resistance of the city of Tyre to the besieging armies of Alexander the Great in the fourth century B.C. Thus he hit on Tyrus as a suitable first name for his son. For no particular reason, the infant was given Raymond for a middle name.[6]

Interestingly, Alexander adds his own twist on the source of Ty's middle name, Raymond, with a quotation that predates the famous Forrest Gump serial quotation by a full decade: *"For no particular reason…."* No reference was given for this assertion.

A prolific history and sports author named Richard Bak from Detroit published another biography of Ty Cobb in 1994 titled *Ty Cobb: His Tumultuous Life and Times*. Bak went to great lengths in his early chapters to expound on the effect that the Civil War had on the family of Ty Cobb and then described the possible effect that the war had on selection of the name Tyrus—a new wrinkle in the discussion. Without attribution he makes this statement:

> It's even possible that the bitter legacy of Sherman's march played a part in William Cobb's naming of Tyrus, because after the war Atlanta often was referred to as "The Tyre of the South," calling to mind the fate of that other unlucky city.[7]

Speaking of names, Bak even delves into the namesake of Ty Cobb's adversary, Commissioner Kenesaw Mountain Landis.[8] He pointed out correctly that Landis was named after the Civil War Battle of Kennesaw Mountain, which was fought in Georgia on and around a pair of small ridges known as Big Kennesaw and Little Kennesaw Mountain, near the Atlanta suburb of Marietta. He also pointed out that Landis' parents misspelled the name of those ridges by dropping an "n" from the usual Anglicization.

However, one must suspect Bak's knowledge of Civil War history, and hence his unreferenced speculations that Ty's parents were thinking of General Sherman when naming him. Bak incorrectly states that Sherman's Union Army won the Battle of Kennesaw Mountain, which was actually a resounding Confederate victory. After losing nearly 3,000 men, Sherman withdrew all forces on June 27, 1864.[9] This is a major error for any historian, bordering on unforgivable. Bak also asserts that Atlanta was often referred to after the Civil War as "The Tyre of the South." Atlanta has been called a lot of things in the last century and a half, including "Gate City of the South," "New York of the South," "Chicago of the South," "Convention City of Dixie Land," "Dogwood City," and others. But except for a single obscure reference in David Power Cunningham's 1865 book *Sherman's March through the South*, I found no other uses of this moniker.[10]

The year 1994 also saw the reemergence of Al Stump, a serious nemesis of Ty Cobb. Stump penned his magnum opus, a biography titled *Cobb: The Life and Times of the Meanest Man Who Ever Played Baseball*.[11] The book was adapted into the movie of the same title, directed by Ron Shelton and starring Tommy Lee Jones as Ty. Stump carries on the war-and-warrior naming theme, discarding the Norse-god-Týr theory and expanding on the City-of-Tyre theory:

> In naming his first son, the senior Cobb dipped into his interest in war and warriors. Tyrus was not named for Týr, a Norse god of arms-bearing, as would later be claimed by members of the sports press. In 332 B.C., sweeping across Asia Minor, Alexander the Great was halted by defenders of the ancient Phoenician city of Tyre. Through seven months of carnage, the Tyrians kept Alexander's army at bay. Thence came the newborn's name. The child's middle name, which he much disliked, came from a distant relative, a gambler by profession, but friendly with the Professor.

Ty with siblings Florence Leslie (center) and John Paul (right) in a photo taken around 1896.

Ever the sensationalist, Stump adds a juicy tidbit, speculating on the source of Ty's middle name as coming from a distant relative, not necessarily a Cobb, who was also a (gasp!) gambler.[12] Throughout his career, Stump peppered his writing with fictional statements to provoke thoughts and speculations about the negative or shady side of his subjects. This is undoubtedly an example.

In 2005 came a second Ty Cobb biography by Richard Bak—*Peach: Ty Cobb in His Time and Ours*.[13] He carries on the story of the city of Tyre and its valiant but unsuccessful defense. Like all the other biographers who propagate this story, no explanation of the leap from Tyre to Tyrus is given.

> William, who was widely read, had always admired the story of the ancient Phoenician city of Tyre, which in 332 B.C. had put up a gallant but doomed resistance to the legions of Alexander the Great. Hence the first-born's unique name.

Charles Leerhsen's myth-shattering and widely read biography titled *Ty Cobb, A Terrible Beauty* was published to great acclaim in 2015.[14] Leerhsen openly admits that the source of the name Tyrus could have been a name that was invented by his parents, and further speculates that the source of Ty's middle name Raymond is anybody's guess.

> Tyrus Raymond Cobb was the baby's full name. Where his parents got "Raymond" is anyone's guess. "Tyrus," though it doesn't sound so strange now (thanks largely to Tyrus Raymond Cobb), may well have been a name of their own invention. (It was only after he started hitting above .300 that people stopped calling him

"Cyrus.") W.H. apparently fashioned it from Tyre, the ancient Phoenician city that in 332 B.C. gallantly held out for seven months before finally falling to Alexander the Great.

Leerhsen does note that Ty's father "apparently fashioned" the name Tyrus from the name of the ancient Phoenician city of Tyre, acknowledging what most earlier biographers failed to note—that there was no historically significant person in the city of Tyre by the name of Tyrus. No prior biography explains how the name Tyrus was derived from the city name Tyre.

Another Ty Cobb biography was published in 2015, this one by Tim Hornbaker titled *War on the Basepaths, The Definitive Biography of Ty Cobb*.[15] Hornbaker makes only a small mention of the source of the name Tyrus, replaying what Ty said in his 1961 autobiography about the Norse god Týr and the city of Tyre, but he does acknowledge that it is a "rather unusual" name:

> Regarding the rather unusual name, Cobb explained that it came from a "Tyrian leader" from Tyre, which today is in modern-day Lebanon. He disavowed a claim that it was from Týr the Norse god of War.

Hornbaker also fails to recognize that there was never a Tyrian leader named Tyrus.

One year later, in 2016, another Ty Cobb biography was published, this one by sociology professor Steven Elliott Tripp of Grand Valley State University, whose earlier fame came as host of the podcast *New Books in Gender Studies*.[16] This biography was titled *Ty Cobb:*

Baseball and American Manhood.[17] Professor Tripp rehashes the City-of-Tyre theory:

> Another indication of William's attachment to Southern culture concerned the name he chose for his first-born—Tyrus. A student of ancient history, William admired the story of the ancient Phoenician city of Tyre which had resolutely defended itself against a number of invading armies during its storied past. Only the massive army of Alexander the Great was able to conquer it after a long and terrible siege. When Alexander finally broke through, he ordered that the entire Tyrian army be put to death and all its citizens sold into slavery. From a Southerner's perspective, the similarity between the history of Tyre and what the South had endured in war and reconstruction could not be plainer. William's choice of Tyrus as a name revealed his allegiance to the cult of the Lost Cause, a growing cultural movement that hoped to keep alive the dream of Confederate nationalism through public rituals and—as in the case of William's choice of a name for his first-born—private acts. Like the ancient Tyrians, William hoped that his progeny would fight the righteous fight against unwelcome invaders.

Professor Tripp adds "the Southerner's perspective," waxing grandiloquent about Professor Cobb's feelings about the Civil War, alleging—based on no stated facts—an ultimate fidelity to the Lost Cause, linking the naming of Tyrus Cobb to his father's supposed allegiance to Confederate nationalism. This is

Ty's parents, William Herschel Cobb and Amanda Chitwood Cobb, circa 1900.

no better than Stump's fantastical inventions. Professor's Tripp's condescending assertion is worse than suspect; it is an ahistorical overreach of massive proportions. Aside from expecting us to believe that he can discern what would be the deeply hidden motivations of a man who had been deceased for more than 12 decades, Tripp completely neglects that Professor Cobb came from a long line of abolitionists and Union sympathizers. Ty's grandfather, John Franklin Cobb, was drafted into the 39th North Carolina Infantry Regiment only two months after President Jefferson Davis authorized the Confederacy's first Conscription Act on April 16, 1862, requiring three years of service from all males aged 18 to 35. He declared to the Confederate officer inducting him in Murphy that he was a Unionist, stating: "I am an American citizen. I am not a rebel," but he was sworn in anyway.[18] He was discharged in August for medical reasons a month before his regiment saw its first combat action.[19] Thus he was not, strictly speaking, a Confederate war veteran, and it seems unlikely he would have either held the Lost Cause mentality or propagated it to his son. Tripp also fails to mention that Professor Cobb's paternal grandfather, William A. Cobb, was a Methodist minister and devout abolitionist who shocked his congregation by preaching against slavery and was run out of the county for his beliefs and his advocacy.[20]

Strange also that Tripp could believe that Professor Cobb's naming of his son in 1886 was a hidden act of allegiance to the Lost Cause when less than 20 years later his public acts promoted the exact opposite: as a Georgia State Senator, Cobb advocated successfully for state funding of Negro education. He later worked as editor of the *Royston Record*, the local newspaper in Ty's hometown, which was owned and controlled by a well-known abolitionist and Universalist minister.

THE BIBLICAL HISTORY OF THE CITY OF TYRE

All but two of Ty Cobb's biographers include the City-of-Tyre theory, but none explain how one gets from Tyre to Tyrus. Only Charles Leerhsen states that Cobb's father "apparently fashioned" it, while Ty himself believed incorrectly that Tyrus was the name of a leader of Tyre. The link between the names Tyre and Tyrus actually comes from the King James Version of the Bible.

The original 1611 edition, with its very old English, was replaced in 1769 by a newer version which became the standard for all English-speaking Christians. This was the Bible in common use by Southern churches around the time of Ty's birth in 1886, and his father, as an educated man and grandson of a minister, was surely familiar with it. This Bible uses both the names Tyre and Tyrus to refer to the ancient Phoenician city. There is no doubt that the two names refer to the same city, and the prominent use of Tyrus in the books of Ezekiel and Zechariah dispel any assumed need for Ty's father to "fashion" one name from the other. The names Tyrus and Tyre were used interchangeably throughout.[21]

Cobb's biographers consistently attribute the Tyrus name selection to the struggle of that city against Alexander the Great, but there is a rich history of the city both before and after—even into the New Testament time—that lead to many mentions throughout the Bible.

The first mention comes in the Old Testament book of Joshua as one of the cities of the tribe of Asher (~1200 B.C.), a seaport in Syria about midway between Sidon and Accho. The city was partially on an island and partially on the shore. It was a center of great commerce, sending goods to the east by land and to the west by the sea. The island part of Tyre was fortified with a wall recorded to be 150 feet high in places, and it held an exceedingly strong defensive position. Joshua had captured Jericho, but was unable to capture Tyre, and the city later rivaled Jerusalem.

In King David's reign (~969 B.C.), Israel formed an alliance with Hiram, the king of Tyre. David's use of stonemasons and carpenters from Tyre, along with cedars from that region, was essential to building his palace. In King Solomon's reign (957–31 B.C.), the construction of the temple in Jerusalem, about 100 miles away, relied heavily on supplies, laborers, and skilled artisans from Tyre. The seamen of Tyre also aided in navigating the ships of King Solomon.

Israel continued its close ties with Tyre during King Ahab's reign (~875–53 B.C.). Ahab married the Phoenician princess Jezebel of Sidon, and their union led to the infiltration of pagan worship and idolatry in Israel. Both Tyre and Sidon were notorious for their wickedness and idolatry, which resulted in numerous denouncements by Israel's prophets, who predicted Tyre's ultimate destruction.

The book of Ezekiel (~592–65 B.C.) laments for the city of Tyrus, identifying the Prince of Tyrus, who claimed that he was a god sitting proudly in God's seat. In Ezekiel's proclamations, God tells the Prince of Tyrus that he is a man and not God. Ezekiel then identifies the Prince of Tyrus as Satan himself. Other curses from God directed at Tyrus that were prophesied by Ezekiel include (among many others): "I am against thee, O Tyrus, and will cause many nations to come up against thee…"; "I shall make thee a desolate city…";

"I bring forth a fire from the midst of thee, it shall devour thee, and I will bring thee to ashes..."[22]

King Nebuchadnezzar II of Babylon laid siege to Tyre for 13 years beginning in 586–85 B.C. During this time, the inhabitants transferred most of their valuables to the island. The king seized Tyre's mainland territories, but was unable to subdue the island fortress militarily and returned to Babylon. Tyre, weakened by the conflict, soon recognized Babylonian authority, which effectively ended the city's autonomy.

After the restoration of Jerusalem in Nehemiah's time, the people of Tyre violated the Sabbath rest by selling their goods in the markets of Jerusalem. Following the Babylonian period, Tyre remained in subjection to Persia from 538 to 332 B.C. In 332 B.C., Alexander the Great besieged and conquered the port city after a seven-month siege. He conquered the island part of the city by building a 200-foot-wide land bridge from the shore which still exists today. Afterwards, the Ptolemies, the Seleucids, the Romans, and the Muslim Arabs all had their turn at rule.

In the New Testament, Jesus mentions Tyre as an example of an unrepentant city (~ A.D. 30). Jesus also ministered in the district of Tyre and nearby Sidon, healing the demon-possessed daughter of a Canaanite woman there.

The persecution that arose after Saint Stephen's martyrdom (A.D. 36) caused the Christians in Jerusalem to disperse. As a result, a Christian church was established in Tyre which is said to contain a stone that Jesus sat upon when he visited there. Saint Paul later spent a week there with the disciples on the return voyage of his third missionary journey (~ A.D. 58).

From the time of Christ up to the Crusades, Tyrus was a flourishing city of commerce, renowned for the great wealth it derived from dyes of Tyrian purple, extracted from shellfish on its coast.

In 1124, Tyre was captured by the first Crusaders, and later was successfully defended by them in the four-month Siege of Tyre by Saladin in 1187–88. It finally fell to the armies of the Mamluk Sultan Khalil in 1291, and the city was completely destroyed by the Saracens, thereby fulfilling Ezekiel's prophecy: "They will destroy the walls of Tyre and pull down her towers..." The island part of Tyre remained a desolate ruin for centuries.

Although not biblical history per se, Shakespeare would later (1609) immortalize the city of Tyre in his play *Pericles, Prince of Tyre*.[23] In this story, the Seleucid King of Syria, Antiochus the Great (222–187 B.C.), had a beautiful daughter who had many suitors. He discouraged all suitors by requiring each to solve a riddle in order to pursue her. If a suitor gave the wrong answer to Antiochus' riddle, he was killed. When Pericles, Prince of Tyre, did solve the riddle, Antiochus attempted to kill him as well. But Pericles was repulsed by his correct answer to the riddle, which was that Antiochus and his daughter were in an incestuous relationship. Fearing death, Pericles fled back to Tyre with Antiochus in pursuit. The play covers the later trials and tribulations of Pericles and his family through many episodes of shipwrecks and tragedy, until Pericles is finally reunited with his own daughter, Marina.

Of course, there is a long tradition of giving children names found in the Bible, perhaps more notably thought of as a Southern practice now, as names like Ezekiel, Josiah, and Zebediah remain more prevalent in the Southeast than elsewhere in the US, but Biblical naming was certainly a popular practice in both North and South at the time of Ty's birth. Given the repeated appearance of the name Tyrus in the Bible, one might expect to find other Tyruses in the historical record. But how does this fit with Ty's own belief that his name was unique or that he might have been the first?

WHAT'S IN THE DATABASES?

While working on a book about the Civil War and looking for roster information about the 8th Regiment of Georgia Volunteer Infantry, I accessed a massive on-line database of military service records of US soldiers from the Revolutionary War onward.[24] On a whim, I did a search on the name Tyrus over the entire database. I was surprised by what I found. My search shows that the name Tyrus was not nearly so unusual as previously supposed. There were actually many soldiers throughout history who bore that name.

Three soldiers fought in the Revolutionary War with the first name Tyrus, and three more in the War of 1812. One soldier in the War of 1812 had the last name Tyrus, and one soldier in the Mexican American War of 1846 had it as his first.

In the Civil War, a total of 28 soldiers had the first name Tyrus, 27 Union and one Confederate. Clearly the popularity of that name was much greater in the North than the South, perhaps explaining why Ty knew no other person who shared his own first name. In addition, there were seven soldiers whose last name was Tyrus, four Confederates and three Union (Exhibit 1, following page). Continuing the search, I found 70 soldiers who served in World War I with the first name Tyrus, 22 soldiers with the last name Tyrus, and 47 soldiers with the middle name Tyrus. These soldiers were contemporaries of Ty, and thus he could not have been

Exhibit 1. Soldiers with the Name Tyrus, 1775–1865

First Name	MI	Last Name	Conflict	Side	Rank	Company	Regiment	State
Tyrus		Turkins	Revolutionary					
Tyrus		Pratt	Revolutionary					
Tyrus		Preston	Revolutionary					
Tyrus		Dresser	1812	Britian				
Tyrus		Ball	1812	US			Volunteers	S. C.
Tyrus		Prouty	1812	US	Pvt			
John		Tyrus	1812	US				
Tyrus		Rhodes	Civil War	Confederate	Slave			
Joseph	B.	Tyrus	Civil War	Confederate	2nd Lt	F	15th Inf	Texas
James	E	Tyrus	Civil War	Confederate	Pvt	A	38th Inf	Tenn
James		Tyrus	Civil War	Confederate	Sgt.	Capt. Gamblin's	Cav	Miss
Fredrick	W	Tyrus	Civil War	Confederate	Pvt	A	38th Inf	Tenn
Tyrus		Adams	Civil War	Union			Navy	
Tyrus		Fidler	Civil War	Union	Pvt	F	173rd Inf	Penn
Tyrus		Lonebaugh	Civil War	Union	Corporal	A	41st Inf	Illinois
Tyrus	M	Rosecrans	Civil War	Union	Pvt	E	1st Light Attillery	Illinois
Tyrus		Adams	Civil War	Union			Ship "New Berne"	
Tyrus		Bell	Civil War	Union	Corporal	F, G, K	74th Col'd Inf	
Tyrus		Dickson	Civil War	Union	Pvt	L	8th Cav	Illinois
Tyrus		Fidler	Civil War	Union				Penn
Tyrus		Fredrick	Civil War	Union	Deserter	Capt. Gamblin's	54th Col'd Inf	Mass
Tyrus		Goodwin	Civil War	Union	Pvt	A	111th Inf	Penn
Tyrus	G	Higgins	Civil War	Union	Pvt	B	12th Inf	Illinois
Tyrus		Higgins	Civil War	Union	Pvt	B	12th Inf	Illinois
Tyrus		Horton	Civil War	Union	Sgt.	I	1st Cav	Illinois
Tyrus		Hurd	Civil War	Union	Capt.	D	15th Cav	Kansas
Tyrus		Longebaugh	Civil War	Union	Pvt		41st Infantry	Illinois
Tyrus	J	Hurd	Civil War	Union	Sgt.	D	9th Cav	Kansas
Tyrus		Lursenbigler	Civil War	Union			54th Inrantry	Penn
Tyrus	C	Lloyd	Civil War	Union	Pvt	F, C	1st Battn Cav	Delaware
Tyrus		Martin	Civil War	Union	Pvt	A	30th Inf	Ohio
Tyrus		McCarger	Civil War	Union	Pvt, Blacks	M	8th Cav	Illinois
Tyrus		Michael	Civil War	Union	Pvt	B	10th Inf	Indiana
Tyrus	J	Nichols	Civil War	Union		Sharpsooters	154th	New York
Tyrus		Page	Civil War	Union	Pvt	G	131st Inf	Penn
Tyrus	H	Page	Civil War	Union	Pvt	D	26th Inf	Iowa
Tyrus		Smith	Civil War	Union				Winsconsin
Tyrus		Talbert	Civil War	Union	2nd Lt	E	22nd Inf	Indiana
Tyrus		Wallace	Civil War	Union	Pvt	F	96th Inf	New York
Marshall		Tyrus	Civil War	Union	Corporal, [	F	5th Col'd Hvy. Art'y	Virginia
John		Tyrus	Civil War	Union	Sgt.	E	68th Col'd Inf	
W	Paul	Tyrus	Civil War	Union				Kentucky

their namesake. Clearly, although the name Tyrus was not a common name, it was not an unheard-of name either (Exhibit 2).

The database yielded more of note: two World War I soldiers with the first name Tyrus and last name Cobb (Tyrus Raymond Cobb of Georgia and Tyrus Anton Cobb of Indiana) plus two with the middle name Tyrus and last name Cobb (Harry Tyrus Cobb and John Tyrus Cobb, their resident states not recorded). Among the 1,216 draft-registered soldiers surnamed Cobb, a total of four had the first or middle name Tyrus..

In World War II, I found even more soldiers named Tyrus. Of course, many of these soldiers were named after Tyrus Raymond Cobb by parents who must have

been baseball fans. There were over 3,000 service records of soldiers with either first or last name Tyrus, and 329 with the name Tyrus Raymond or Raymond Tyrus. Nineteen actually had the name Tyrus Raymond Cobb, without a doubt a tribute to Ty Cobb, and of these, two had this three-name tribute to Ty preceding a different surname. In the Korean War I found only 122 soldiers with the first or last name Tyrus.

Other sources of names I found include the Social Security Death Index (SSDI), the Social Security Birth Name database, and several other online databases. SSDI shows first, middle, and last names with birth year and death dates. Seven people with the first name Tyrus were born before Ty Cobb's birth in 1886. (SSDI also shows one individual named Tyrus Raymond

Cooke born in Missouri in 1889.) As expected, the number of people with the first name Tyrus increased dramatically beginning in 1909, matching the rise of Ty Cobb's baseball fame. In all, there are 957 records for persons with the first name Tyrus, 224 with the middle name Tyrus, and 122 with the last name Tyrus, although there are some duplicate records within this data.

I was unable to gain direct access to the Social Security Administration Birth Name database, but did find a website which provided a visualization of selected names from that data.[25] Exhibit 3 shows a plot of babies named Tyrus from 1900 through 2020, although the website cautions that data before about 1935 are not necessarily accurate. As expected, the plot shows rapid increase beginning after 1905 when Ty Cobb began to gain fame in baseball. Interestingly, it shows another significant increase around 1961, the year of Ty's death. And finally, it shows a marked decrease in the late 1990s which might be attributed to the negative myths that were fabricated and popularized by Al Stump in his 1994 book and in the subsequent movie about Ty Cobb.[26]

ANALYSIS AND CONCLUSION

Firm conclusions about century-old individual actions and feelings are simply not possible. But this study has shown that several widely believed facts regarding the

---

Exhibit 2. World War I Soldiers with the Name Tyrus

Last names of 70 soldiers with first name Tyrus

Bailey, Bateman, Benton, Berry, Bingham, Caswell, Clide, Cobb (2), Collins, Conklin, Cooke, English, France, Freeman, Frost, Garrett, Gray, Habegger, Harris, Heindel, Heinmann, Hewet, Hill, Hilton, Holmes, Holt, Howard, Hunker, Hunter, Jefferies, Johnson, Joyce, Kehmier, King, Lane, Larson, Lemon, Lengle, Lesley, Lindsay, McCargar, McEwan, Meyer, Meyers, Middleton, Nuss, Peck, Peters, Phillips(2), Pittman, Price, Price, Ruston, Settle, Shaffer, Sims, Strohl, Syng, Thompson, Thorpe, Ulysses, Walters, Whitehorn, Youngblood, Youse

First names of 22 soldiers with last name Tyrus

Archie, Arthur, Cleveland, Clyde, Forrester, Gail, Henry, James, Joe, John (2), L. B., Lindsay, Marion, Robert (2), Rogers, Tidor, Timpko, Tom, Ulysses, Willie

Last names of 47 soldiers with middle name Tyrus

Barnard, Blacklock, Broadhead, Clark, Cash, Cobb (2), Epler, Flanders, Harper, Heimann, Hollon, Hovan, Hower, Jacobsen, Jones, Leigh, Lemaire, Lindsay, Long, Mainer, Martin, McChargue, Meimann, Money, Muggridge, O.Malley, Page, Pempin, Poska, Ray, Rhoad, Savage, Sharp, Shoener, Smith, Sooy, Sunderland, Tidwell, Vaughan, White, Wilfong, Wilfong, Willington, Wimberly, Wolf, Wyckoff

---

Exhibit 3. Babies Named Tyrus, 1905–2020

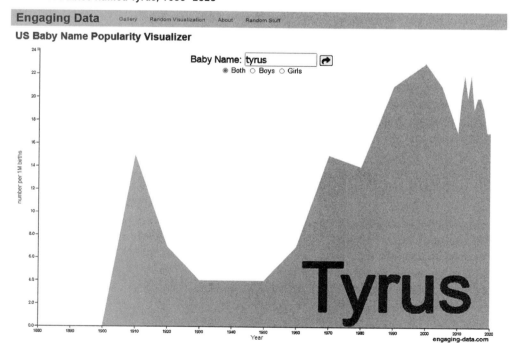

Ty would name his eldest son Tyrus, shown here (left) with siblings Herschel and Shirley.

name Tyrus are either not true, or are not likely, and lead to one new piece of analysis. Here is a summary of what I have gleaned from this study:

Ty was quoted by John McCallum in 1956 as purportedly saying that he believed he was the first person in the US to be named Tyrus.[27] The data reviewed here show he was definitely not the first in the country with that name. Ty's own 1961 autobiography stated he was named after a leader of the city of Tyre by the name of Tyrus. This cannot be correct, as there was no historical person named Tyrus who led the city of Tyre in its defense against Alexander the Great, and Ty's statement includes several other historical mistakes including Alexander the Great leading a "Roman invasion" (Alexander was Greek). Ty did offer the caveat, "I am not exactly sure," when describing how his father picked his name, yet he seemed to be quite emphatic he was not named for the Norse god Týr. Given that Týr was actually a pretty good guy, it might not be completely out of the question that Ty's father could have chosen Tyrus based on that.

Cobb's biographers all parroted the City-of-Tyre theory in some form, many citing the city's resistance to Alexander the Great as the supposed inspiration.[28] Two tried to create a presumed link between the name Tyrus and the Southern Confederacy, neither of them credible. None recognized that "Tyrus" was actually the name of the city as written in several books of the King James Version of the Bible. Presumably, following the convention of using biblical names, Professor Cobb might have taken it from the KJV Book of Ezekiel, where the name Tyrus is used exclusively and appears a dozen times in chapters 26–28 alone. But given the

centuries-long condemnation of the wickedness of the city of Tyre described in the Bible, why would Professor and Mrs. Cobb would even consider naming their firstborn after Tyre at all? Not to mention that cities don't seem to be typical sources of baby-naming at all?

The final conclusion of this study is that we don't know why Prof. Cobb and his wife named their first son Tyrus, and even Ty himself, as he clearly stated, did not know. However, it seemed to me a striking coincidence that in World War 1 there were two soldiers with first name Tyrus and last name Cobb (one of which was Tyrus Raymond) and also two soldiers with middle name Tyrus and last name Cobb. To examine this further, I asked the SABR Statistical Analysis Committee for assistance in analyzing these WW-1 name probabilities.

Here is how they posed the statistical problem: Assume a random distribution of the names of the 4.6 million soldiers which we know were in service in World War I. Of these 4.6 million soldiers, we also know there were a total of 117 soldiers with the first or middle name Tyrus—70 with first name Tyrus and 47 with middle name Tyrus.

It happens that 1,261 of the 4.6 million soldiers were surnamed Cobb. The probability that any specific one of the soldiers named Tyrus would be surnamed Cobb is easily calculated as 1261/4.6 million, or 1 in 3648. But, of the 117 soldiers with first or middle name Tyrus, there were actually 4 surnamed Cobb. What then is the probability that at least 4 of the 117 Tyruses in WWI were surnamed Cobb? That answer, assuming as usual a binomial distribution, turns out to be 1 in 26 million.[29]

The extremely low probability that 4 of the 117 Tyruses in WWI would be surnamed Cobb means that it is not merely a coincidence. I postulate that these Tyrus Cobbs were actually related to each other in some way. If this is true, then the source of the name Tyrus for the baseball player was from within the Cobb family and actually came from an ancestor or relative named Tyrus Cobb, not an ancient city cursed for centuries by the Judeo-Christian God and not the benevolent Norse god of war, law, and honor. ∎

Notes

1. John McCallum, *The Tiger Wore Spikes, An Informal Biography of Ty Cobb* (New York: A.S. Barnes and Co., 1956), 18.
2. Ty Cobb with Al Stump, *My Life in Baseball, The True Record* (New York: Doubleday, 1961), 34.
3. William R. Cobb, "The Georgia Peach: Stumped by the Storyteller," *The National Pastime: Baseball in the Peach State* (Society for American Baseball Research, 2010).
4. A recent Internet search for "Famous people named after cities" has proven me wrong, at least for modern glitterati and their children—obviously a present-day phenomenon. Here are just a few from those search results, most of whom are completely unknown to me: Paris Hilton, Paris Brosnan, Orlando Bloom, Bristol Palin, Brooklyn Decker, Brooklyn Beckham, Cheyenne Jackson, London Hudson, Chicago West, Kingston Rossdale, Bronx Wentz, Milan Mebarak, Savannah Guthrie, Santiago Cabrera… The US Baby Name Popularity Visualizer (https://engagingdata.com/baby-name-visualizer) which draws data from the Social Security Administration's baby Names website (https://www.ssa.gov/OACT/babynames/background.html) shows Paris to have been a popular choice pre-dating the 1880 start of the database, perhaps more due to the name of the Trojan War hero Paris than the French city, although I will note that Memphis suddenly came into use as a baby name in 1990 and has had a meteoric rise since.
5. John McCallum, *Ty Cobb* (New York: Praeger Publishers, 1975).
6. Charles Alexander, *Ty Cobb* (New York: Oxford University Press, 1984), 9.
7. Richard Bak, *Ty Cobb, His Tumultuous Life and Times* (Dallas: Taylor Publishing Company, 1994), 5.
8. "More Trouble in Mudville," *Sports Illustrated*, May 28, 1973, https://vault.si.com/vault/1973/05/28/moretrouble-in-mudville, accessed August 31, 2023.
9. The Confederates lost fewer than 1,000.
10. David Power Cunningham, *Sherman's March Through the South* (Bedford: Applewood Books, 1898), 238. Originally published in 1865.
11. Al Stump, *Cobb, The Life and Times of the Meanest Man Who Ever Played Baseball* (Chapel Hill: Algonquin Books of Chapel Hill, 1994), 32.
12. The 1880 Census does list four individuals named Raymond Cobb, a six-year-old in Missouri, a one-year-old in Florida, a 30-year-old in Pennsylvania, and a two-year-old in New York. None of these were listed in the Census with the occupation of gambler.
13. Richard Bak, *Peach: Ty Cobb in His Time and Ours* (Ann Arbor: Ann Arbor Media Group, 2005), 14.
14. Charles Leerhsen, *Ty Cobb, A Terrible Beauty* (New York: Simon and Schuster, 2015), 24.
15. Tim Hornbaker, *War on the Basepaths, The Definitive Biography of Ty Cobb* (New York: Sports Publishing, 2015), 2.
16. https://www.imdb.com/title/tt12986326/fullcredits?ref_=tt_ov_st_sm, viewed July 2022.
17. Steven Elliott Tripp, *Ty Cobb, Baseball, and American Manhood* (Lanham: Rowman & Littlefield, 2016), 8.
18. Leonora Cobb Spencer, *Cobb Creek: An Account of the Cobb Family and Pioneer Days, with a Biographical Sketch of Tyrus Raymond Cobb* (Murphy: Southwest North Carolina Genealogical Society, 1982), 29. Leonora was Ty's Aunt Nora, sister to his father and the daughter of John Franklin Cobb. Based on dates referenced in the text, the text of *Cobb Creek* was written around 1920 and survived within the family and community until it was bound and printed in 1982 by the Southwest North Carolina Genealogical Society. Nora's quotes about John Franklin Cobb's Confederate service were likely from her recollections of stories she was told as a youngster.
19. Leonora Cobb Spencer, *Cobb Creek*, 29.
20. Leerhsen, 29.
21. As part of my investigation, I checked out an earlier Latin Bible to see what term it used for Tyre and Tyrus. Much to my surprise, there were even more variations of the name. A total of five variations were present in the 26th chapter of Ezekiel alone: Tyrus, Tyre, Tyro, Tyrum, and Tyri. I consulted a Latin expert who explained that the Latin language has cases, meaning that nouns take different forms depending on their role in a sentence. English also has cases, but to a much lesser degree, i.e., the *book* and the *book's* cover. Latin has six cases, and five of them appear in this chapter of Ezekiel. They include nominative case (Tyrus); vocative case, used when talking directly to someone (Tyre); genitive case, the same as the English possessive (Tyri); accusative case, showing the object of the sentence (Tyrum); and dative case, showing the indirect object (Tyro). I don't claim to understand all this well, but describe it here to further illustrate that the forms Tyrus, Tyre, and others in Latin all refer to the same thing: an ancient Phoenician coastal city, not to a person.
22. Ezekiel, Chapter 26, KJV
23. William Shakespeare, *Pericles, Prince of Tyre* (London: Henry Goffon, Publisher, 1609).
24. Fold3, a service of Ancestry.com, at https://go.fold3.com, accessed July 2022. Fold3 includes the military service records of the US, UK, Canada, Australia, and New Zealand.
25. US Baby Name Popularity Visualizer, Engaging Data, https://engaging-data.com/baby-name-visualizer/, July 2022
26. I examined several other online databases, such as Ancestry.com, but found that they provided so many conflicting and duplicate name listings that they were not useful to my study.
27. It cannot be said with certainty that Ty ever actually made this statement, since McCallum's 1956 biography was "unauthorized." It is doubtful that Ty would have given this quotation to McCallum for use in an unauthorized biography, though he might have made the statement in an earlier conversation when McCallum was a sportswriter for several northwestern newspapers in the early 1950s.
28. One wonders why Professor Cobb would have been so impressed by the *unsuccessful* defense of the city of Tyre against Alexander's seven-month siege, which resulted in its complete destruction. Does it not seem likely that Professor Cobb might be more impressed by the city of Tyre's *successful* defense in a 13-year siege by King Nebuchadnezzar II, which failed to capture the island fortress of Tyre, and after which the disheartened Babylonian king packed up and went home?
29. Private Communication from Phil Birnbaum, Chairman of the SABR Statistical Analysis Committee, email dated September 1, 2022.

Softball and Swastikas

The Riot at Toronto's Christie Pits

Stephen Dame

Toronto's worst incident of civil unrest happened in one of its most storied ballparks. More than six hours of brawls, bloodbaths, and beatings were unleashed at the corner of Bloor and Christie streets because of tensions built during 15 years of postwar animus. It was a race riot, it was a lawless free-for-all, it was a surge that menaced the innocent. It was also the oppressed launching a counterstrike against their oppressors during nine innings of junior softball. The riot at Christie Pits Park permanently scarred the city of Toronto and its perennial branding as tolerant, orderly and just.

FROM SANDPIT TO SANDLOT

Ball diamonds were a late addition to the landscape north of Toronto's downtown Bloor Street. Garrison Creek ran freely through what is today Christie Pits until the City of Toronto turned the creek into a storm sewer before the turn of the twentieth century. A natural sand mine was then established within the steep creek valley. The Christie Street sandpit was used to combat icy walkways and thoroughfares. The sand was also mined to repair eroded beachfronts, create abrasives, produce cement, and, of course, lay baseball infields. There was even a rush on city sandpits during an ill-advised fad of people eating sand to clean out their stomachs and toughen their skin.[1] To both the municipality and the "sand eaters," the desert in the Christie sandpit was preferable to the sands of Lake Ontario, which often included shells, refuse and avian waste. Colloquially and immediately, the city facility became known as Christie Pits, complete with its extraneous final "s."

In the winter of 1905, the City of Toronto was under pressure to create more civic spaces for families, specifically playgrounds. Mayor Thomas Urquhart told interested parties that converting sandpits was the most convenient and affordable option.[2] A year later, the city purchased and demolished the two houses bordering the edge of the Christie Street sandpit for a total of $3,020. A plan was announced to convert the pit and its immediate surroundings into a public park.[3]

The conversion from pit to playground took time and gruelling work. Piles of sand needed to be hauled out of the pit and dispersed along the city's beaches, using shovels and wagons. Grading work would then need to fill holes and flatten earth. A few months into the arduous tasks, James Swan was standing on low ground, shoveling sand into a pile above his head. The mound he'd created gave way, covering him in an avalanche of sand. He was pronounced dead after his comrades pulled him from the debris.[4]

After a year of hard labor, the area was ready to be graded in December 1907. The city allotted $1,000 so that "the unemployed" and a number of horses could level the pit floor.[5] The effort was divided into three-day contracts. Men could submit their name into a pool of workers, with 30 to 50 men chosen for each 72-hour work period. Demand was so high that hopefuls were routinely turned away. More than 225 names were added to the waiting list.[6] The city announced plans for three baseball diamonds, a swimming pool, a lawn tennis court and children's playgrounds on site.[7] Another year passed as men toiled in the Pits. By the end of 1908 the city removed the workhorse stables and prepared the park for public use. While grading work was still in progress, the city announced a new name and park designation. The *Daily Star* editorial board mocked the announcement as premature: "The Christie sandpits will now be called Willowvale Park," the editors wrote. "But that willowvale nothing towards making them fit for playgrounds."[8]

The name change never did stick. Before the grounds were even officially opened, a reader of the *Globe* submitted a condemnation. "Why change the name from what it has been for a generation?"[9] he asked. Three years after the official name change, it was accepted in Toronto that "what is now known as Willowvale Park is far and wide known to youngsters as the Christie sandpits."[10] Two decades later, locals in the Annex, Harbord and Christie Street neighborhoods of Toronto were still calling the park "Christie Pits."[11] In 1983, the City of Toronto finally abandoned the Willowvale moniker and rechristened Christie Pits officially.

The Pits baseball grounds were completed in May 1909. The Senior City Amateur League hosted the first reported game there on one of three diamonds ready for play. A team calling themselves the Ideals beat a group of ballplayers known as the Centennials by a score of 16–9. The Adair brothers, identified only by their initials, "S" and "B," served as the battery for the Ideals.[12] Teams bearing the monikers Kent, St. Andrew's, Harbord, and St. Peter's, named for various schools, streets, and churches, played baseball and softball in the Pits. After the completion of the first season of ballgames, two local aldermen led debate over the quality of the grounds. Alderman Dunn expressed regret that more had not been done to improve the quality of grass and infield dirt. He requested an additional $5,000 so that the diamonds could reach their potential. Alderman McBride was blunt in his reply: "It is just a sandpit and we can't spend that much." The City Council voted down Dunn's request for more funds.[13] McBride, however, was wrong. Christie Pits would prove to be much more than just a sandpit.

SOFTBALL IN THE PITS

In the era before television, entertainment often required a journey. Torontonians living between the city's two embracing rivers could travel by streetcar to theaters, arenas and newfangled movie houses. If the radio serial wasn't enough to keep them home, car owners could motor their way into the downtown core and attend any number of spectacles. Circuses, professional sporting events, and the last gasps of vaudeville were all enticing Toronto's ticket buying public. Baseball was one of the greatest forces pulling people out of their homes. Maple Leaf Stadium, home to Toronto's professional ballclub starting in 1926, was not the only baseball hotspot that routinely drew crowds in excess of 10,000.

People flocked to Christie Pits to see games. They would then, as they do now, sit on blankets or place chairs on the most welcoming parts of the grassy slope. The largest crowds turned up for senior men's amateur baseball games, especially during playoff season. With multiple games happening simultaneously in the Pits, members of the crowd could shift from one diamond to another if their original game ended or became laborious. Games featuring men, women, and children, both baseball and softball, gained spectators as the days and evenings wore on. Big crowds were reported, but exact counts were hard to come by in the ticketless and seatless Pits. "Over 10,000"[14] and "capacity attendance"[15] were oft-reported attendances for

various ballgames throughout the years. Charity softball matches, especially those featuring the National Hockey League Maple Leafs vs. the International League Maple Leaf baseball club, were highly attended events each year.[16]

By the end of the Roaring Twenties, at least 21 local softball organizations were recognized by the Toronto Amateur Softball Association.[17] The TASA existed to collect fees, rent and allot diamonds, and ensure the amateurism of its softballers. The Exhibition League hosted games in the southwest, the Beaches League operated out east, while the Olympic, Intercounty, Danforth, and Elginton leagues all carved out their own sanctioned territories.[18] The Playgrounds, Churches, and Western City leagues were the three TASA outfits operating in Christie Pits. The results of games and exploits of amateur softball players received consistent coverage in the *Toronto Daily Star*, a few column inches away from the professional baseball results. Even legendary sportswriter Lou Marsh, he of the formerly eponymous trophy awarded annually to Canada's best athlete, devoted attention to softball and its many players. Great intrigue was added to the softball coverage in the early 1930s as the TASA sought to eliminate "shamateurism"[19] and unaffiliated outlaw softball leagues[20] from the diamonds of Toronto.

A reader of the sports page could also, at a glance, see the social fissures simmering in Toronto during the spring of 1933. Mixed in among the box scores, listed alongside softball teams called the Native Sons, Businessmen, Aces, Oaks, Lakesides, and Zion Benevolent, was a team in the TASA St. Clair League that had named themselves the Swastikas.[21]

ANTISEMITISM IN TORONTO

Owing to Canada's deliberately Eurocentric immigration policies, the earliest Jewish immigrants to Toronto had been, for the most part, British subjects and merchants.[22] At the turn of the twentieth century, the Jewish population in all of Canada was estimated to be just 16,401.[23] That population remained small because the country's immigration policy had always been as ethnically selective as it was economically self-serving. It entailed an unofficial descending order of ethnic preference, with Jewish and Black people at the bottom.[24]

The great majority of Jewish immigrants headed to large cities, where they rapidly formed an urban proletariat and began to fill crowded, often poverty-stricken neighborhoods in Winnipeg, Montreal, and Toronto.[25] Toronto's most prominent Jewish neighborhood could be found one block south of Christie

Pits. The nearby Spadina Avenue garment industry employed many Jews who were excluded from other professions in the city.[26] Numerous garment workers resided in homes north of Front Street, south of Harbord Street and west of Spadina.[27] Harbord Collegiate Institute was the local high school. By 1919, there was a common belief among students that Jews and Italian Catholics were considered unwelcome in Christie Pits by the resident WASP majority.[28]

After the First World War, Toronto's population was not immune to the concoction of anti-Semitic conspiracy theories and stereotypes infecting the Western world. "No Jews Allowed" and "Gentiles Only" signs could be seen hanging in the windows of restaurants, shops, and country clubs across the city.[29] Ontario had practices in place known as Restrictive Covenants, which could prevent the sale of houses and property to anyone who was not Christian. The restrictions, struck down by the Supreme Court of Canada in 1948, were outlawed not because they were discriminatory, but because it was difficult to accurately assess the religion of potential buyers.[30] Jews in Toronto were not just excluded from general society by their religion. They were also widely deemed to be a threat to that society.[31]

A pamphlet called *The Protocols of the Elders of Zion*, debunked as Russian propaganda by 1921, was widely read and considered responsible for the rapid rise of antisemitism in Canada. Available first at retailers and libraries, it was further disseminated when Henry Ford distributed 500,000 free copies across Canada and the United States via affiliated service stations and his network of auto dealerships.[32] *The Protocols* presented itself as a record of meetings in which Jews from around the world plotted to subvert Christianity and gain world domination. By 1933, pro-Nazi pamphlets, some funded by the German party itself, were being distributed and read in Toronto. Both anti-Semitic and fascist groups formed in Ontario during that same year.[33] So extensive was Canadian antisemitism that the American chargé d'affaires remarked on "the rapidity of its spread." He informed his superiors in Washington that "Canadians had no desire to have Jews emigrate to their country" and that antisemitism was increasingly "finding expression in private conversations."[34] In 1930s Toronto, one did not need to be a devotee of fascism or Nazism to become suspect of Jews.[35] Antisemitism was a common and accepted facet of everyday life.

On January 30, 1933, Adolf Hitler was appointed chancellor of Germany. His National Socialist German Workers Party won a minority government in the March 5 election. The German political scene was chaotic. Hitler consolidated support by framing his nationalist movement as a bulwark against Jews and communists. His speeches and statements were loaded with antisemitic untruths.

Hitler's words and actions were closely followed by the daily papers in Canada. Within weeks of his selection, swastika clubs had formed and placed recruitment ads in Montreal and Toronto newspapers.[36] These clubs espoused the political beliefs of their German inspiration. They placed antisemitism at the fore and used the new Nazi flag as their symbol. In April, shortly after Hitler issued the first of his more than 400 anti-Jewish laws and decrees, Andre Laurendeau became the first political figure in Canada to formally endorse the Nazi vision. He wrote in a Montreal newspaper that Jews constituted a social danger in Canada. His message was syndicated across the country.[37] By the summer of 1933, Hitler and his policies were being widely discussed and debated on radio, in the newspapers, and on the streets of Toronto.[38]

The mere presence of Jews at areas of public recreation, including as softball spectators in the Pits, led to protests against Jewish use of public beaches and parks.[39] The Balmy Beach Swastika Club was formed with the avowed intention of keeping Toronto's largest beach free of "obnoxious visitors." In early August 1933, the club paraded along Woodbine Avenue, 200 strong, with Nazi flags and "Hail Hitler" banners—a common representation of the slogan at that time, substituting the English word "hail" for "heil." They said the symbol of the German Nazi party was for good luck, and would help their organization gain its objective. They sang as they marched: "Oh, give me a home, where the Gentiles may roam. Where the Jews are not rampant all day. Where seldom is heard, a lone Yiddish word. And the Gentiles are free all the day."[40]

There were a few public voices directly condemning the swastika clubs. Jewish alderman—and future mayor—Nathan Phillips was the most prominent. "The whole principle is all wrong," Phillips said. "I don't think it will gain any prominence in an enlightened city like Toronto. This sort of rot simply won't go."[41] Al Kaufmann, a Jewish resident from nearby Kew Gardens, formed an "up-town gang" to counter the swastikas. He and a number of Jewish youths marched the beach boardwalk looking for members of swastika clubs. "We couldn't find any" he said. "If there had been trouble, I think we could have taken care of ourselves."[42]

On August 2, 1933, the *Daily Star* ran a story with the headline "Feeling Tense." It reported that for some time, "a real attempt at organizing a fascist movement aimed against the Jews has been in progress."[43] Evil that had been just below the surface was now in the open. The swastika banner that had been so prominently displayed at Balmy Beach would soon be unfurled during a softball game at Christie Pits.

HARBORD AND ST. PETER'S 1933 SOFTBALL CLUBS

St. Peter's Church has stood at the corner of Bathurst and Bloor Streets in Toronto, six blocks east of Christie Pits, since 1907. It was expanded in 1925 to accommodate a growing number of Catholics in the area. The youth and young adult ministries at the church had been fielding softball teams in the TASA-affiliated Church League since games began in the Pits. By 1930, the St. Peter's club had developed a reputation as speedsters. Nicknamed the "Galloping Ghosts," they played a small ball brand of softball, winning games by virtue of their so-called snappy style.[44] The team, in the Junior Division of the Church League, was also playing well defensively in 1933. Managed by William Carroll, St. Peter's often allowed three or fewer runs[45] and occasionally won games in a romp, such as their 11–1[46] drubbing of Westmoreland to cap the regular season.

By mid-August, St. Peter's had successfully advanced through a series of playdown games. They were recognized by the TASA as champions of the Church League and scheduled to meet the winners of the Playgrounds League, with whom they shared the Pits.

The Playgrounds championship was decided during a best-of-three series played between teams representing Harbord Collegiate and North Toronto high schools. Harbord, coached by Bob Mackie, swept the series with a convincing 5–0 victory in Game Two.

Sammy Brookes, the Harbord pitcher, was described as "sensational" by the *Daily Star*.[47] Brookes had been involved in a game earlier that season when the free-hitting Harbord team smashed multiple home runs, including a grand slam, in a 24-run affair over a team from John Dunn Community Centre.[48] The Harbord lads represented a school that first opened in 1892. It was a large and imposing Jacobethan Revivalist structure three blocks south of Christie Pits. Nearly 90% of its student population was Jewish.[49]

The Playgrounds and Church divisions of the TASA had produced their playoff teams for 1933. The city-wide quarterfinal series was set to begin in Christie Pits on Monday evening, August 14. It would be a best-of-three showdown between the hard-hitting Jewish boys from Harbord and the speedy, small-ball Catholics of St. Peter's. The religious affiliations of each team would overshadow their ballplaying abilities during the series. Five days before their first game, an omen appeared just beyond the left-field line.

A newly formed Willowvale Swastika Club paraded the Nazi banner down Bloor Street on Wednesday, August 9. Five Jewish men, residents of nearby Euclid Avenue, attacked the marchers, who retreated into the Pits. Sydney Adams, father of one of the Swastikas, dismissed the whole affair as "foolish nonsense and a lot of tomfoolery."[50]

HARBORD VS. ST. PETER'S: THE RIOT AT CHRISTIE PITS

On August 14, over 11,000 people attached themselves to the steep sides of Christie Pits. Most of the crowd, described as one of the largest in the history of the park, came to see the Western City Baseball championship between the Vermonts and Native Sons.[51] Several thousand spectators eventually crossed the pit

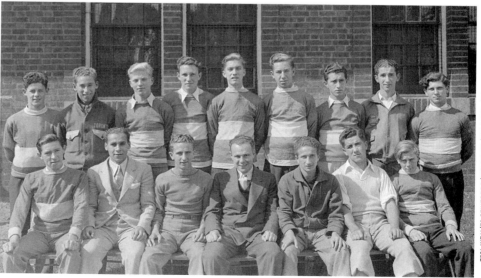

The 1933 Playgrounds champions came from the Harbord school, three blocks south of Christie Pits. Built in 1892, the school's student population was 90% Jewish.

to see the first game of the Harbord and St. Peter's softball playoff.[52] By this time, Harbord supporters had become aware of something more sinister in large crowds such as these. "Every time you went to watch a ballgame," a Harbord fan later said, "these guys with swastikas would yell 'Hail Hitler' and all this."[53]

The *Toronto Telegram* reported that a five-foot-long swastika banner, sewn in white cloth on a black sweater coat, was repeatedly unfurled by some St. Peter's supporters whenever Harbord players came to bat. This continued throughout the game, "amid much wisecracking, cheering and yelling of pointed remarks."[54] The Harbord players managed to keep their cool, maintain their focus, and play well enough to tie the game in the bottom of the ninth inning. The top of the 10th saw no scoring, giving Harbord a chance to end it. Sensing their opportunity, the St. Peter's supporters began flaunting their swastika banner. Shouts and epithets were hurled across the diamond as supporters of both teams found themselves on the verge of violence.

With a runner on second and animosities dangerously escalating, a Jewish boy came to the plate for Harbord. He looked not at the pitcher, but at the symbol of Nazi hatred being held aloft by his own countrymen. When the ball was nearly over the plate, he gripped his bat and swung it—not at the ball, but at them. He connected, hammering a double and winning the game for Harbord in dramatic fashion.[55]

Supporters of both teams filled the field as the players themselves retreated from the scene. Spectators, sure that a fight would follow, were surprised to see the two sides screaming at each other as they were pulled in separate directions.[56] A young Jewish spectator told the *Daily Star*, "There will be trouble when the teams play here again on Wednesday evening."[57]

Hours after Game One, during the early morning of August 15, members of the Willowvale Swastikas returned to the park with ladders, brushes, and white paint. On the roof of the communal clubhouse, in the center of Christie Pits, they painted a huge swastika above the words "Hail Hitler." One of the painters was later found by a *Daily Star* reporter. Although he would not give his name, he admitted to the graffiti job and said, "We want to get the Jews out of the park."[58] William Carroll of St. Peter's was eager to separate the actions of his supporters from those of his players. He stated that hoodlums beyond his control had started a sideshow. He then went on to defend those hoodlums: "Why should St. Peter's supporters get the blame for it any more than the supporters of the Harbord team, or in fact, any other team in the park?"[59]

Game Two was scheduled for Wednesday, August 16. Two of Toronto's daily newspapers printed warnings. The *Mail and Empire* quoted "Jewish boys" who said, "Just wait until the same teams meet again!"[60] The *Daily Star* concluded its coverage of the painting incident by quoting a Harbord fan: "We won't go to the next game to make trouble, but if anything happens, we will be there to support our players."[61] Another anonymous source told the paper that opposition to the swastikas would be more fearsome on Wednesday night.[62]

James Brinsmead, a municipal civil servant, visited the Ossington Avenue police station on Wednesday morning and informed constables there of the potential for violence. The police would eventually dispatch only a single officer to each of the two ballgames in the Pits that evening.[63] Toronto's chief of police, Dennis Draper, did not believe the second game of a softball series constituted a serious threat.[64]

It did not take long for a threat to materialize. Another "crowd of 10,000 citizens"[65] was reported in Christie Pits. The western baseball final continued on the northeast diamond and the second Harbord vs. St. Peter's game took place on the northwest softball field. Before the opening pitch of the softball game could be thrown, an altercation occurred between a member of the Swastikas and a Jewish spectator. The Swastika was hit in the head with a club while the spectator was thrown downhill into the cyclone fence of the backstop. Both men required medical attention.[66]

The first major incident of violence took place during the second inning. A group of Willowvale Swastikas approached an area of Christie Pits that was lined with 1,000 Jewish Harbord supporters. The Swastikas began to yell, "Hail Hitler" in unison. Incensed, a group of the Harbord supporters lunged at the chanters and told them to "shut up!" When the Swastikas persisted, a sawed-off lead pipe appeared and various members of the hate group were struck with it.[67]

A brawl ensued, with batons, more pipes, and other concealed weapons. Blood flowed freely as the fighters moved up the north hill towards Pendrith Avenue.[68] They eventually brawled away from the Pits and found themselves fighting in nearby backyards. The softball game, which had paused to watch the fracas, resumed. The single police officer assigned to the neighboring baseball game ran across to support his softball associate. Order was temporarily restored.[69]

With the game tied after three innings, more cries of "Hail Hitler" rang out. Four Jewish youths drew sawed-off lead pipes and headed for two men they believed to be leading the Nazi sympathizers. Supporters rushed to the assistance of both groups of fighters.[70] Three additional police officers, having arrived by motorcycle, joined the original patrol duo and helped defuse the skirmish.[71] The atmosphere remained tense, but without incident, as St. Peter's took a late lead. Harbord prepared for its final turn at bat in the ninth, down by a single run. It was not yet dusk as St. Peter's secured a 6–5 victory by catching a deep fly ball from the last Harbord batter.[72]

As the crowd of thousands milled about after the game, two young men unfurled a large white blanket bearing a black swastika. In the words of the *Daily Star*, "a mild form of pandemonium broke loose," and, as the *Telegram* put it, "The sign stood out like a red flag to a bull."[73] The antagonists bearing the flag were rushed by Jewish youths. One of the flag bearers was knocked out cold and another scurried away. The swastika flag itself was captured and torn in a pique of vengeful satisfaction by Walton Street resident Murray Krugle. What followed next was described as a "general inrush"[74] of male youth who began to fight with fists, then with boots, and eventually with bottles, pipes, broomsticks, and baseball bats. The "Bloor Street War"[75] was underway. The first bike pedalling recruiters feverishly cycled to adjacent neighborhoods pleading for reinforcements.

As word of the fighting spread, Jewish backup arrived by car and pickup truck from areas southeast of the Pits near Spadina Avenue. Next, carloads of Italian Catholics arrived from directly south of the Pits on College Street. The handful of police on site attempted to intercept the rolling cavalries, but they were quickly and badly outnumbered. Vehicles carried not only fighters but their weapons as well. A seven-foot-long piece of lumber with a spike driven through it was later found in an abandoned truck near the war zone.[76]

Brawling continued unabated for an hour before mounted and motorcycle police arrived. Their authority and presence did not immediately dissipate the rumble. The fighting merely tapered for another 90 minutes. Just before 10 PM, the battle poured out of Christie Pits and onto Bloor Street as thousands of brawlers blocked the roadway. Streetcar bells and automobile horns added to the cacophony.[77] Shortly after 10:30 PM, the assembled police force was finally large enough to end the assaults.

The peace did not last. During the initial fighting, Joe Goldstein, a Jewish teenager, was chased across the Pits and knocked unconscious. He was carried first to the nearby home of his sister-in-law, and then by police escort to hospital. Goldstein was badly injured, but his wounds were not life threatening. Rumors began to spread around Jewish neighborhoods that Goldstein had died. Organization only took a few minutes, and soon, truckloads of shouting Jewish youths, armed with anything they could lay their hands on, were speeding back toward the softball grounds.[78]

Several of these trucks, each jammed with about 25 young men, were met by a column of police on horseback. The trucks broke through and soon found a large group of swastika-wearing enemies. The two groups attacked each other with black jacks, broom handles, stones, and steel and lead pipes.[79] Hundreds

The only known photo from the Christie Pits riots.

of fighters who had already exhausted themselves and their original quarrels jumped right back into this new fray. The police were helpless. An eight-block section of Toronto—including one of its largest parks and downtown's main northwestern thoroughfare—was lawless and out of control.

Both sides were accused of reckless irresponsibility during the riot. One eyewitness said he was horrified to see "a gentleman, passed middle age, who was taking no part in the violence, struck on the head with a baseball bat." Joe Brown, a young witness to the fight, said he was walking home from the Pits when five youths jumped out of a passing car and assaulted him with clubs. A 21-year-old named Solly Osolky rushed in to help a fallen youngster on Bloor Street and was attacked for his efforts. "They belaboured me with their clubs," he added. David Fischer had been a spectator at the ballgame. "I was preparing to go home," he said. "Some fellow then hit me over the head and started to shout Hail Hitler."[80]

Fighting continued in and around Christie Pits after 11:30 PM. Injuries, fatigue, and a growing police presence began to divide the uprising into smaller and smaller battles. A crowd of rioters again blocked Bloor Street, causing the police to devise a new tactic. The motorcycle brigade would charge toward groups of fighters. When they were close enough to be effective, the officers would turn their exhaust pipes towards the combatants, spreading heavy, choking fumes throughout the crowd. By midnight, there were fewer than 200 people within 100 yards of the park. Occasional fistfights persisted. The police patrolled Christie Pits and the streets around the ball diamonds until the riot was officially declared over at 1:30 AM, six hours after it started[81].

Somewhat miraculously, no fatalities occurred during the riot at Christie Pits. Osolky, Brown, Fischer, Goldstein, and two men named Al Eckler and Louis Kotick were reported to have been the worst of the injured. They all suffered cuts, abrasions, and trauma about the head and neck. A few had broken bones. Most were released from hospital within a day. Undoubtedly, countless other street fighters kept their injuries to themselves.

Only two arrests were made during the riot. Russel Harris of Bloor Street was held on a charge of vagrancy, later dismissed. He'd been caught with a fishing knife. Magistrate Browne advised Harris to leave his knife at home unless he was scaling fish. Jack Roxborough was held on a charge of carrying offensive weapons. He'd been seen wielding a metal club above his head. He was given the option of paying a $50 fine or serving two months in jail.[82] His decision has been lost to history.

Following the riot, Jack Turner, secretary of the TASA, announced that no more league games would be played in Christie Pits until the present trouble had been cleared up. The managers for both the Harbord and St. Peter's teams denied responsibility for the riot and stated that none of their players had participated in the disturbance.[83] Both teams would need to continue the series with new bats, owing to their equipment having been stolen and weaponized by the mob.

The TASA scheduled the third and final game in the series for Wednesday, August 23, at Conboy Soccer Stadium, an enclosed field with grandstand at the corner of Ossington and Dupont, about 12 blocks northwest of Christie Pits. The organization also announced that the game would be a ticketed affair. The TASA thought the cost of admission, and the park being a privately owned enclosure, would keep away the undesirables.[84] A squad of police from the Ossington Avenue division surrounded the stadium and kept a strict watch on all points of entry. Police also forced a number of onlookers on a nearby rail bridge to vacate their unsanctioned seats. A few hundred others were said to have watched the game from nearby factory rooftops and household windows.[85]

Only 71 loyal spectators paid to see the rubber match at Conboy Stadium. It was described as one the finest exhibitions of softball ever witnessed in Toronto. The game went into the bottom of the 11th inning when "Red" Burke hit a walk-off home run to give the series to St. Peter's by a score of 4–3.[86] After losing a heartbreaking game, the Harbord team, "like true sportsmen, shook hands with the winners and wished them good luck in their future games."[87] St. Peter's would go on to lose to a team known as the Millionaires, who were in turn bested by a team sponsored by the Cities Service oil and gas company (today known as Citgo). The Cities Service team claimed its trophy as Junior Softball Champions of Toronto during a ceremony held at the Royal York hotel on October 19, 1933.[88]

THE AFTERMATH

After the riot, the swastika symbol was cast in even darker shadow throughout Toronto. The Balmy Beach Swastika Club knew enough to abandon the symbol and change its name within 24 hours of the riot. At an emergency meeting, members were conciliatory, voting to allow Jews and gentiles to serve together on a new committee devoted to cleaning and protecting the beach.[89] Other swastika clubs persisted but declined in favor and fidelity as the decade wore on. By 1936, Toronto's newspapers were free of their mention.

Toronto Mayor William Stewart met the media a few hours after police had regained control of Christie Pits. He warned all citizens that people displaying the swastika would be liable to prosecution. "The repeated and systematic disturbances in which the swastika emblem figures provocatively, must be investigated and dealt with firmly," said the mayor. "The responsibility is now on the citizens to conduct themselves in a lawful manner."[90]

Toronto Police made three more arrests related to the riot the following Friday. 17-year-old Jack Pippy, 18-year-old Charles Boustead, and 21-year-old Earl Perrin were charged with unlawful assembly. In the Crawford Street garage owned by Pippy's parents, police found the white paint and paraphernalia used to smear the swastika on the Pits clubhouse.[91]

When senior baseball returned to Christie Pits two days after the riot, the police presence was noticeable inside the park. About 100 teenagers mingled in the vicinity of the Pits, many of whom were said to have weapons and pieces of pipe concealed inside their coats.[92] Though police said the boys were looking for trouble, they found none as "calm prevailed in the swastika war zone."[93] Police claimed that most of the youth had been drawn to the park out of curiosity. Both Harbord and St. Peter's continued to field teams in the Christie Pits softball league for decades to come. There were no further overt incidents of antisemitism involving the two teams.

On September 10, 1939, six years and 25 days after the riot, Canada declared war on Nazi Germany and its swastika flag. By 1945, more than 10% of Canada's population had joined the army. Over 1.1 million Canadians suited up and shipped out. Toronto supplied 2,000 recruits within 48 hours of the declaration of war and over 70,000 more as the conflict endured.[94] Given the high number and youthful demographic of the rioters in Christie Pits, it would be reasonable to assume that many answered the call of king and country. The economic realities of the area around the riot zone make it even more likely. More than 60 men who died fighting for Canada during the Second World War lived in the immediate vicinity of Christie Pits.[95]

In 2008, the city installed a permanent plaque near the Bloor Street entrance to Christie Pits. It reads in part, "On August 16, 1933, at the end of a playoff game for the Toronto junior softball championship, one of the city's most violent ethnic clashes broke out in this park."[96] Joe Goldstein, the boy whose rumoured death reignited the riot, now 88 years old, was present for the plaque unveiling.[97] Another living Jewish witness to the riot, who wished to remain anonymous, remembered that August night quite clearly.

"When we got to the Pits, it seemed to me that half of the Jews and half of the goyim of the city were there," he recalled. "There were a lot of heads broken. There was a tremendous confrontation, and I would definitely say that we won. We were proud. I think for a week we were higher than a kite."[98] ∎

Notes

1. "Sand Eaters Are in Toronto," *Toronto Daily Star*, June 5, 1906, 1.
2. "A Check on the Proposed Civic Park in Sand Pits," *Toronto Daily Star*, December 8, 1905, 6.
3. "City Buys Sandpits," *Toronto Daily Star*, November 13, 1906, 1.
4. "Met Death Under Cave-In of Sand," *Toronto Daily Star*, July 18, 1907, 8.
5. "For the Unemployed," *Toronto Daily Star*, December 10, 1907, 9.
6. "Three Days Work for Only 225 Men," *Toronto Daily Star*, December 11, 1907, 1.
7. "City Hall Comment," *Toronto Daily Star*, June 27, 1908, 9.
8. "Little of Everything," *Toronto Daily Star*, October 3, 1908, 2.
9. "A Name Suggested for the Playground at Christie Street," *Globe* (Toronto), July 4, 1908, 9.
10. "Garrison Creek Will Be No More," *Globe*, April 7, 1911, 9.
11. Ted Staunton and Josh Rosen, *The Good Fight*, (Toronto: Scholastic Canada Ltd., 2021), 7.
12. "Amateur Baseball," *Toronto Daily Star*, May 10, 1909, 9.
13. "In Willowvale Park," *Toronto Daily Star*, April 22, 1910, 2.
14. "Native Sons Double Score on Pat Downing's Vermonts," *Globe*, August 15, 1933, 11.
15. "Benefit Game," *Toronto Daily Star*, July 12, 1930, 11.
16. "Scribes to Convort Down at Sunnyside," *Toronto Daily Star*, June 7, 1933, 11.
17. "Softball Scores," *Toronto Daily Star*, July 10, 1930, 11.
18. "Softball Results," *Toronto Daily Star*, July 12, 1930, 11.
19. "Shamateurism," *Toronto Daily Star*, July 5, 1933, 16.
20. "Three Men Re-Enter Organized Softball," *Toronto Daily Star*, April 26, 1933, 9.
21. "Softball Scores," *Toronto Daily Star*, May 23, 1933, 10.
22. "Softball Scores," May 23, 1933, 26
23. Ira Robinson, *A History of Antisemitism in Canada* (Waterloo: Wilfrid Laurier University Press, 2015), 36.
24. Irving Abella, Harold Troper, *None Is Too Many: Canada and the Jews of Europe 1933–1948* (Toronto: University of Toronto Press, 1983), 5.
25. Robinson, 37.
26. "Antisemitism," Ontario Jewish Archives. accessed March 8, 2023, https://www.ontariojewisharchives.org/Explore/Themed-Topics/Antisemitism.
27. Jamie Michaels, Doug Fedrau, *Christie Pits*, (Toronto: Dirty Water, 2019), 102.
28. Staunton, Rosen, 7.
29. "Antisemitism."
30. "Antisemitism."
31. Robinson, 64.
32. Robinson, 64.
33. Robinson, 94.
34. Abella, Troper, 51.
35. Robinson, 94.
36. Michaels, Fedrau, 62.
37. Robinson, 90.
38. Michaels, Fedrau, 34.
39. Robinson, 66.

40. "Swastika Emblems Vanish from Beach," *Toronto Daily Star*, August 2, 1933, 11.
41. "Hint Beach Ban Part of Vast Propaganda," *Toronto Daily Star*, August 2, 1933, 12.
42. "Swastika Emblems Vanish," 11.
43. "Feeling Tense," *Toronto Daily Star*, August 2, 1933, 12.
44. "St. Peter's at Greenwood," *Toronto Daily Star*, July 17, 1930, 11.
45. "Softball Scores," *Toronto Daily Star*, June 23, 1933, 11.
46. "Softball Scores," *Toronto Daily Star*, August 3, 1933, 11.
47. "Two Softball Titles Won in Playgrounds," *Toronto Daily Star*, August 3, 1933, 13.
48. "Harbord Wins," *Toronto Daily Star*, June 7, 1933, 12.
49. Marcus Gee, "Harbord Collegiate Celebrates 125 Years as Toronto's Famous Immigrant Launching Pad," *Globe and Mail* (Toronto), April 7, 2017, https://www.theglobeandmail.com/news/toronto/harbord-collegiate-celebrates-125-years-as-torontos-famous-immigrantlaunching-pad/article34637778/.
50. Cyril Levitt, William Shaffir, *The Riot At Christie Pits* (Toronto: New Jewish Press, 2018), 118.
51. "Swastika Painted on Roof of Club," *Toronto Daily Star*, August 15, 1933, 27.
52. "Native Sons Double Score," 11.
53. Levitt, Shaffir, 117.
54. Levitt, Shaffir, 117.
55. "Trouble Narrowly Averted at Ballgame as Hitler Emblem Hoisted," *The Mail and Empire* (Toronto), August 15. 1933, 1.
56. Levitt, Shaffir, 118.
57. "Swastika Painted on Roof of Club," 27.
58. "Swastika Painted on Roof of Club," 27.
59. Levitt, Shaffir, 119.
60. "Police Warned of Ball Riot," *Toronto Daily Star*, August 17, 1933, 1.
61. Levitt, Shaffir, 119.
62. "Police Warned," 1.
63. "Police Warned," 1.
64. "Draper Admits Receiving Riot Warning," *Toronto Daily Star*, August 17, 1933, 1.
65. "Six Hours of Rioting Follows Hitler Shout, Scores Hurt, Two Held," *Toronto Daily Star*, August 17, 1933, 1.
66. Levitt, Shaffir, 119.
67. Levitt, Shaffir, 120.
68. "Six Hours of Rioting, Scores Are Injured," *Toronto Daily Star*, August 17, 1933, 3.
69. "Six Hours of Rioting, Scores Are Injured," 3.
70. Levitt, Shaffir, 121.
71. "Six Hours of Rioting, Scores Are Injured," 3.
72. Levitt, Shaffir, 121.
73. Levitt, Shaffir, 121.
74. "Swastika Feud Battles in Toronto Injure 4," *Globe*, August 17, 1933, 1.
75. "Swastika Feud Battles in Toronto Injure 4," 1.
76. "Hail Hitler Is Youths' Cry," *Globe*, August 17, 1933, 2.
77. "Six Hours of Rioting, Scores Are Injured," 3.
78. Levitt, Shaffir, 124.
79. "Six Hours of Rioting, Scores Are Injured," 3.
80. "Six Hours of Rioting, Scores Are Injured," 3.
81. Levitt, Shaffir, 127.
82. "Draper Admits Receiving Riot Warning," 1.
83. Levitt, Shaffir, 133.
84. "On Again," *Toronto Daily Star*, August 22, 1933, 10.
85. "Flare Up Possibility Draws Curious Crowd," *Globe*, August 24, 1933, 10.
86. "Only 71 Spectators See Pete's Triumph," *Toronto Daily Star*, August 24, 1933, 16.
87. "Flare Up Possibility Draws Curious Crowd," 10.
88. "Softball Champions Honoured at Banquet," *Globe*, October 20, 1933, 8.
89. "New Organization Will Take Place of Swastika Club," *Globe*, August 18, 1933, 9.
90. Levitt, Shaffir, 129.
91. "Police Question Other Members of Alleged Gang," *Globe*, August 19, 1933, 1.
92. "Calm Prevails Again in Swastika War Zone," *Globe*, August 18, 1933, 1.
93. "Thousands in Park Wait Watchfully," *Globe*, August 18, 1933, 2.
94. Ian Miller, "Toronto's Response to the Outbreak of War, 1939," *Canadian Military History, Vol 11*, 2002, 10.
95. Patrick Chan, "Grief's Geography," *Global News*, November 4, 2013, https://globalnews.ca/news/932833/griefs-geography-mapping-torontonians-killed-three-wars/.
96. "Riot at Christie Pits," Local Wiki, accessed on March 24, 2023, https://localwiki.org/toronto/Christie_Pits_Riot/_files/riot-at-christie-pits-heritage-toronto-2008-plaque.jpg/_info/.
97. "Riot at Christie Pits."
98. Levitt, Shaffir, 129.

Alex Johnson and Tony Conigliaro

The California Angels' Star-Crossed Teammates

Paul Hensler

When the American League expanded for a second time in 1969 and split into a pair of divisions, the California Angels could be excused for still thinking of themselves as an expansion team, since they had come into existence only eight years earlier. Over the course of this brief lifespan, the Angels had compiled a desultory track record, forging a won-lost record of 614–679 (with one tie), a winning average of .475.

Trying to establish themselves in Southern California while the specter of the Los Angeles Dodgers loomed large, the Angels had moved to new quarters in Anaheim in 1966. But when the Angels dropped to 67–95 in 1968, their poorest record to date, and began the divisional era by going 11–28, Bill Rigney was relieved of his duties as skipper. New manager Lefty Phillips tried to right the listing ship, winning 60 while losing 63 (with another tie) and bringing the Angels in at third place in the AL West, but 26 games behind the division champion Minnesota Twins. California had much work to do to become a contender.

Lackluster Angels production in 1968—the team outscored only the Chicago White Sox and came in seventh or eighth (out of 10 teams) in several other offensive categories—was eclipsed by even worse numbers in 1969: The Angels finished last (now out of 12) in runs scored, hits, doubles, home runs, walks, batting average, slugging percentage, on-base percentage, and on base-plus-slugging. Expansion-year pitching had delivered no advantage to California batters.

Over the next two seasons, general manager Dick Walsh used the trade market to try to fortify the weak Angels offense, and in the course of doing so brought together two compelling figures who, by their most recent performances, should have brought a new degree of potency to the Angels lineup. This essay will show how those players, Alex Johnson and Tony Conigliaro, in their individual ways, failed to build on the stepping stone of an ostensibly successful 1970 campaign.

TRYING TO IMPROVE: STEP 1

In late November 1969, Walsh acquired Johnson and utility infielder Chico Ruiz, a close friend of Johnson's, from the Cincinnati Reds in exchange for three pitchers. Johnson's early career showed glimpses of promise: Breaking in with the Philadelphia Phillies in 1964, he put up a .303/.345/.495 slash line in 43 games, for an OPS+ of 135. The following season he hit .293/.337/.443 over 97 games, an OPS+ of 120. But he had a track record as a poor defensive player, having committed 30 errors in 321 games in the minors. Johnson confessed to being jittery when in the outfield, and although his work with the glove got better, his *"perceived* lack of effort and poor attitude" grated on Phils manager Gene Mauch, and in late October 1965 the outfielder was packaged in a trade to the St. Louis Cardinals.[1]

Johnson did little to distinguish himself in his early tenure with his new team, batting only .186 before being sent to Triple-A Tulsa in mid-May 1966. The following season, in which St. Louis ultimately captured the World Series, the right-handed Johnson was platooned in right field with newly acquired Roger Maris, but Johnson again faltered while playing in only half of the regular-season games and accumulating just 39 hits in 175 at-bats for a .223 average, one home run and an anemic 68 OPS+.

As his malcontent behavior became more of a detriment to the team, the 25-year-old once more was on the trading block. "We tried everything to bring out his potential," said an exasperated Dick Sisler, the Cardinals hitting coach.[2] This time he was dispatched to the Cincinnati Reds.

Upon his 1968 arrival at Crosley Field, Johnson transformed from bust to boom, with Reds manager Dave Bristol seeming to be the reason for the turnaround. Rather than nagging his temperamental player about his comportment, Bristol was content to leave Johnson to his own devices. Johnson became the everyday left fielder, appearing in 149 games and contributing a .312/.342/.395 line (116 OPS+), with little power but 16 stolen bases, earning him Comeback

Player of the Year honors from *The Sporting News*, although Breakout Player of the Year would have been a more appropriate label.

As if to prove his rightful place as a prime-time player, Johnson improved in every meaningful offensive category in 1969, including 17 home runs, more than twice his previous career high. But just as the Reds were about to emerge as the Big Red Machine under new manager Sparky Anderson in 1970, their outfield became crowded with prospects Hal McRae and Bernie Carbo, who could platoon in left field. That made Johnson expendable. The Angels anticipated his production would continue to trend upward.

Phillips's first full year at California's helm was infused with a modicum of hope: The Angels had equaled their young franchise record of 86 victories in 1970 and resided in second place for most of the season before settling into third on Labor Day. By remaining within hailing distance of the Twins, who would repeat as division winners, California could lay claim to status as contenders in the AL West. However, this joy and optimism were tempered by the baggage that accompanied the acquisition of Alex Johnson.

While the Angels were pleased with the statistics generated by their new left fielder in 1970—named to the American League All-Star team, Johnson had his best offensive season and won the league batting title (by a whisker over Carl Yastrzemski) with a .329 average—his brooding and moodiness never deserted him. The enigmatic player was fined for lack of hustle, and while he led the Angels by grounding into 25 double plays, some of these may have been the result of his batting in the heart of the order. (Recall that Jim Rice of the Boston Red Sox led both leagues in GIDPs for four straight years in the 1980s.) He yelled at teammates and reporters who attempted to engage him in conversation. "There is venom in his bat and on his tongue," noted *The Sporting News* of Johnson's hitting ability and demeanor. His actions became an increasingly serious distraction.[3]

For his part, Phillips was held in high regard for somehow weathering the storm swirling around Johnson. The manager was credited with working psychological wonders in stroking the egos of several of his players who needed coddling, and although Phillips was quick to deflect the praise directed his way, the results, in the AL West standings and in Johnson's performance at the plate, more than hinted at Phillips's ability to hold up in a difficult situation. By writing Johnson's name in the cleanup slot and leaving him in the game rather than replacing him with a late-inning defensive outfielder, Phillips gave

Alex Johnson had "venom in his bat and on his tongue."

Johnson much latitude in the hope of letting the ends of his production justify the means.

But as the summer of 1970 progressed, Johnson was trying the patience of too many of his teammates and, ultimately, his manager. Club officials worried over the negative impact that Johnson might have on younger players who would be better served by a more appropriate role model. According to *The Sporting News*, "His recent taunting of an Angel pitcher nearly precipitated a clubhouse free-for-all," and "acknowledging his malevolent disposition, his wife, Julia, has apologized to the other Angel wives for the way her husband treats their husbands."[4]

By season's close, it seemed a miracle that California forged the win total it had reached. In the final weeks of September, Johnson and Ruiz "exchanged words and punches in a brief skirmish at the batting cage.... This outburst followed a reported melee of the previous night that left the clubhouse in disarray."[5] Through all this turbulence, Johnson was documenting his plight so that he could take his own complaints to the Major League Baseball Players Association, whose director, Marvin Miller, later observed, "Two things became quite clear. Many of Johnson's grievances were legitimate, and he had serious emotional problems."[6]

Turning the corner of the disruptive campaign, the Angels, on paper at least, possessed the means to build on their success. Yet the stat sheet failed to account for all the characteristics of what underpinned the roster and contributed to—or detracted from—the chemistry among the players and their relationship with the manager. And with the book barely closed on the 1970 season, Dick Walsh was already at work to add more power to the lineup, sending three players to the Red Sox for catcher Jerry Moses, pitcher Ray Jarvis, and outfielder Tony Conigliaro.

TRYING TO IMPROVE: STEP 2

"Tony C," as Conigliaro was affectionately known to hometown fans, was the embodiment of a local kid made good. A native of Revere, Massachusetts, he burst onto the scene in 1964 as a 19-year-old who slugged 24 home runs and then led the American League in that category the next year with 32. With handsome looks to boot, Conigliaro also was a budding pop singer, with several recordings on the RCA label to his credit by early 1965. He had the world as his oyster even though he was playing for a team that was less than mediocre, the BoSox finishing ninth in the American League in 1966. As his power numbers continued to draw attention, he became the second-youngest player to belt 100 career homers, achieving the mark in July 1967, but as a batter who crowded the plate, he missed playing time due to HBP-related injuries that included broken bones in his left arm and wrist.

When Boston made an unexpected challenge for the AL pennant in 1967, Conigliaro was prominent in the lineup, batting cleanup for rookie manager Dick Williams's "Impossible Dream" team and earning a berth on the AL All-Star squad. But the outfielder would not be on hand to relish the pennant that the Red Sox eventually captured: He was beaned on the evening of August 18 in a game against the Angels at Fenway Park. Hit in his left eye by a Jack Hamilton pitch and suffering a broken cheekbone, Conigliaro was relegated to the sidelines with the fear that he might lose sight in the eye, and his rehabilitation would cost him the entire 1968 season.

Diligence and persistence paid off for Conigliaro in 1969, when he earned AL Comeback Player of the Year honors. In 141 games, he tallied a modest .255 batting average but showed that his ability to hit the long ball remained in his arsenal, stroking 21 doubles and 20 home runs while driving in 82 runs, though his triple slash line of .255/.321/.427 and his OPS+ of 103 were all a big step down from his peak years in Boston. An even brighter season in 1970—"with one good eye," according to Conigliaro's biographer, he batted .266 in 146 games, with 36 home runs and 116 RBIs—seemed to lay to rest any doubts about his hitting ability, if not his recovery.[7]

But fourth- and third-place finishes in 1968-69 cost Williams his job, and the manager was rankled by strife in the clubhouse and by Conigliaro's tendency to enjoy the nightlife. Friction between management and a few notable mainstays, among them Reggie Smith and George Scott, eventually led to the trades of several players, but Tony C's circumstances were peculiar in their own way. Shortstop Rico Petrocelli said that Conigliaro "wanted to be treated like a superstar. It was his hometown…. He felt he should have been the guy, the man."[8]

An internecine imbroglio between Smith, Red Sox newcomer Billy Conigliaro—Tony's younger brother—and Yastrzemski, was the source of much angst. As the Sox elder statesman at the age of 30, Yaz incurred the wrath of Boston fans when the team foundered early in the 1970 season, and the former Triple Crown winner was accused of cultivating too personal a relationship with Boston owner Tom Yawkey.[9]

In the wake of the 1970 season, the Red Sox sought to address shortcomings with their pitching staff and pulled off several trades that allowed them to deal away some of their surplus offensive power. One of the prime subjects sent packing was Tony Conigliaro. His trade to the Angels provoked a firestorm of protest from Boston fans. "It was, however, a trade that took advantage of Conigliaro's post-beaning value at the time it had peaked," in the view of one baseball historian. Another opinion had it that Yastrzemski was a driving force behind getting his fellow outfielder off the Boston roster.[10]

Still cautiously optimistic about furthering what they had accomplished in 1970, the Angels were hoping that Conigliaro's bat would bolster their offense—if, that is, he could overcome the shock of being let go by his now former team. There may have been some reactionary enthusiasm on the part of the Angels in response to the crosstown Dodgers' acquisition of Dick Allen, who arrived via trade on October 5, 1970, from the St. Louis Cardinals. Six days later, the Angels countered with an exchange that gave them their own high-profile slugger.

Tony Conigliaro would win the Comeback Player of the Year award, but never truly regain the potential he'd shown prior to the severe injury of the beaning.

Conigliaro's new club exuded such confidence in him that his visage appeared on the cover of the Angels' 1971 media guide along with the team's three other headliners from the previous season: Clyde Wright, Jim Fregosi, and Alex Johnson. Even his mellifluous nickname, "Tony C," graced the back of his road uniform instead of the traditional last name reserved for that spot. In its preview of the coming season, The Sporting News touted the outfield of Johnson, Conigliaro, and newly added Ken Berry as "the best in [the] club's history."[11] So, what was *not* to like about the team's prospects in the new year?

For one thing, the Angels finished spring training with an uninspiring 10–15 record, and Johnson had already been fined and pulled in the first inning of one contest for failing to run out a groundball. He was giving no indication of any change to his work ethic or improvement in his play in the outfield.

As Johnson perpetuated his annoyances, Conigliaro was settling in quite nicely in the sunny environs of Southern California. He worked to cultivate a cordial relationship with the local press, continued to appear as a singer, dreamed of a future in Hollywood movies, and picked up extra cash through commercial endorsements. That his next-door neighbor was Raquel Welch only burnished the luster of his new venue. Conigliaro's reported $76,000 salary and the Cadillac El Dorado he drove were other perks that he enjoyed as the hero in search of something to conquer.

But for all the material trappings Conigliaro enjoyed, the real harbinger of his days as an Angel may have been the weak .186 batting average he compiled in spring camp as well as playing time missed due to back spasms and flu. More ominously, the closeness of family that underpinned his life in Boston was no longer available to him, his father Sal and brother Billy still ensconced back East. Though Tony worked hard as a professional ballplayer, "He was the new kid in the neighborhood…he needed to win everyone over with baseball heroics."[12] This was a tall order considering that the fans at Anaheim Stadium were generally less passionate about their team than the denizens of Fenway Park.

FOR WANT OF A SPARK

As the 1971 season began, the confluence of Johnson and Conigliaro did not deliver the offensive punch the Angels had hoped for. The former hit decently, though not of batting-title quality, but the home fans persisted in vocalizing their displeasure with choruses of boos. The latter seemed destined for alienation from his teammates because of various ailments or inauspicious conditions, ranging from discomfort with his injured eye, which he attributed to the brightness of the West Coast sun, to pains in his neck, legs, and back. Pitcher Tom Murphy noted that the right fielder "always seemed to be hurt," but Conigliaro wanted to dispel the notion that he was seldom up to the task, and, unlike Johnson, he strove to improve his defensive play so that center fielder Berry, already famed for his glove work, would have fewer worries.[13]

Through the first three months of the season, Conigliaro played in an average of 22 games each month but missed 15 contests. His batting average peaked at .264 in mid-May, but the power stroke that had been his signature was in short supply. California's mediocre standing in the AL West in the early going was due in large part to the quality of its pitching, which ranked in the middle of the league, whereas the offense was second from the bottom.[14]

Conigliaro's name never appeared on the disabled list, but an unwelcome amount of tarnish was accumulating on his reputation because of the time he was unavailable. Despite receiving numerous shots of cortisone for relief of back pain, Conigliaro could not convince his teammates of his woes. They took an increasingly dim view of what they were starting to believe was more hypochondria than the impact of actual injuries. Clubhouse pranksters greeted Conigliaro in early June with a display comprising "a stretcher set up in front of his locker with his uniform spread out on it and a pair of crutches wrapped in Ace bandages forming a coat of arms."[15] Offended by the exhibit, which was soft-pedaled by manager Phillips as just mischief that ballplayers perpetrate, Conigliaro retreated, fittingly enough, to the sanctity of the trainer's room. None of his teammates had endured the near-fatal episode of being hit in the head and worked so diligently to return to the game, and it was impossible for any of them to understand his circumstances.

Try as he might to regain the form he displayed in 1970, Conigliaro only struggled more and found that his fellow Angels were labeling him a slacker. About the only persons in whom he could confide were Jerry Moses, the catcher who had accompanied Conigliaro in the trade from Boston, and, curiously, Johnson. The defending batting champion shunned the press for the most part, and he continued to exasperate his manager with aloof and indifferent play, yet Johnson now found a sympathetic companion in Conigliaro. It may well have been that the Angels were leading the league in malcontents, and this was prior to the Oakland Athletics gaining distinction as a team whose clubhouse became branded with its own infighting.

Early in the season, Johnson agreed to an interview with a new publication, *Black Sports* magazine, and in his conversation with journalist Bill Lane, he chided fans who reveled in booing him yet would instantly begin cheering him with the next base hit. Johnson, an African American from Detroit, confessed that some of his white teammates "get along with him very well," but he was blunt in his assessment of the differences between the races. "I've been bitter ever since I learned I was Black. The white-dominated society into which I was born, in which I grew up and in which I play ball today is anti-Black. My attitude is nothing more than a reaction to their attitude.... The white society actually rejects the Black in everything. What we often take for true equality is smiling toleration."[16] Johnson had to have felt some degree of comfort in speaking freely to a reporter likely with a sympathetic ear.

As the 1971 season progressed, Angels players and team management found themselves in an increasingly untenable position. In trying to tolerate Johnson's behavior, Phillips alternated between fining and benching the outfielder, then reinstating him, all to no avail as the half-hearted base-running and loafing after fly balls continued. Frustrated teammates—Berry and Wright in particular—wearied of trying to reason with Johnson and nearly touched off locker-side brawls. Ruiz, who "had an agreeable personality and was well-liked by...teammates and opponents alike," as well as a lengthy and close relationship with Johnson, became the focal point of a notorious incident in which the infielder allegedly pulled a gun on Johnson in the clubhouse.[17]

Press photos of Johnson sitting alone on the dugout bench told the sad story of a man ostracized by those with whom he should have been relishing the opportunity and privilege of playing baseball at the highest level. Instead, the problem continued to fester as long as Johnson remained a member of the club.

An end of the tribulations was believed to be in sight when GM Walsh thought he had a deal worked out with the Milwaukee Brewers. Johnson would be traded for outfielder Tommy Harper. But when the latter's bat showed signs of emerging from a lengthy slump as the mid-June trade deadline approached, the Brewers nixed the transaction.

Johnson played his last game for California on June 24. The Angels suspended him for 30 days without pay beginning in late June, and the expiration of that penalty dovetailed into his placement by commissioner Bowie Kuhn on the restricted list. Johnson's case was taken up by the players' union, which filed a grievance to be submitted to arbitration. In a *Sports*

Illustrated profile that ran shortly after Johnson's suspension began, the outfielder fingered Ruiz as "the cause of the dissension," but the magazine placed blame in the most obvious place, citing "Johnson's curious rebellion" and a "mockery of the game that cut his fellow players doubly deep. In a world of performance, to refuse to perform seemed to make fools of those who did, seemed to make nonsense out of the pure patterns of the game they played."[18]

Dick Miller later reported in *The Sporting News*, "The number of fines and Johnson's behavior, it was contended, should have indicated to General Manager Dick Walsh and Manager Lefty Phillips that Johnson was under extreme mental distress." The final tally for the season came to 29 fines totaling $3,750.[19] The adjudication of the grievance, however, came out in Johnson's favor.

MLBPA director Marvin Miller, who was on the front line of Johnson's defense, said, "I think it's fair to say that most of the Angels didn't grasp the depths of Johnson's psychological problems."[20] Subsequent examinations by a pair of psychiatrists confirmed Johnson's compromised mental state, and he won his case, as arbitrator Lewis Gill found that the player's condition warranted a spot on the disabled list rather than a disciplinary suspension. The financial payout would be back salary minus the amount of the fines imposed by the ballclub, and Johnson was given a new home on October 5 when he and Moses were traded to the Cleveland Indians.

For Conigliaro, his ignominious finale came on July 9 in a marathon, 20-inning game at Oakland, when he went hitless in eight trips to the plate, including five strikeouts, yet these few statistics hardly tell the full story. A prelude occurred in the 11th inning when he fanned on a pitch that eluded the catcher, but with first base occupied and less than two outs, Conigliaro was automatically out. Still, he irrationally ran to first and argued with the home plate umpire about the play. Eight innings later came the ugly coda: Upon striking out after an unsuccessful bunt attempt—even trying after the bunt sign was removed with two strikes—Conigliaro "exploded" at plate ump Merle Anthony, who walked away to avoid worsening the confrontation. When the outfielder removed his batting helmet and swatted it fungo-style toward first base, he was ejected from the game, but not before "heav[ing] his bat over [first base umpire George] Maloney's head."[21]

Frustrated at losing 1–0 in the wee hours of the morning, Phillips grumbled to the press about Conigliaro's actions, which exacerbated a deteriorating situation. The manager complained about his player's lack of knowledge of the rules and his penchant for ignoring signals from the dugout, but then Phillips stunned the gathering by saying, "The man belongs in an institution."[22]

Phillips's blunt opinion was followed mere hours later by Conigliaro's departure from the team. The embattled player confessed that headaches, coupled with vision that never fully recovered after his August 1967 beaning, had rendered him a shell of the player he had once been. Conigliaro's emotional outburst was a sad denouement, and he immediately retreated to the safety of his home turf and family in Boston.

Conigliaro referred to his exit as a retirement, and with Johnson still suspended, one might have believed the air to be clearer for the California roster. But the Angels played roughly .500 ball for the remainder of the season—they went 36–37 after the late-inning meltdown on July 9—and fell to fourth place in the AL West, leading to the predictable dismissal of Phillips and his coaching staff.

As Johnson had filed a grievance over his treatment by the ballclub, so too did Conigliaro, who, after originally acknowledging that he was forfeiting about half of his salary by retiring, revived the claim that since a medical condition had forced him from the game, he was entitled to $30,000, which was eventually paid by the team.

Speculation in *The Sporting News* about the 1971 Angels having one of their best outfields ever had been predicated on the anticipated synergy created by the defending AL batting champion followed in the batting order by a power hitter who, to all appearances, had overcome his eyesight issue. Yet their statistics and the team's won-loss record show that no chemistry emerged from this pairing, whether in the form of enhanced individual performance or in the club's ability to gain in the standings.

Table 1. Angels Games in Which Alex Johnson and Tony Conigliaro Appeared

	PA	R	H	HR	RBI	OPS
Johnson	215	16	54	2	18	.672
Conigliaro	200	16	44	4	13	.714
Total	415	32	98	6	31	.692

Games	Won	Lost	Pct.
52	22	30	.423

Source: Baseball-Reference.com

Johnson hit third in the order, where he remained for most of the games in which he played; Conigliaro started out in the cleanup slot, but as ailments took their toll, he was dropped to sixth. In some instances,

the pair were in the same contest only because one of them appeared as a pinch-hitter or a late-inning replacement. In any case, a combined batting average of a tepid .263 with an accompanying RBI total that would project to merely 50 (based on a 600 at-bat season) was not what the Angels had anticipated.

There is a curious intersection of what was acknowledged as Johnson's "emotional illness," in Miller's words, and the dismissive comment by Phillips about Conigliaro being ripe for institutionalization. Through the 1970s, it was not uncommon in public discourse to hear references to "mental retardation," "funny farm," or other unkind vernacular related to behavioral issues; an editorial in *The Sporting News* went so far as to diagnose Johnson as "a social schizophrenic."[23]

Thankfully, modern sensibilities and better medical knowledge have come to recognize behavioral illnesses that can be treated by trained professionals who today are better equipped—and supported by the general public—than they were decades ago. For example, yesteryear's "shell shock" is better understood today as post-traumatic stress disorder. Johnson and Conigliaro's respective circumstances—behavioral in the case of the former, behavioral (to a lesser degree) *and* the difficulties of recovery from a ghastly head injury for the latter—demand our attention and understanding.

SUMMARY

Through the vicissitudes of the baseball world, two All-Star players were paired up in the corners of the 1971 California Angels outfield, and optimists among baseball observers could only dream of the possibilities. That Johnson and Conigliaro both departed by midseason only adds to the intrigue, and their exits created a void similar to when a conflict ends: Peace has been achieved, but the effects fail to dissipate quickly. Picking up the pieces of a shattered campaign, the Angels won about half of their remaining games beyond early July, but the "one step forward" taken by the club in 1970 clearly yielded to "two steps back" by the end of the following season. Even the appointment of a new GM, Harry Dalton, whose success with the "Oriole Way" in building Baltimore as the most formidable team of the late 1960s and early 1970s set the standard of the era, could not correct the course of a franchise steeped in mediocrity.

Granted that the issues faced by California were deeper than the shortcomings of two outfielders upon whom so much rested. But there were lessons to be learned by the time Alex Johnson won his grievance case: Emotional issues, unremittingly part of the human condition, should not be given short shrift; and players suffering from physical injuries, especially the type of damage from one of the worst head injuries ever sustained, may likely endure long-term complications and perhaps only experience a tentative recovery.

It is to his credit that Johnson continued to play for several more years beyond his pair of volatile seasons with the Angels and that Conigliaro also persisted beyond August 18, 1967, a date after which his baseball career would be forever marked as a comeback. For the few months of 1971 when they both wore Angels uniforms, the bats of Johnson and Conigliaro yielded unremarkable production rather than the expected one-two punch, and their departures created the challenge for Dalton of having to fill a pair of vacancies in the outfield and in the heart of the California batting order. ■

Acknowledgments

The author wishes to thank the peer reviewers and editor King Kaufman for their suggestions and work on this essay.

Sources

In addition to sources cited in the endnotes, the following were also used:
Baseball-reference.com
1971 California Angels News Media Guide
The Sporting News
Bill Nowlin, "Tony Conigliaro," Society for American Baseball Research, https://sabr.org/bioproj/person/tony-conigliaro/.
Jeff Pearlman, "Catching Up With…Alex Johnson, Angels Outfielder," *Sports Illustrated*, March 9, 1998.
Daniel E. Slotnik, "Alex Johnson Dies at 72; Deft Batter Won a Key Ruling," *The New York Times*, March 5, 2015.

Notes

1. Mark Armour, "Alex Johnson" Society for American Baseball Research, https://sabr.org/bioproj/person/alex-johnson/. (*Emphasis added*.)
2. Armour, Alex Johnson.
3. John Wiebusch, "Don't Try to Chat with Alex—Just Let Him Hit," *The Sporting News*, May 2, 1970.
4. Ross Newhan, "Alex of Angels Is Falling from Realm of Glory," *The Sporting News*, August 15, 1970.
5. Newhan, "A Lot of Wrongs Dot Wright's Leap to 20," *The Sporting News*, October 3, 1970.
6. Marvin Miller, *A Whole Different Ball Game: The Sport and Business of Baseball* (New York: Birch Lane Press, 1993), 135.
7. David Cataneo, *Tony C: The Triumph and Tragedy of Tony Conigliaro* (Nashville: Rutledge Hill Press, 1997), 190.
8. Cataneo, *Tony C*, 190.
9. Bill Nowlin, *Tom Yawkey: Patriarch of the Boston Red Sox* (Lincoln: University of Nebraska Press, 2018), 289.
10. Nowlin, 288; Cataneo, *Tony C*, 193.
11. C.C. Johnson Spink, "Spink's Forecast: Orioles and Dodgers to Win," *The Sporting News*, April 10, 1971.
12. Cataneo, *Tony C*, 198.
13. Cataneo, *Tony C*, 198.
14. American League batting and pitching statistics, *The Sporting News*, July 12, 1971.
15. Cataneo, *Tony C*, 200. The tasteless addition of ketchup-stained sanitary napkins also was part of the scene.
16. Bill Lane, "Alex at the Bat," *Black Sports*, July 1971. This publication was ahead of its time: Not until well into the 21st century was "Black" capitalized in the mainstream media.
17. Jerome Holtzman, "'71 Saw Gate Up, Short Move, Alex Angry," in Paul MacFarlane, et al, *Official Baseball Guide for 1972* (St. Louis: The Sporting News, 1972), 281.
18. Ron Fimrite, "For Failure to Give His Best…," *Sports Illustrated*, July 5, 1971.
19. Dick Miller, "Johnson Fined 29 Times 19 in '71; Total: $3,000," *The Sporting News*, September 11, 1971, 32; Armour, "Alex Johnson."
20. Marvin Miller, *A Whole Different Ball Game*, 137.
21. Cataneo, *Tony C*, 201–02.
22. Cataneo, *Tony C*, 202.
23. "Better to Fight Than to Talk," *The Sporting News*, July 31, 1971.

Dick Such's Hard-Luck Season

Going 0–16 for the York (PA) White Roses

Barry Sparks

When he stepped on the mound at Municipal Stadium to face the hometown Waterbury Giants on Sept. 3, 1967, Dick Such of the York White Roses carried the burden of an 0–16 record. It was his last chance that season to snap his winless streak. The 6-foot-4 right-hander got off to a rocky start as Bobby Bonds crashed a two-run homer in the bottom of the first inning and Francis DeGold slammed a solo shot in the second.

Trailing 3–0 after two innings, a dejected Such walked off the mound and took a seat in the dugout. Completing his shortest stint of the season, he had no chance of earning a win. He received a no-decision because his teammates staged a rare late-inning rally and downed Waterbury, 6–3.

The dismal season and his 0–16 record, however, were hardly his fault. Such compiled a respectable 2.81 ERA and lost eight games when the White Roses, a Class AA affiliate of the Washington Senators, were shut out. As a whole, the team went 43–95. His season of futility is unmatched in the history of the Eastern League, which dates back to 1923.[1] Looking at the severity of the streak, few might predict that Such would make the major leagues and serve nearly 20 years as a major league pitching coach.

Such—a Sanford, NC, native—was drafted by the Senators in the eighth-round of the January secondary draft in 1966, and went 6–8 in 14 starts for the Burlington Senators of the Carolina League (A). The following year he was moved up to York, and despite serving a two-week stint in the National Guard, he started a team-high 20 games. He registered eight complete games (tied for first on the team) and hurled 128 innings. A lack of control hurt him—he issued 70 walks and hit 10 batters while striking out but nearly every other pitching stat other than his won-loss record had improved from the previous season (Table 1).

Washington, perhaps recognizing Such's record was deceiving, called him up after the Eastern League season ended. Although he never got into a game, he said it was a thrill to sit in the bullpen, warm up, and meet manager Gil Hodges, pitching coach Rube Walker, and slugger Frank Howard. "The call-up was a message from the Senators that they believed in me," said the 79-year-old Such in a phone interview from his home in Sanford. "Mentally, it had been an excruciating year for me. The call-up boosted my confidence."

Washington Post reporter William Gildea interviewed Such late in the 1967 season and described him as "good natured and not depressed. He's not chain-smoking or staying awake at night. He's a hard worker with a dogged resolution and no illusions."[3]

A York sportswriter observed, "Such has a million-dollar arm, but his luck isn't worth two cents."[4] Such was a victim of both bad luck and ineptness. The 1967 York White Roses were a minor league version of the infamous 1962 New York Mets. The club, which finished more than 30 games behind Elmira in the Western Division of the Eastern League, couldn't hit or field. The infield was a porous mess. White Rose shortstops committed 43 errors, while the team muffed 188 chances for a .962 fielding average.

The club's lack of offensive punch bordered on incredible. York was shut out 29 times, including being no-hit on four occasions. The team batting average was a puny .217. First baseman Joe Klein led the team with a .268 average and was one of only two position players to bat .250 or better. Dick Billings and Brant Alyea were the top RBI men with just 34 each. The club knocked more triples than home runs (30 to 27).

York's cavernous Memorial Stadium definitely favored pitchers. Left field was 375 feet (with a 24-foot high fence), center field measured 440 feet, and right field was 335. The White Roses managed just five four-baggers at home, all to right field.

1. Dick Such Pitching Statistics

Year	Team	Level	W	L	ERA	CG	IP	WHIP	H9	HR9	BB9	SO9
1966	Burlington	A	6	8	3.13	4	92	1.467	7.9	0.6	5.3	6.8
1967	York	AA	0	16	2.81	8	128	1.391	7.6	0.4	4.9	5.3

The club featured future Washington Senators outfielders Del Unser, Brant Alyea, and Barry Shetrone, catcher Dick Billings and pitcher Bill Gogolewski.

When asked about his hard-luck season, Such said, "It's gotten so bad it's amusing. We hit, but right at people. When we get a couple runners on and need a timely hit, we never get it. I know the guys behind me aren't trying to make errors. It's amazing how a team can be so unlucky."[5]

In a 1970 interview during spring training with the Senators, Such admitted he developed a losing attitude about midway through his season in York. "It took about a year or so to realize that the mental approach to baseball is as important as the physical," he said.[6]

Warren Hamilton of York was one of the few die-hard White Roses fans in 1967. (Attendance totaled only 27,826, averaging 400 fans per game.) In 2004 he recalled, "Such was an excellent pitcher. He was one of the better pitchers on York's staff. He was considered potentially as good as Dick Bosman or Joe Coleman, Jr., who went on to enjoy a fair amount of success with the Senators."[7]

Despite the mounting losses, Hamilton never remembered Such getting upset on the mound or in the clubhouse. Hamilton became friends with several Senators during their stints in York, occasionally visiting them in the clubhouse at DC Stadium. Through his trips to Washington, he also got to know Senators manager Gil Hodges. "Hodges was following Such and I tried to keep him informed," said Hamilton. "After one of Such's late-season 1–0 losses, I called Hodges at his hotel in New York and told him that Such had lost again. Hodges was disappointed that he didn't snap his losing streak. Everyone was rooting for Such."[8]

After his playing career, Such held various coaching and instruction positions for several organizations, including the Minnesota Twins, Boston Red Sox, and Long Island Ducks.

How unlucky was Such?

The White Roses were shut out eight times in his 20 starts. He lost four 1–0 games and another game by a 2–1 score.

Here are some details of Such's hard-luck season:

May 14 – Loses 1–0 at Waterbury as the Giants score a run in the bottom of the ninth inning on a single, stolen base, and a single. Such surrendered just three hits going into the ninth.

June 4 – Leaves the game against Pawtucket after 11.1 innings with two men on and two outs and the score tied, 2–2. Reliever Dick Bates uncorks a wild pitch, allowing the go-ahead run to score. A single plates an insurance run.

June 9 – Loses 1–0 against Elmira on back-to-back doubles in the sixth inning.

June 13 – Loses to Williamsport, 3–1. The game was tied 1–1 going into the top of the eighth. A single, sacrifice fly, and a single snapped the tie. The third run scored on two errors.

June 27 – Carries a three-hitter and a 1–0 lead into the eighth inning at Waterbury. Jose Morales, Waterbury's 1966 home-run leader, clouts a solo shot to tie the game. Such leaves in the top of the ninth for a pinch-hitter. York goes on to lose 2–1 in 10 innings.

July 5 – Loses 1–0 against Pittsfield. Such gives up the lone run in the first inning on a walk, double, and single.

August 4 – Hooks up in a scoreless pitching duel with Williamsport's Gary Gentry. Such pitches shutout ball for 8.1 innings, surrendering just three hits, before tiring and being relieved by Gene Baker. York scores the game's only run in the top of the 11th inning on a walk and a two-out triple. Gentry goes the distance for Williamsport, allowing four hits, three walks and fanning 11.

August 10 – Gives up two runs in the second inning against Reading on a double, single, and two errors. Loses 2–1.

August 16 – Limits Waterbury to four hits in eight innings but three of them come in the seventh inning when the Giants score two runs. Such loses, 2–0.

August 28 – Loses 1–0 at Binghamton. The only run was a man he walked, who stole and then was singled home.

September 3 – Surrenders two home runs and leaves the game trailing 3–0 after two innings, his shortest stint of the season. Down 3–2 entering the ninth inning, York stages one of its rare late-inning rallies, plating four runs to secure a 6–3 win…for reliever Rube Toppin.

Such tried to convince himself he was a good athlete, despite his record. "I felt like I was a winner, and if I gave it my best every time out, eventually good things would happen. My record wasn't good, but my numbers were okay, so you just find all the positives you can and move on. I had to learn that."[9]

Washington called Such up to the major leagues in September, then after never getting into a game, he finished out the year in the Florida Instructional League, where he went 0–2.

Washington kept a close eye on Such in 1968 as he pitched for Class A Burlington in the Carolina League, posting a 10–17 mark with a 3.47 ERA. The following season, he pitched for Class AAA Buffalo in the International League, Class AA Savannah in the Southern League, and in the Florida Instructional League.

The Senators invited Such to spring training in 1970. The tall right-hander admitted he had spent the previous two seasons trying to shake off the negative effects of his 0–16 season at York. During that spring training, Such demonstrated the potential to help the Senators' pitching staff and made the opening day roster. Manager Ted Williams wasted little time using him. Such hurled the eighth and ninth innings against the Detroit Tigers on Opening Day, April 6, in Washington. The rookie didn't allow a hit while surrendering three walks and fanning three.

Such recorded his only major league win in a four-inning relief stint against the Milwaukee Brewers on April 28. He pitched the best game of his major league career on May 21 against the New York Yankees in Yankee Stadium. He started the game, pitched six innings and surrendered just two hits, one of them Danny Cater's two-run homer. The Senators lost, 2–0.

Such was 1–5 with a 7.56 ERA when the Senators shipped the 25-year-old to Class AAA Denver in late July. Recalling the 1970 season with the Senators, Such said, "I enjoyed my short time in Washington. I got to meet President Nixon, who said he had been reading about me during spring training, and Ted Williams was my manager. I have a lot of good memories."[10]

While on the mound in Denver, he heard something pop in his elbow and his pitching arm was never the same. He hurled three more disappointing seasons before he ended his career in 1974 after three pinch-hitting appearances for the Class AA Pittsfield Rangers in the Eastern League.

Table 2. Dick Such's 1967 Season

Date and Team	Record	Inn	H	R	ER	BB	SO	Result
April 25 vs. Elmira	(0–1)	5	2	4	1	8	5	Lost 5–0
May 3 at Elmira	(0–2)	6	3	2	1	3	5	Lost 2–0
May 10 at Reading	No decision	8	7	2	2	3	5	York lost 3–2 in 10
May 14 at Waterbury	(0–3)	8.1	5	1	1	2	4	Lost 1–0
May 20 vs. Pittsfield	(0–4)	4.2	7	7	4	4	0	Lost 7–6
May 27 at Pittsfield	(0–5)	2.1	4	4	4	2	2	Lost 9–5
May 31 vs. Waterbury	(0–6)	6.1	7	2	2	3	5	Lost 3–0
June 4 vs. Pawtucket	(0–7)	11.1	8	4	2	7	9	Lost 4–2 in 12
June 9 vs. Elmira	(0–8)	7	4	1	1	2	0	Lost 1–0
June 13 vs. Williamsport	(0–9)	9	5	3	2	6	7	Lost 3–1
June 20 at Williamsport	(0–10)	3.2	6	5	5	5	0	Lost 6–3
June 27 at Waterbury	No decision	8	5	1	1	2	4	York lost 2–1 in 10
July 5 vs. Pittsfield	(0–11)	7	7	1	1	2	6	Lost 1–0
July 12 at Pittsfield	(0–12)	6	9	6	1	4	7	Lost 6–0
Aug. 4 at Williamsport	No decision	8.1	3	0	0	3	6	York won 1–0
Aug 10 vs. Reading	(0–13)	7	7	2	1	3	6	Lost 2–1
Aug 16 vs. Waterbury	(0–14)	8	4	2	2	3	4	Lost 2–0
Aug 23 vs. Binghamton	(0–15)	3.2	6	6	5	4	1	Lost 8–1
Aug 28 at Binghamton	(0–16)	6	4	1	1	3	1	Lost 1–0
Sept 3 at Waterbury	No decision	2	5	3	3	1	0	York won 6–3

THE SENATORS DISMAL HISTORY IN YORK

York's five-year affiliation with Washington, from 1963 through 1967, was marked by a lot of bad baseball and fan apathy. The York White Roses compiled an overall Eastern League record of 29–406 (.417 winning average), never posting a .500 season. Their best mark was 67–72 in 1965 when they finished third. In five seasons, the White Roses finished an average of 24 games out of first place.

Here are the team's records, finish, games out of first place, and attendance:

Year	W-L	Place	GB	Attendance
1963	63–77	fifth	20	42,827
1964	55–85	sixth	27	35,540
1965	66–72	third	17.5	53,345
1966	62–77	sixth	26	42,588
1967	43–95	fourth	30.5	27,826
		(two four-team divisions)		

Consider that a sold-out game at Nationals Park (capacity 41,546) would exceed the number of fans the York White Roses drew in two of their five seasons affiliated with the Washington Senators. Here's an indication of how minor league baseball's popularity has changed. In 1967, the eight-team Eastern League drew a total of 429,381 fans. In 2016, a single team in the Eastern League, the Reading Phillies, attracted more: 445,023.

Despite his hard-luck season at York and lack of major league experience, Such enjoyed a long and productive career instructing others. From 1975 through 1982, Such served in various capacities for the Texas Rangers, including as a roving pitching instructor in the Rangers' farm system. He joined the major league club as pitching coach in 1983 and served until early May 1985. The Minnesota Twins named him their pitching coach in September 1985. He held that position until 2001. His stint included World Series championships in 1987 and 1991.

The Florida Marlins hired Such in 2002 to coach the AAA Calgary Cannons pitchers. After one season, he was out of baseball until 2006, when he joined the Long Island Ducks in the independent Atlantic League. He later served as pitching coach for the Atlantic League Camden Riversharks. In 2009, he accepted an offer to be a pitching coach in the Boston Red Sox minor league system. He worked with the organization until his retirement in 2021.

"In retrospect," Such said of his struggles, "it helped me as far as becoming a coach and figuring out that everyone has to deal with failure in the game of baseball. I certainly did that and got through it somehow or another."[11] In 2012, *Bleacher Report* named him the 16th best pitching coach of all-time.[12] ∎

Notes

1. The Eastern League was previously known as the New York-Pennsylvania League, then was renamed in 1938 when New Jersey joined the league. Joe Trezza, "Then and Now: The Eastern League" MiLB.com, March 21, 2022; https://www.milb.com/news/eastern-league-overview, accessed September 6, 2023.
2. Phone interview with Dick Such, July 6, 2022.
3. William Gildea, "Such Brings a Perfect Record To Senators—Incredible 0-16," *Washington Post*, Sept. 3, 1967, D4.
4. "York, Reading Split Stadium Twin Bill," *York Dispatch*, Aug. 11, 1967, 14.
5. Gildea, "Such Brings Perfect Record...".
6. George Minot, "Dick Such to Pitch Today As Senators Meet Yankees," *Washington Post*, March 5, 1970, E1.
7. Barry Sparks, "York's hard-luck loser," *York Sunday News*, Sept. 19, 2004, 37.
8. Sparks.
9. Kevin Czerwinski, "Such's Life," *Ball Nine*, Feb 12, 2021; https://ballnine.com/2021/02/, accessed February 14, 2021.
10. Sparks.
11. Czerwinski.
12. Doug Mead, "The 50 Best MLB Pitching Coaches of All Time," *Bleacher Report*, February 1, 2012; https://bleacherreport.com/articles/1047146-the-50-best-mlb-pitching-coaches/, accessed September 7, 2023.

Erasing Moments and Memories

Iconic Games Reconsidered with the Automatic Runner

Francis Kinlaw

In recent decades, rules in several professional sports have been revised with a goal of reducing the length of games or matches. Both pro and college football have changed their timekeeping rules repeatedly to shorten games. In hockey, five-minute overtime periods, often followed by shoot-outs, have become routine in non-playoff games. Tie-breakers are played in tennis. Most of these changes have occurred without significant controversy, but attempts to alter procedures in the tradition-bound sport of baseball have been met with strong criticism from many quarters.

A relatively new rule, the automatic placement of a runner on second base in extra innings, has affected strategy—as well as outcomes of games—since its adoption by Major League Baseball in 2020.[1] The automatic runner's introduction was initially opposed by many observers, and it remains a frequent subject of debate among players and fans. Detractors have called it a "gimmick" and argued that it contradicts the "timeless nature of the sport."[2]

The rule has served its intended purpose of reducing the length of games and preventing numerous contests from extending into multiple extra innings. Unfortunately, those developments will come at a future cost since many of the sport's most memorable games *became* memorable because results were delayed in coming.

Four games, each of which is considered a classic, stand as evidence that several extra innings can increase the "memory factor":

- Harvey Haddix's 12 innings of pitching perfection against the Milwaukee Braves in 1959 that resulted in a heartbreaking defeat for the southpaw and the Pittsburgh Pirates.

- A 22-inning marathon between the New York Yankees and Detroit Tigers in 1962 decided by Jack Reed's home run.

- A 16-inning pitching duel in 1963 matching Warren Spahn of the Milwaukee Braves and Juan Marichal of the San Francisco Giants that was finally brought to an end by a Willie Mays blast.

- The tense 12-inning Game Six of the 1975 World Series that concluded with the infamous "midnight homer" off the bat of Carlton Fisk.

By reviewing plays from each of these games, we can determine how significant placement of runners would have been in the 1950s, 1960s, and 1970s. (Plays that occurred in inconsequential half-innings of the games will not be discussed.)

MAY 26, 1959: BRAVES 1, PIRATES 0, 13 INNINGS (COUNTY STADIUM, MILWAUKEE)

No individual performance in a regular-season game from the 1950s compares with that of Haddix, a solid but unsensational left-hander. He retired 36 consecutive Braves—and his streak of perfection would have been extended further if Pirates third baseman Don Hoak had not committed an error on an infield grounder by the Braves' Felix Mantilla leading off the 13th inning. Hoak's low throw to first baseman Rocky Nelson was followed by a successful sacrifice bunt by Eddie Mathews, an intentional walk to Henry Aaron, and an apparent game-winning home run by Joe Adcock that was reduced to a double because of a base-running mistake by Aaron. Haddix's unfortunate and unique fate was viewed sympathetically throughout the baseball community.

How would this game have turned out if it had been played with runners placed on second base at the beginning of each extra inning? The answer: The Pirates would have secured a perfect game by Haddix with a winning tally in the top of the 10th frame after the Pirates' Bob Skinner assumed the role of runner at second base, owing to his having made the last out in the ninth. Skinner would have been able to advance to third base when Bill Mazeroski hit a grounder to the right side of the infield and score on Hoak's single to left field.

Harvey Haddix on the mound for Pittsburgh.

Even if Pittsburgh had not won the game in the 10th, the Bucs would have had another splendid opportunity to score a decisive run in the top of the 11th. An exception in the new rule allows the pitcher to avoid being the runner if he made the last out in the previous inning. The previous hitter can be used instead. Because Haddix had grounded out to end the 10th inning, he would have been able to conserve his energy as outfielder Joe Christopher trotted out to second base. Dick Schofield's single to left might have enabled Christopher to cross the plate but, if not, the Pirates would have likely taken the lead when Bill Virdon subsequently hit into a force play at second base.

Then, under the modern rule, a *third* opportunity for victory would have come Pittsburgh's way in the top of the 12th! Smokey Burgess (Haddix' batterymate) would have been the runner on second base as the inning began. After Rocky Nelson hit a fly ball to Braves left fielder Wes Covington and Skinner lined out to first baseman Adcock, Mazeroski ripped a single to center field that could have brought Burgess home.

Following each of these offensive threats by his teammates, Haddix continued to retire every Milwaukee hitter in order.

So, without a doubt, the rule adopted more than six decades later would have prevented this game from becoming the extraordinary show that it is still considered to be.

But what about a seemingly endless game played on a Sunday afternoon (and early evening) three years later in Detroit?

JUNE 24, 1962: YANKEES 9, TIGERS 7, 22 INNINGS (TIGER STADIUM, DETROIT)

This game lasted exactly seven hours. The Tigers used 22 players in a losing effort, and 21 Bronx Bombers

participated. Each team posted seven runs in the first nine innings of play and, since so many runs were being scored in a hitter-friendly ballpark, it seemed highly unlikely that several hours would pass before a conclusion was reached. But that is exactly what occurred.

Under the current rule, the Tigers could have nailed down a victory in the bottom of the 10th inning. With Chico Fernandez handling the running duty at second base, Mike Roarke reached on a throwing error by Yankees third baseman Clete Boyer. Even if Fernandez couldn't have advanced to third on the error, he would have remained on the basepaths and scored the winning run on either a single to left by Steve Boros or one to right by Billy Bruton. Without a zombie runner, however, the game went on.

The modern rule would have eliminated 12 innings of memorable baseball, and all of the rallies that might have happened if those innings had included an automatic runner would have been impossible. But that's no fun, so let's take a look at them anyway. We'll take a look at each half inning as if it started with the same leadoff hitter, ignoring any changes that might have resulted from the ghost-runner rule.

The Tigers would have certainly wrapped up a victory in the bottom half of the 11th stanza. Purnal Goldy would have been the runner on second when Rocky Colavito smashed a triple to deep center field.

In the top of the 13th, with Boyer, the eighth hitter in the Yankees batting order, taking the place of pitcher Tex Clevenger on second base, it would have been New York's turn to take a lead. After Tom Tresh was called out on strikes, Bobby Richardson's double to left field would have put his team ahead. The Tigers, however, might have responded when they came to bat in the bottom of the inning because it would have been their good fortune to have the fleet-footed Bruton on second base when Goldy hit a fly ball to center that was corralled by Roger Maris. If Bruton could have advanced to third on the putout (which is questionable), he would have scored when shortstop Tresh was unable to throw out Colavito on an infield hit.

There would have been more action—and possibly decisive scoring—in both halves of the 14th. Yogi Berra singled leading off the inning. John Blanchard, who would have been the ghost runner, was no speed merchant, but he might have been able to turn on the burners sufficiently to score. Even if he couldn't, he would have scored from third when Bill Skowron hit into a force play at second base for the first out of the inning, or when Boyer flied to deep left field for the second.

But the Tigers would have responded with a third scoring opportunity in the bottom of the 14th. Dick McAuliffe would have been on second base when Dick Brown singled to center field. There can be little doubt that McAuliffe would have hustled home with a run that would have either tied the score or sent the fans to the stadium exits.

But most of the 35,368 spectators remained, and scoring opportunities continued to occur for both teams. In the top of the 15th inning with Boyer filling in for pitcher Bud Daley as the runner on second base, Tresh's single to center field would have put the Yankees ahead. New York's lead would have been short-lived, however, because the Tigers roared back upon returning to their dugout. Boros would have inherited second base and moved to third on Bruton's grounder to first baseman Skowron. Boros would have presumably trotted home soon afterward when Colavito reached first safely on a groundball down the third-base line. The score would have been tied again, and at least one more extra inning would have been in store.

In the 16th, the Yankees' Jack Reed would have been on second when Skowron singled to right field. Reed could have been expected to scramble home on Skowron's hit, but if third-base coach Frank Crosetti had held him, Boyer would have broken the tie with another single to right. With Goldy fielding the ball since Al Kaline was out of action with a separated shoulder, Reed's chances of scoring would have been enhanced.

In the 18th, Maris would have been the automatic runner when Berra singled to right field, and it can be assumed that Maris would have sped home and tilted the score in New York's favor.

None of these hypothetical runs scored, though, so play continued…

In the top of the 19th, the Yankees would have again benefited from the current rule. Skowron would have been leading off of second base when Tresh singled to center field to give New York a run that would have eventually decided the game.

In the 21st frame, Blanchard would have been on second base when Boyer singled to right field, and it is conceivable that the Yanks would have grabbed the lead on Boyer's hit.

The outcome of the game was finally determined for real in the top of the 22nd inning when Reed homered into the left-field stands. The fact that the round-tripper by Reed occurred with Maris on first base after being walked by Phil Regan invites mention of an incidental

but inevitable consequence of the "2020 rule" that affects baseball statistics. The final score of the game was 9–7, but in more modern times Tresh would have been on second base, 90 feet ahead of Maris, and the final score would have likely been 10–7, assuming the Tigers didn't score in the bottom of the 22nd. Furthermore, Reed would have been credited with three RBIs instead of two, and Tresh would have been credited with an additional run scored during the 1962 season. Regan's earned-run average would not have increased since Tresh's presence on second base was not due to Regan's performance as a pitcher.

In summary, if a "Manfred Man" had been placed on second base at the beginning of each half-inning of this game, the Tigers would have scored in as many as five of the 12 extra innings preceding the 22nd (i.e., the 10th, 11th, 13th, 14th, and 15th) and the Yankees would have scored in seven of the innings (the 13th, 14th, 15th, 16th, 18th, 19th, and 21st). Most significantly, when the influence of additional runners is merged with play-by-play accounts of the actual game, it becomes obvious that the Tigers would have won the "22-inning" game in the 10th!

JULY 2, 1963: GIANTS 1, BRAVES 0, 16 INNINGS (CANDLESTICK PARK, SAN FRANCISCO)

This lengthy affair was remarkable in that two legendary hurlers (Spahn and Marichal) were both in top form. Their standoff on the mound remained scoreless until Mays homered with one out in the bottom of the 16th inning, four hours and 10 minutes after the first pitch. As in the previously cited games, however, the number of innings played would have been drastically reduced if the automatic-runner rule had existed—and each team would have been on the brink of victory much earlier in the evening.

The first such threat would have occurred in the bottom of the 10th with Orlando Cepeda of the Giants on second base. He would have advanced to third when Ed Bailey grounded into a second-to-first putout and then possibly scored on a bunt by Ernie Bowman. (Bowman bunted for a single in the "real" game.)

Another scoring opportunity for San Francisco would have occurred in the 11th inning with eighth-place hitter Chuck Hiller occupying second base while Marichal rested in the dugout. Harvey Kuenn led off by grounding to Braves shortstop Roy McMillan but, because Kuenn was extremely adept at hitting balls to the right side of the diamond, it should be assumed that he would have attempted to do so in order to advance Hiller. With Hiller on third, Mays' fly ball to left would have produced the winning run.[3]

Milwaukee would have had its first chance for an overtime victory in the top of the 13th with McMillan leading off of second base. After Lee Maye hit a fly ball to right fielder Felipe Alou that might have enabled McMillan to tag up and go to third, Frank Bolling singled to right field for what would have likely been an RBI. But the Giants might have erased that advantage and tied the game in the bottom half of the inning when Bowman rapped a single with Bailey running from second.

As the game progressed, the Giants would have definitely put the game away in the bottom of the 14th when Kuenn doubled to center field with Hiller (again replacing Marichal) running from second base.

Finally, in the top of the 16th inning (the Braves' last turn at bat prior to Mays' decisive home run), Bolling flied out to Alou in right for the first out with automatic-runner Maye on second base. Regardless of whether Maye could have tagged up and reached third before the arrival of Alou's throw, Dennis Menke's subsequent single to left field could have produced a very significant run.

With automatic runners in this game, Milwaukee would have had two opportunities to score in extra innings (the 13th and 16th). San Francisco could have tallied four times (in the 10th, 11th, 13th, and 14th). But, because no one in the major league universe had yet dreamed of the modern rule's creation, neither team broke the deadlock until Mays hit his home run.

As in the case of Jack Reed's homer in the Yankees-Tigers game, several baseball records would have been affected by placement of an automatic runner on second base. Because Hiller would have been on the base paths when Mays took Spahn's pitch deep, the final score would have been 2–0 rather than 1–0, assuming the Braves also had not scored their Manfred Man in the top of the inning. Mays would have been credited with two RBIs instead of one, and Hiller would have scored an additional run during the 1963 season. Spahn's ERA would not have been revised for the same reason that Regan's ERA would have been unaffected by the automatic runner in the Tigers-Yankees contest.

OCTOBER 21, 1975: RED SOX 7, REDS 6, 12 INNINGS (FENWAY PARK, BOSTON)

Although Commissioner Rob Manfred has said that the sport's traditional rules will continue to be applied in playoff and World Series games, it should be understood that flirtation with change could affect not only results of individual games but also the determination of championships.

With three victories in the first five games of the 1975 Fall Classic, the Cincinnati Reds were one win away from closing the door on a strong Boston club. The Red Sox and much of New England firmly believed that a comeback was still possible with Game Six and Game Seven (if necessary) scheduled to be played in Fenway Park. The Boston franchise ultimately fell short of its long-sought goal in an unforgettable seven-game series, but a review of critical plays in the *sixth* game reveals that the Big Red Machine would have closed out their eventual Series victory one night earlier if zombie runners had been employed in the mid-1970s.

In that sixth game, the two teams were locked in a 6–6 tie after playing nine innings of perhaps the most entertaining baseball ever seen in postseason

Warren Spahn (left) and Juan Marichal (above) faced each other in a marathon game on July 2, 1963. in which Marichal pitched 16 innings and Spahn 15⅓.

competition. If automatic runner Tony Perez had been placed on second base in the top of the 10th inning after making the final out in the ninth, the Reds would have likely taken a lead on a single to center field by Davey Concepcion. After the Red Sox were retired in a routine manner in the bottom of the 10th, southern Ohio would have erupted into a state of celebration. (Six consecutive BoSox hitters were retired in the 10th and 11th innings preceding Fisk's game-winning blast off the left-field foul pole.)

In the unlikely event that Perez would have stumbled on the basepaths in the 10th inning and been tagged out, the Reds would have gained another advantage two innings later. Speedy Joe Morgan would have been stationed on second base in the top of the 12th, and with one out he would have darted home on Perez's single through the middle of the infield. (Even if Morgan had somehow not scored on Perez's single, he would have strolled home when George Foster subsequently blooped a single to left.)

Therefore, if the automatic-runner rule had been in effect at the time, Cincinnati would have almost certainly scored a critical run in the 10th inning of Game Six, the most memorable moment of Fisk's career would never have occurred, and a nerve-racking Game Seven would never have been played!

CONCLUSION
Although people in the baseball industry and fans of the sport have expressed differing opinions about this controversial rule, it was unanimously adopted on a permanent basis in February 2023 by a Major League Baseball joint competition committee consisting of six management officials, four players union representatives, and one umpire.[4] This retrospective glance at a quartet of celebrated games indicates clearly, however, that the potential effects of automatic runners on results of games and entire seasons cannot be overstated. Furthermore, such a determination should raise a logical question in the minds of today's thoughtful fans: If amazing moments such as these could have been eliminated by the rule change, what memorable moments will we be deprived of in the future? ∎

Sources
http://www.retrosheet.org.
The Sporting News: June 3, 1959, 5.
The Sporting News: July 7, 1962, 11.
The Sporting News: July 13, 1963, 40.

Notes
1. MLB's rulebook does not assign a new term to the automatic runner, but in common parlance this player is often referred to as the "ghost" runner or "zombie runner," as well as the "Manfred Man"—a reference both to the commissioner of baseball and South African keyboardist Manfred Mann—with two n's—of the eponymous rock bands Manfred Mann and Manfred Mann's Earth Band. SABR does not use the term "ghost runner" as that term already refers to something else: in sandlot baseball a "ghost runner" is an imaginary runner placed on base when the real baserunner has to leave the base for some reason, such as taking a turn at bat when there are not enough players per team (as when playing three-on-three), or when one's parents have declared it is suppertime, etc. See "New Rules, Features, Protocols for 2020 MLB Season," https://www.mlb.com/news/mlb-announces-new-features-for-2020-season.
2. Evan Drellich and Eno Sarris, "MLB Makes Extra-Inning Ghost-Runner Rule Permanent, Per Sources: How Has It Changed the Game?" *The Athletic*, February 13, 2023, https://theathletic.com/4191908/2023/02/13/mlb-extra-innings-position-player-rules/; Mike Axisa, "MLB debuts new extra innings rule: Shohei Ohtani makes history, but A's walk off on grand slam home run," *CBS Sports*, July 25, 2020, https://www.cbssports.com/mlb/news/mlb-debuts-new-extra-innings-rule-shohei-ohtani-makes-history-but-as-walk-off-on-grand-slam-home-run/; Joe Rivera, "MLB Rule Changes for 2022: Why Controversial Extra-Inning Ghost Runner Is Sticking Around (For Now)," *The Sporting News*, March 23, 2022, https://www.sportingnews.com/us/mlb/news/mlb-rule-changes-2022-extra-inning-ghost-runner/pfawy4fmbxzcdl-noolo2bd3p.
3. Dale Voiss, "Harvey Kuenn," Society for American Baseball Research https://sabr.org/bioproj/person/harvey-kuenn/; Jack Lang, "National League Manager Confidential Player Ratings," *Sport*, July 1963, 87.
4. Drellich and Sarris, "Ghost-Runner Rule Permanent;" Axisa, "MLB Debuts New Extra-Innings Rule;" Rivera, "MLB Rule Changes for 2022;" Ronald Blum, "Ghost Runner in Extra Innings Made Permanent by MLB," Associated Press, February 13, 2023, https://apnews.com/article/mlb-sports-baseball-los-angeles-dodgers-rob-manfred-fcbe340bfcc21dffe7f6af314c06063e.

The 1945 Pennant Races

Douglas Jordan, PhD

From a historical perspective, the primary event that took place in 1945 was the conclusion of World War II. But the war was still raging at the end of 1944, and additional manpower was needed to ensure victory over the Axis powers. Because of this, in December 1944, the director of War Mobilization and Reconversion, James Byrnes, ordered all dog and horse racing tracks to be closed in January 1945.[1] He argued that people working in the industry would be better employed in the war effort, and that the fuel used by the industry, and by patrons getting to the races, was needed by the armed forces.

The order made the status of the upcoming baseball season uncertain as the calendar turned to 1945. Would the same edict be applied to other sports, including baseball? On New Year's Day, Byrnes assured reporters that other sports would not be shuttered, but that the policy for 4-F draft deferments for athletes would be tightened.[2] That could be a big problem for major league baseball: At one point in 1944, 260 out of 400 players (65 percent) were designated 4-F.[3] How would teams replace players if more of them were draft eligible in 1945?

Uncertainty associated with the answer to this question persisted through Opening Day. A directive was issued on January 20 that required War Department review of all 4-F professional athletes.[4] Some players were still considered 4-F after these reviews but many were not. There was also uncertainty about 4-F players working in war related industries. Their status wasn't clarified until March 21, when the War Manpower Commission issued a directive allowing professional baseball players to leave their jobs until October to play.[5] With many major league players already serving, the end result was that the rosters of major league teams when the season opened on April 17 consisted of a mixture of men too young or too old to serve, plus some 4-F players.

A detailed discussion of the composition of major league rosters during World War II is beyond the scope of this article. However, there is a general perception that the overall quality of play was inferior to non-war years, especially in 1945. During that year, H.G. Salsinger of the *Detroit News* wrote, "Even the most charitable and amiable of men must admit that the quality of major league baseball in the current season is the poorest in more than 50 years."[6]

The perception of low-quality play is not shared by all. SABR member Renwick Speer argues against the notion.[7] He notes that major league players such as Lou Boudreau, Frank Crosetti, Babe Dahlgren, Phil Cavarretta, Al Lopez, Marty Marion, and Mel Ott did not miss a full season during the war years. Speer concludes, "We maintain that a good brand of baseball was played in the major leagues during World War II without pretending to imply that it was the same without Pee Wee, the Yankee Clipper, Rapid Robert, and the Kid."

Regardless of the quality of play, what cannot be disputed is that there were two exciting pennant races in 1945. After play on Sunday, September 23, the two American League contenders were separated by a single game. The leaders in the National League were 1½ games apart. The World Series contestants were decided over the last week of the season. The purpose of this article is to examine and discuss the 1945 season to see what led to its exciting conclusion.

METHODOLOGY

Pennant races are usually described verbally based on the number of games separating teams. Fans are very comfortable with this convention, but there are two drawbacks associated with it. First, the standings in terms of games behind on any given day do not show what has happened over time. In addition, games behind is a relative measure because it is based on how far each trailing team is behind the leading team. The relative positions can change because the trailing teams are playing well, or because the leading team is playing poorly, but fans can't know from looking at the standings on a particular day how the teams have fared recently.

Both of these drawbacks can be alleviated by using a graph of the standings over time. Unfortunately, a graph of games behind over time does not solve the relative position issue. That problem can be fixed by graphing the number of games over .500 for teams instead of games behind. A level line from data point to data point means the team played exactly .500 ball over the time period. A line with a positive or negative slope means the team played better or worse than .500 ball. Therefore, the discussion of the 1945 pennant race in this paper will be based on graphs of games over .500 for the teams under consideration. The more familiar number of games behind is always just half the difference in games over .500. Unless otherwise noted, all data are taken from Baseball-Reference.com.

SETTING THE STAGE

No baseball season exists in a vacuum. Teams and players that fared well the previous year are usually expected to do well again during the current season. Therefore, a brief discussion of the 1944 season and a few broader items will set the stage for the 1945 campaign.

With the exception of New York City, it is rare for two teams from the same city to play in the World Series. The only time that happened in St. Louis was in 1944. In the American League, the St. Louis Browns went 14–3 over their last 17 games that year. The Detroit Tigers went 13–4 over the same period. The two teams were tied with one game left in the season. The Browns won and the Tigers lost on the final day of the campaign to give the Browns the only pennant they won in over 50 years in St. Louis (the franchise moved to Baltimore in 1954). The Washington Nationals came in last with a 64–90 record.

There wasn't a pennant race in the National League in 1944. The St. Louis Cardinals dominated the league with 105 wins. The Pittsburgh Pirates' 90 victories were second best. It was the third consecutive year the Cardinals had won the NL pennant and won more than 100 games. The only other team with three straight 100-win seasons before the Cardinals was the Philadelphia Athletics from 1929–31.[8] The Cardinals won the World Series four games to two. One notable aspect of the Series was that every game was played in the same ballpark, since the two teams shared Sportsman's Park as their home field.[9]

The Cardinals' chances for a fourth consecutive pennant were reduced when three 1944 All-Stars had to serve in the military in 1945. Stan Musial missed the entire season, and catcher Walker Cooper and hurler Max Lanier played briefly before being called up. The pitching staff took another blow when 22-game winner Mort Cooper, who had feuded with St. Louis owner Sam Breadon over his salary, was traded to the Boston Braves early in the season for nine-game-winner Red Barrett.

The two pitchers switched roles in 1945. Barrett collected 21 wins for the Cardinals while an elbow injury limited Cooper to 11 starts for the Braves.[10] In addition to the surprise performance from Barrett, the Cardinals got an unexpected contribution from rookie pitcher Ken Burkhart, whose 18 wins and 2.90 ERA helped keep the Cardinals in contention through the year. In light of what happened in 1945, it should be noted that the Chicago Cubs finished the 1944 season 30 games out of first place with a 75–79 record.

The 1945 baseball schedule contained an unusually high number of doubleheaders. This was done in order to minimize team travel in response to wartime travel restrictions.[11] Table 1 shows the dates of 1945 doubleheaders for the top two teams in each league.

The schedule was a success in in minimizing travel, but it made the season a relentless grind for the players. This was justified as a wartime necessity, but it exhausted the players, especially pitchers, and made the last two months of the season as much a test of survival as a race for the pennant.[12] The American League contenders got the worst of it. Detroit played six doubleheaders in May and July. This was followed by nine in both August and September for a total of 36 doubleheaders over the course of the season.

The Nationals had it even worse. The team played seven doubleheaders in both June and July, and then had an incredible 14 twin bills in August, with nine

Table 1. Dates of Doubleheaders in 1945 for Contending Teams

	April	May	June	July	August	September	Total
Detroit	29	6,13,19, 20,27,30	3,10,16, 17,24	1,4,8,18, 20,22	5,6,8,12,13, 19, 20,21 26	3,5,6,9,10, 12,15 16,26	36
Washington	29	6,13,19, 20,27,30	3,5,15,17, 19,24,30	1,4,6,16, 18,20,22	1,2,3,4,5,12, 13,19,20,22, 25,26,29,31	2,3,5,6,9, 10,15,16,23	44
Chicago (NL)	29	6,20,27,30	3,10,14, 15,24,29	1,4,6,8,12, 15,18,22,29	3,5,8,12,19	2,3,5,9, 14,16,27,29	33
St. Louis (NL)	22,29	2,6,13,16, 20,27,30	3,10,17, 24,27	1,4,8,13,15,18, 19,22,29,31	5,12,15,19	2,3,6,9, 14,16,29	35

more in September. The Nationals played a double-header on five consecutive days at the beginning of August (going 9–1 over those 10 games), and a total of 44 over the course of the campaign. Why did the team play so many games the last two months of the season? In addition to wartime travel restrictions, the Nationals owner, Clark Griffith, had agreed to let the Washington professional football team use the field during the last week of the baseball season, so the Nats had to finish their schedule on September 23 instead of September 30.

It's likely that Washington was able to stay competitive in spite of having to play so many games during the last eight weeks because the pitching staff had four knuckleball pitchers. Dutch Leonard (17–7), Roger Wolff (20–10), Mickey Haefner (16–14), and Johnny Niggeling (7–12) all featured the easier-on-the-arm knuckleball. Griffith's early adoption of night baseball (the Nationals played more night games than any other team), which allowed wartime workers to go to games and increased attendance, also helped the knucklers. "The knuckler has the edge under the lights," Wolff said. "Leonard and Niggeling and myself ought to do all right."[13]

Wolff was right. Data from the 1945 season show the four pitchers had a combined 2.84 ERA during the day vs. 2.20 at night. The day/night split for batting average against was .243/.218. But these better pitching numbers didn't translate into more wins. The Nationals had a .550 winning average at night against a .570 winning average during the day.[14] The overall quality of play may have had something to do with the quartet's success. Collectively weaker hitting in 1945 may have enabled Washington to rely on a primarily knuckleball-pitching staff.

The history of night baseball is tangential to this story. However, a short digression will be of interest given the modern tendency to play games at night. The first night game was played in Cincinnati in 1935. But baseball was very slow to adopt the innovation. Why was that? The short answer is because of the attitude of the owners. "Why, this night game is baseball's ruination. It changes baseball players from athletes to actors. It's nothing more than a spectacle," said Tigers owner Frank Navin. Sportswriter H.G. Salsinger, summarizing the attitude of the time, wrote, "Baseball was made to be played in the daylight. It just isn't as good at night, it

can't be. Infielders can't get a jump on the ball at night. Ground balls go through the infield that would be fielded in daylight. You cannot see the spin of the ball at night—only a white object sailing at you. Night baseball is a much inferior game."[15]

THE FIRST FOUR MONTHS OF THE 1945 SEASON

The performance in terms of games over .500 for the American League over the first two-thirds of the 1945 season is shown in Figure 1.

Figures 1 and 2 (below and following page) are a little confusing because they show the performance of all eight teams in each league. The easiest way to understand each graph is to start with the team names on the right side and follow the line for a particular team from right to left in order to see what happened to the team earlier in the season. In Figure 1, the data points for Boston and St. Louis are on top of each other. Therefore, there are two lines coming out of the sixth data point and there are seven (instead of eight) final data points on the far right side.

In 1945, the season opened on Tuesday, April 17. The AL standings after play on Sundays at approximately monthly intervals are displayed in Figure 1. One month into the season the New York Yankees and Chicago White Sox led the league with the Tigers just a game behind, and the defending champ Browns three games in arrears with a .500 record.

However, the standings that day were of minor importance compared with the news that Germany had surrendered on May 8. In addition to the national jubilation that followed V-E Day, the implications for baseball were significant. Two million soldiers, including many major league players, were to be released

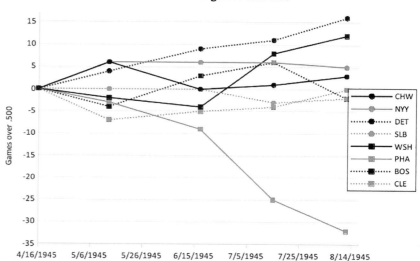

Figure 1. 1945 AL Pennant Race Before August 12
Games behind is half the difference in games over .500

within the next year, and War Department reviews of 4-F professional athletes were suspended.[16] This resulted in many players returning to their teams over the course of the 1945 season.

By mid-June, the Tigers had moved into first place and the White Sox had fallen off the pace. The Yankees trailed Detroit by 1½ games while the Nationals were four games under .500 and 6½ games behind. Two of the most important events of the season (from an AL pennant race perspective) occurred between mid-June and mid-July. The Nationals went 18–6 over the month to move into second place, just 1½ games behind Detroit, on July 15. The most surprising aspect of this run was that most of it took place on a 19-game road trip.

Both teams got some excellent news in this timeframe. Hank Greenberg, one of the first major league players to go into the service, returned to the Tigers on July 1. He hit the 250th home run of his career in his first game back. The Nationals got an offensive boost from the return of Buddy Lewis on July 27. Although Lewis did not have Greenberg's power, he batted .333 with 37 RBIs over 69 games to provide an offensive boost to a Nationals team that batted .258 on the season. These two teams continued to play well over the next month. They had separated themselves from the rest of the league by August 12, with the Tigers leading the Nats by two games.

The race in the National League prior to August 12 is shown in Figure 2.

The two NL teams in New York got off to fast starts in 1945. The New York Giants went 16–5 over the first month to lead the Brooklyn Dodgers by two games just after V-E Day. Both teams fell back to the rest of the NL pack over the following month, so by mid-June, the top six teams in the NL were separated by just 3½ games, with Brooklyn on top.

As in the AL, the next month was significant for the pennant race. The Cubs went 21–7 (which included a 13–3 road trip) to take a four-game lead over the Cardinals by mid-July. The Dodgers were just a game behind St. Louis. Chicago continued to play well for the next month, going 21–8 from July 16 to August 12. This increased their lead over St. Louis to six games with Brooklyn trailing the Cardinals by just a half game at the end of play on August 12.

THE FINAL SEVEN WEEKS IN THE AMERICAN LEAGUE

Although the war in Europe had ended in May, the conflict with Japan continued as the calendar turned to August. Thousands of men were sent to the Pacific Theater in preparation for an invasion of the Japanese mainland. Casualties on both sides were expected to be very high during the invasion. But a new weapon of war and the Soviet Union's declaration of war against Japan on August 8 changed the course of history. Japan surrendered on August 14 after atomic bombs were dropped on Hiroshima on August 6 and Nagasaki on August 9.

From a baseball perspective, the end of the war meant that all of the former players would be coming back. The only question was whether they would return in time for them to play in 1945. Two prominent examples were Bob Feller and Joe DiMaggio. Feller's highly anticipated return occurred on August 24 against the Tigers in Cleveland. It seemed as though he'd never been away. The Indians beat the Tigers 4–2 behind Feller's complete game four-hitter (with 12 strikeouts). But the War Department didn't discharge DiMaggio in time. His return would have to wait until 1946.

The last seven weeks of the pennant race in the AL are shown in Figure 3.

There are several differences between the first roughly two-thirds of the race in Figure 1 and the last third in Figure 3. First, in order to focus on the contest for the pennant, only the top four teams in the league are shown. In addition, the results are shown weekly, rather than monthly.

Figure 2. 1945 NL Pennant Race Before August 12
Games behind is half the difference in games over .500

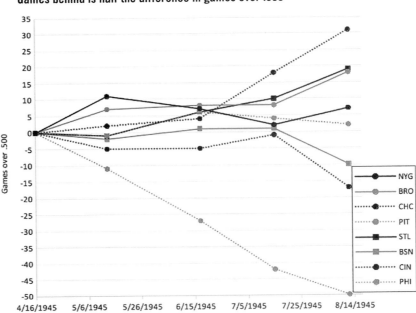

Figure 3 shows that the league-leading Tigers stayed 16 games over .500 between August 12 and September 2, while the Nationals moved from 12 to 14 games over .500. This left Washington one game behind after play on the second day of September. The Nationals made up some of that ground by winning three out of four during a series in Detroit August 15–18. Although it is not shown in Figure 3, Washington trailed by just a half game on August 22 and August 24.

In spite of the heavy workload, Washington went 9–3 in the 12 games after September 2. But unfortunately for the Nationals, Detroit (which played five doubleheaders in the same timeframe) also played very well that week, so the Tigers maintained a one game lead after play on Monday, September 10. Detroit's lead was reduced to a half game as the Tigers entered a crucial five-game series (back-to-back doubleheaders on Saturday and Sunday, with another game on Tuesday) against the Nationals in Washington starting on Saturday, September 15. The Nationals' chances to move into first place were improved because Greenberg could not play due to injury.[17]

Pitching, which had been the strength of the Washington club all season, did not perform well during the Saturday twin bill. The Nationals allowed seven runs in both games and were swept, leaving them 2½ games back. A split on Sunday and a victory on Tuesday left them 1½ games behind with just five more away games on their truncated schedule.

Washington still trailed by 1½ games entering its final two games, against the A's in Philadelphia on

September 23. The Tigers lost to the Browns that day, so a sweep by the Nationals would have put them into a virtual tie for first place. The Nationals won the nightcap, but the first game has gone down in infamy for Washington fans. Leading 3–0 in the middle of the eighth inning, two consecutive Nationals errors put men on first and second with no outs. That led to three unearned runs for the Athletics, and the game went into extra innings.

In the top of the 12th inning, the A's center fielder, Sam Chapman, was having trouble with the sun so he requested timeout to have his sunglasses brought out. Bingo Binks, the Nationals center fielder, didn't take the hint. He went out for the bottom of the 12th without sunglasses. With two outs, Binks lost an easy popup in the sun, and the batter, outfielder Ernie Kish, reached second base. Kish scored on a single by George Kell to give Philadelphia a walk-off victory, leaving Washington one game behind the Tigers as their season ended.[18]

Detroit had four games scheduled for the following week. If the Tigers lost three of four they would be tied with the Nationals. They split the first two games before traveling to St. Louis for a season-ending doubleheader against the Browns on September 30. Had the Browns swept, there would have been a one-game playoff in Detroit for the pennant.[19] The first game of the twin bill is arguably the most well-known game played in 1945.

It was raining in St. Louis for the 10th straight day on September 30.[20] The field was a quagmire, and the game probably would not have been played if the pennant were not at stake.[21] The contest commenced after a 50-minute delay, with Virgil Trucks, just a few days after being discharged from the Navy, starting for the Tigers.[22] Trucks allowed a run in the bottom of the first, but the Tigers took the lead with single tallies in the fifth and sixth innings. The Browns scored single runs in the seventh and eighth to take a 3–2 lead going into the ninth. Pete Gray, the Browns' one-armed outfielder, scored the go-ahead run in the eighth.

Nels Potter, the starter for the Browns, was still pitching in the ninth. A single, fielder's choice, bunt, and intentional walk brought Greenberg to the plate as a pinch-hitter with the bases loaded. Greenberg described what happened next:

Figure 3. 1945 AL Pennant Race After August 12
Games behind is half the difference in games over .500

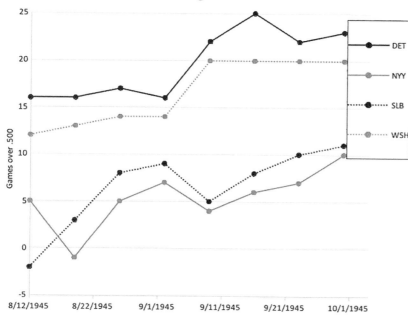

As he wound up on the next pitch, I could read his grip on the ball and I could tell he was going to throw a screwball. I swung and hit a line drive toward the corner of the left-field bleachers. I stood at the plate and watched the ball for fear the umpire would call it foul. It landed a few feet inside the foul pole for a grand slam. We won the game, and the pennant, and all the players charged the field when I reached home plate and they pounded me on the back and carried on like I was a hero.[23]

The Browns failed to score in the bottom of the inning, and the second game was not played.

From a modern perspective, another interesting aspect of the story is that the Tigers would have won the pennant even if they had lost the first game. The weather conditions and darkness would have precluded the second game being played. There was no rule at the time saying a team had to complete its schedule, even if any unplayed games had bearing on the pennant race. Since the second game could not have been played, even with a loss, the Tigers would have won the pennant by a half game.[24]

THE FINAL SEVEN WEEKS IN THE NATIONAL LEAGUE

The last seven weeks of the pennant race in the NL are shown in Figure 4, which shows that the Cubs had a comfortable lead over the Cardinals and the Dodgers on August 12. Brooklyn went 2–8 over their next 10 games, including losing three out of four to the Cubs at Ebbets Field, which essentially ended their bid for the pennant. Chicago and St. Louis faced off seven times in late August and early September. The Cubs got swept in three games at home, and then lost three out of four in St. Louis. This put the Cardinals just 1½ games behind Chicago after play on September 2.

Both teams had favorable schedules in September. The Cardinals were at home almost the entire month before finishing the season with six away games starting on September 25. The Cubs had an 18-game home stand from September 3–17, with eight away games in the latter part of the month. They both took advantage of playing at home. The Cardinals won seven straight from September 6–12. But unfortunately for St. Louis, Chicago went 13–4 from September 3–16 to increase

its lead to four games after play on Sunday, September 16. A Cardinals victory and a Cubs loss on the 17th meant the teams were separated by three games as the Cubs went to St. Louis for a three-game series starting on the 18th. The two teams were also scheduled to play two games in Chicago the following week.

The Cardinals had good reason to be confident that they could catch the Cubs. The three-time defending NL champs were 13–4 against Chicago for the season, and had won three of their last four games going into the September 18 contest. St. Louis won the game on the 18th to close to within two games. A late-season acquisition by the Cubs had a big impact on half of the remaining games between the two clubs.

The Cubs purchased pitcher Hank Borowy from the Yankees for $97,000 (an immense figure at the time) on July 27.[25] Borowy, who went 108–82 in a 10-year major league career, is not well remembered today, but he was the ace of the Yankees staff in 1944. He had 10 wins for the Bronx Bombers in 1945 before he was sent to the Cubs, and he made an immediate impact on the NL pennant race. Borowy went 8–2 with a 1.96 ERA for Chicago before starting against the Cardinals on September 19.

George Dockins was on the mound for St. Louis for the contest on the 19th. The game was a classic pitchers' duel. The Cubs put a runner on second in the first and fourth innings, but failed to drive in the run. The Cardinals loaded the bases in the sixth inning but Borowy ended the threat by inducing a double play, so the game was scoreless after seven innings. In the home half of the eighth, Borowy walked Dockins (who

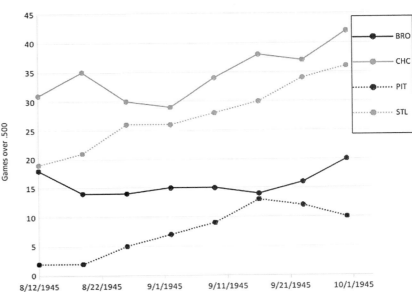

Figure 4. 1945 NL Pennant Race After August 12
Games behind is half the difference in games over .500

Pitcher Hank Borowy was crucial to the Cubs down the stretch in 1945.

was batting ninth) with one out. The Cardinals hurler scored on consecutive singles to put St. Louis ahead, 1–0, entering the ninth.

Dockins got the Cubs leadoff hitter in the ninth to ground to third, but an error by St. Louis third baseman Whitey Kurowski allowed Don Johnson to reach first.[26] A sacrifice bunt by Peanuts Lowrey put pinch-runner Ed Sauer in scoring position. The Cubs were down to their last out after Phil Cavarretta popped out. With one more out the Cardinals would be within a single game of the Cubs. But a single by Andy Pafko drove in the tying run, and the game went to extra innings after Borowy set the Cardinals down in order in the bottom of the ninth. The Cubs scored three times in the top of the 10th and won the contest 4–1, with Borowy again retiring the side in order in the home 10th.[27]

With the benefit of hindsight, the race likely turned on the outcome of the game on the 19th. St. Louis won the third game of the series, but Borowy's victory meant the Cubs lead was still two games with just eight games left in the season. St. Louis trimmed a half game from that lead entering a two-game series in Chicago the next week. A sweep would put the Cardinals in first place with five games remaining. But St. Louis would have to beat Borowy in the first game to make that happen.

Borowy was not as sharp as he had been in the last game, and the Cardinals led 3–2 in the middle of the seventh. But the Cubs pushed four runs across the plate in the bottom of the inning to take a 6–3 lead. St. Louis made it close with two runs in the eighth, but couldn't get the hit that would tie the game. The

Cardinals won the second game of the series, but for the second consecutive week, Borowy had notched the win against St. Louis in a crucial game.

The Cubs won their last five games of the season to win the pennant by a final margin of three games over the Cardinals. Borowy was 11–2 with a 2.13 ERA after he was acquired by Chicago. It needs to be mentioned that Borowy was not the only Cubs pitcher to make a big contribution to securing the pennant. The wartime player shortage compelled Chicago to turn to 38-year-old Ray Prim in an effort to bolster their rotation. Prim responded with a career year that was topped by a tremendous run during the final three months of the season. From July 6 to the end of the season Prim went 11–4 with a 1.27 ERA. His 2.40 ERA overall led the league.

CONCLUSION

The main point of this article is to describe the 1945 pennant races, not the 1945 World Series. That said, it is appropriate to conclude the article with a brief description of what happened after those two exciting races.

The playoff structure in major league baseball was very simple before 1969. The pennant winners faced off in the World Series. So after two tight pennant races, Chicago, with a 98–56 record, played the 88–65 Tigers in the Fall Classic. Detroit's chances against the Cubs had been boosted by the September return of Vigil Trucks, who started two games against the Cubs in the World Series, winning one and getting a no-decision in the other. Given the drama of the two pennant races, it seems appropriate that a World Series between these two teams would come down to a winner-take-all game. The Tigers scored five runs in the first inning of Game Seven and went on to win the contest 9–3. It was the second World Series victory for Detroit. The Tigers had won their first championship with a victory over the Cubs in 1935.

Finally, it would be a dereliction of duty to summarize the 1945 World Series and not mention one of the most famous animals in baseball history. For over 70 years, until the Cubs reached the promised land in 2016, many Chicagoans believed that a goat was preventing the Cubs from winning the World Series. Legend has it that a Chicago tavern owner cursed the team when he and the goat he had brought to Game Four of the 1945 World Series were thrown out of the ballpark. The Curse of the Billy Goat was born. But there is more to the legend than that. Glen Sparks tells the rest of the story in SABR's *Wrigley Field: The Friendly Confines at Clark and Addison*. The author was part of a small group of SABR members who had the opportunity to visit the Billy Goat Tavern during the 2023 SABR convention in Chicago. ■

Acknowledgments
Many thanks to two anonymous peer reviewers. Their suggestions significantly improved the final product.

Notes
1. Bertram D. Hulenspecial, "All Racing Banned on Call of Byrnes to Aid War Effort," *The New York Times*, December 24, 1944, 1.
2. Dan Daniel, "Washington Doesn't Plan to Halt Game," *The Sporting News*, January 4, 1945: 1.
3. William Marshall, Baseball's Pivotal Era, 1945–1951 (Lexington, University Press of Kentucky, 1999), 16.
4. "50 Percent of 4-F's Accepted," *The Sporting News*, March 8, 1945: 1.
5. "Greenest of All Green Lights for Game," *The Sporting News*, March 29, 1945: 10.
6. John Klima, *The Game Must Go On*, (New York, St. Martin's Press, 2015), 344.
7. Renwick W. Speer, "Wartime Baseball: Not That Bad," *Baseball Research Journal* 12 (1983), http://research.sabr.org/journals/wartime-baseball-not-that-bad, accessed May 15, 2023.
8. Four more teams have won 100 or more games in three consecutive years since the Cardinals did it. They are the 1969–71 Baltimore Orioles, the 1997–99 Atlanta Braves, the 2002–04 New York Yankees, and the 2017–19 Houston Astros.
9. The 1921 and 1922 World Series were also played in one stadium, the Polo Grounds in New York City.
10. Gregory H. Wolf, "Mort Cooper," Society for American Baseball Research, https://sabr.org/bioproj/person/mort-cooper/.
11. Klima, *The Game Must Go On*, 269.
12. Klima, 324.
13. Noah Scott, "Knuckleheads: The 1945 Senators and the First All-Knuckleball Rotation," *Pitcherlist*, July 20, 2020, https://www.pitcherlist.com/knuckleheads-the-1945-senators-and-the-first-all-knuckleballrotation/, accessed August 25, 2023.
14. Scott.
15. Steven P. Gietschier, *Baseball: The Turbulent Midcentury Years* (Lincoln, University of Nebraska Press, 2023), 235.
16. Dan Daniel, "Fewer U.S. Calls, Some Will Return," *The Sporting News*, May 10, 1945: 1.
17. Greenberg injured his ankle sliding into second base on September 9. The injury was severe enough that he could not start in the crucial series against Washington. He did pinch-hit three times during the Washington series. See Klima, *The Game Must Go On*, 364.
18. Rob Neyer, "A Last Great Season: The Senators in 1945," ESPN, March 14, 2002, https://www.espn.com/page2/wash/s/2002/0314/1351582.html, accessed May 28, 2023.
19. Neyer, "A Last Great Season…" Neyer writes, "So as the last day of the season dawned, the Tigers still owned a one-game lead over the Senators heading into a twin bill against the third-place Browns in St. Louis. Win either game, and they would clinch the pennant. Lose both, and the Tigers would head back to Detroit, where Dutch Leonard was already waiting to pitch in a one-game playoff for the American League pennant."
20. Marshall, *Baseball's Pivotal Era*, 34.
21. Fred Lieb, "Browns Again Shape History in Final Game," *The Sporting News*, October 4, 1945: 27.
22. Neyer, "A Last Great Season."
23. Neyer.
24. Neyer.
25. The details of the Yankees-Cubs Borowy transaction sound like a soap opera. Yankees GM Larry MacPhail sold Borowy to the National League Cubs deliberately so that the American League Nationals (and their owner, Clark Griffith) would not get the pitching help they desperately needed down the stretch. It was also done to make it harder for the Cardinals to catch the Cubs in revenge for the Cardinals victory over the Yankees in the 1942 World Series. See Klima, *The Game Must Go On*, 326–27.
26. Frederick G. Lieb, "Hard-Fighting Cards Open Hard-Way Drive," *The Sporting News*, September 27, 1945: 8.
27. Play-by-play for this game is not complete. The incomplete Retrosheet account was used to describe the game action. "Chicago Cubs 4, St. Louis Cardinals 1," Retrosheet, https://www.retrosheet.org/boxesetc/1945/B09190SLN1945.htm, accessed June 9, 2023.

Going Downtown with a Golden Sombrero

Combining Baseball's Best and Worst True Outcomes

Herm Krabbenhoft

For a batter or pitcher, the best—or worst—of the "Three True Outcomes" is a home run or a strikeout.[1] The rates of the both home runs and strikeouts have increased substantially over the years. To illustrate, let's compare 1949 and 2019. In the National League in 1949, 42,711 at bats resulted in 935 homers and 4,587 in strikeouts, while NL batters in 2019 collected 3,298 homers and whiffed 21,408 times.[2] Tables 1 and 2 summarize the comparative information (absolute and relative, respectively) for the 1949 and 2019 seasons.[3]

These data show an 81.3% increase in home runs and a 139.9% increase in strikeouts from 1949 to 2019. The rate of strikeouts per homer is also up substantially: 32.2%.

Turning the focus to specific players, I thought it would be interesting to see which players have compensated for multiple strikeouts in a game by hitting a key home run. In the baseball lexicon one term seems particularly appropriate—the "Golden Sombrero," which, according to *The Dickson Baseball Dictionary*, is "A mythical award given to a batter who strikes out four times in a game."[4] And since "Going Downtown" is a commonly used expression to describe hitting a home run, I've dubbed the combination of four strikeouts and a homer in the same game a Downtown Golden Sombrero (DGS). My research here has two objectives: First, find all players with a Downtown

Golden Sombrero.[5] Second, find out were any of those downtowners redemptive—i.e., a game-winning or a game-saving homer?

RESEARCH PROCEDURE

Using the Stathead search engine on the Baseball-Reference.com website, I ascertained all players who assembled (I hesitate to use the term "achieved") a Golden Sombrero and also went Downtown in the same game, during the regular seasons from 1901 through 2023 in the American League and National League seasons, and in 1914–15 in the Federal League. I also searched the Game-By-Game statistics generated by Information Concepts, Incorporated (ICI sheets) for the 1891–1900 National League seasons.[6] A complete list (with the pertinent details) of all the DGSs found is provided in the Supplement to this article (available on the SABR website). Using these lists of DGSs, I then examined the Play-By-Play (PBP) files on the Baseball-Reference and Retrosheet websites as well as the game descriptions presented in relevant newspapers to obtain the critical details of the game.

RESULTS

According to my research, there were 175 DGS performances in the regular season—including five times when the player merited the "Downtown Platinum Sombrero" (the player struck out *five* times). There

Table 1. The Three True Outcomes (Absolute) for the 1949 and 2019 National League Seasons

Year	AB	HR	SO	W	HBP
1949	42,711	935	4,587	4,405	199
2019	83,094	3,298	21,408	7,979	1,048

Table 2. The Three True Outcomes (Relative) for the 1949 and 2019 National League Seasons

Year	HR/100 AB	SO/100 AB	SO/HR	W/100 AB	HBP/100 AB
1949	2.19	10.74	4.91	10.55	0.47
2019	3.97	25.76	6.49	9.60	1.26
△	1.78	15.02	1.58	− 0.95	0.79
% Change	81.3	139.9	32.2	− 9.0	168.1

have also been four DGSs in postseason play. Table 3 presents a chronological breakdown by decade of regular-season DGSs 1891–2023.

After a paltry seven DGSs during the 79 seasons from 1891 through 1969, the number of DGSs has increased dramatically in the 54 seasons since 1970—168 more. The twenty-first century has been extraordinarily explosive—112 DGSs in just 23 seasons. And there have already been 29 DGSs in the first four seasons of the 2020s decade (including the pandemic-abbreviated 2020 campaign of only 60 games).

While the main focus of my research effort was to identify the DGS awardees who came through with game-clinching downtowners, I also uncovered a number of other interesting notes. Accordingly, the following topics are presented in the Appendix (pages 63–66):

(A-1) The first DGS for each NL and AL franchise

(A-2) DGS grand slams

(A-3) Players with multiple DGS games

(A-4) Players with multiple-homer DGS games

(A-5) Players who led off with a homer

(A-6) Downtown Platinum Sombrero awardees

(A-7) Postseason DGSs

There are two types of last-inning game-winning homer, the "pseudo" walk-offs (hit in the top of the inning) and the "bonafide" walk-offs. For a pseudo walk-off homers, the lead produced by the downtowner has to be protected in the bottom half of the frame. As it has turned out, there have been eight DGSs featuring pseudo walk-offs and nine DGSs with bonafide walk-offs. The 17 DGS players who achieved these phoenix-like performances are highlighted in this article (see Tables 4 and 5).[7]

A. THE DGS PLAYERS WITH PSEUDO WALK-OFF DOWNTOWNERS

Willie McCovey of the 1970 San Francisco Giants was the first player to come through with a game-winning downtowner after striking out in four prior at bats. In the game on April 16 against the Astros in Houston, Stretch was K'd in his first four plate appearances—Jim Bouton got him in the first, third, and fifth, while Jack Billingham fanned him in the sixth. In the eighth, Willie Mac drew a base on balls from Fred Gladding. In the top of the tenth, with the game tied, 9–9, McCovey stepped into the batter's box with Bobby Bonds on third base and two outs. Houston skipper, Harry "The Hat" Walker, made a pitching change from right-hander Dan Osinski to southpaw Jack DiLauro. On DiLauro's second pitch, McCovey drove the ball downtown, giving the Giants an 11–9 lead, which San-Fran reliever Ron Bryant protected by setting down the Astros 1–2–3 in the bottom of the frame.[8]

Larry Herndon clouted his phoenix-like downtowner on July 22, 1980. The game-winning blast came in the 15th inning of the game that had started the day before, on July 21, in the Windy City. After having grounded out in his first two trips to the plate, Herndon was struck out by Cubs starter Rick Reuschel in the sixth. In the ninth, Bruce Sutter struck him out. And in the eleventh, Dick Tidrow sent him back to the dugout via the strikeout. The game, still scoreless, was suspended after the twelfth inning and resumed the next day. Facing Bill Caudell in the thirteenth, Herndon struck out to merit the Golden Sombrero. Redemption, however, came in the fifteenth—with one man on and

Table 3. Chronological Summary of the Number of Regular-Season DGSs (1891–2023)

Period	1891–99	1900–49	1950–59	1960–69	1970–79	1980–89	1990–99	2000–09	2010–19	2020–23
DGSs	1	1	4	1	13	16	23	47	40	29

Table 4. "Pseudo Walkoffs": DGS Players with Game-Winning Homers—Top of the Last Inning

DGS #	Game Yr/Mo/D (G)	Player	TM	OPP	HR I (BR)	IS	FS
8	1970–04–16	Willie McCovey	SFG	HOU*	10 (1)	11–9	11–9 (10)
21	1980–07–21	Larry Herndon	SFG	CHC*	15 (1)	2–0	2–0 (15)
34	1987–09–19	Garry Templeton	SDP	HOU*	14 (0)	2–1	2–1 (14)
54	1998–08–20 (2)	Devon White	ARZ	PHP*	11 (2)	12–9	12–9 (11)
65	2001–05–01	Alex Gonzalez	TOR	OAK*	10 (0)	5–4	5–4 (10)
99	2008–08–13	Wladimir Balentien	SEA	LAA*	12 (2)	10–7	10–7 (12)
101	2009–06–07	Mark Reynolds	ARZ	SDP*	18 (2)	9–6	9–6 (18)
137	2018–08–05	Daniel Palka	CWS	TBR*	9 (1)	8–6	8–7

one man out, Herndon took Caudill downtown to give the Giants a 2–0 lead. San Francisco reliever Gary Lavelle gave up a leadoff single in the bottom of the 15th, but then set down the next three batters to secure the win.

Garry Templeton was playing for the San Diego Padres in a game against the Astros in Houston. He had struck out three times against starting pitcher Nolan Ryan and once against reliever Larry Anderson. He also grounded out in the twelfth while facing Rocky Childress. Then, in the top of the 14th, with the game still knotted, 1–1, with two down and the bases empty, Templeton went downtown to give the Padres a 2–1 advantage. San Diego's mound corps of Dave Leiper and Lance McCullers preserved the victory (despite giving up a couple of hits). After the game, San Diego skipper Larry Bowa was exuberant about Templeton's downtowner, exclaiming, "Templeton called that home run; can you believe it? He was running around the dugout telling everybody he was going to leave the yard; leave the yard! Told about five people. Can you believe it?" When told what Bowa had said, Templeton replied, "What? I'd have to be some kind of stupid to call my own shot. Especially in this ballpark. All I told everybody was, 'I'm going to hit the ball hard.' Maybe it just sounded like 'yard.'"[9]

Devon White earned two DGS awards in his big-league career, the first one coming with Arizona in 1998. After not playing at all in the first game of the August 20 twin-bill in Philadelphia, White had "two different games" in the second game of the double header. In his "first game," White struck out in each of his four at bats—two swinging Ks versus starter Ken Ryan and two looking versus Jerry Spradlin and Yorkis Perez, one each. Then, in his "second game," with the Diamondbacks trailing by a 4–9 score going into the top of the eighth, White rose from the ashes, hitting a 2-RBI single off Wayne Gomes to make the score 8–9, and then coming around to tally the run that knotted the score, 9–9. After being stranded following a leadoff double off Ricky Bottalico in the tenth, he came to bat in the eleventh with two outs and runners on first and second. Bottalico was still on the hill. The count went to 1 ball, 2 strikes. Instead of becoming a five-time K-victim, White connected for a homer "on a hanging breaking ball which barely cleared the fence in front of the Phillies bullpen." With a 12–9 lead, D-Backs reliever Alan Embree then held the Phillies scoreless in the bottom of the inning to secure the victory. After his phoenix-like game, White said, "I can't

explain it. I just put the first couple of at bats out of my mind. You can't think about it; that's the stuff that wears you down. You keep battling."[10]

Alex Gonzalez was baffled by an assortment of breaking pitches, striking out swinging four times in the May 1, 2001, game against the Oakland A's. The Blue Jays shortstop was victimized three times by forkballer Cory Lidle and once by reliever Jim Mecir. With the game tied, 3–3, in the top of the tenth, Gonzalez stepped in to face Jason Isringhausen. He homered on Isringhausen's first pitch to give Toronto a 5–4 advantage, which the Toronto bullpen protected in the bottom of the tenth. Here's what Gonzalez said about his DGS game: "That forkball was giving me trouble tonight. When Isringhausen came in, I knew he has a good fastball, but the forkball isn't a pitch he has. I was able to put that forkball out of my mind and swing hard."[11]

Wladimir Balentien of the Seattle Mariners struck out in his first three at bats against Angels starter Ervin Santana on August 13, 2008. After grounding out in his fourth trip to the plate, he took a called third strike from Darren Oliver in the 10th. Then, in the top of the twelfth, with two down and runners on first and third, he powered a 1–1 pitch from Justin Speier into the seats in deep center field for a home run, giving the M's a 10–7 lead, which Roy Corcoran converted into a win by tossing a perfect bottom of the 12th.

Mark Reynolds collected three DGSs in his major-league career, his second coming in 2009 with the Diamondbacks, in an 18-inning game in San Diego on June 7. He had face-to-face encounters with seven pitchers... and one infielder. In his first two plate appearances he grounded out (in the 2nd) and drew a base on balls (in the 5th) versus Padres starting pitcher Josh Geer. He also received a free pass (in the 6th) from reliever Joe Thatcher. Then he struck out swinging in his next two trips to the batter's box, against Cla Meredith (in the 8th) and Heath Bell (in the 10th). In the 12th, with the game still deadlocked, 6–6, Edward Mujica retired him on a flyout. It was back to the swing-and-miss strikeouts again in the 14th (by Luke Gregerson) and 16th (by Chad Gaudin). With San Diego having gone through nine pitchers, manager Bud Black selected infielder Josh Wilson to start the 18th inning. [Wilson had entered the game in the 12th inning in a double-switch.] Wilson—who actually had begun the 2009 season as Reynolds' teammate on the Diamondbacks before being claimed on waivers by the Padres on May 15—proceeded to retire two D-Backs while giving up a hit and issuing a walk before facing Reynolds. Wilson quickly got Reynolds in an 0–2 hole. But Reynolds managed to work the count full. On the eighth pitch, Reynolds took Wilson downtown, giving Arizona a 9–6 lead, which Leo Rosales saved with a perfect bottom half. After the marathon, Reynolds said, "It's tough because No. 1, he's a position player and you don't want him to get you out, and No. 2, you don't know what he's going to throw." That said, Reynolds did have a small clue: "When he pitched for us [one inning to mop-up a game on May 11] he threw all fastballs, so you figure he has some kind of wrinkle. He threw a curveball up there and I laid off some high fastballs; he left one out over and I was able to barrel it up."[12]

Daniel Palka of the 2018 White Sox achieved the most-recent DGS featuring a pseudo walk-off downtowner. In the August 5 game against the Rays, he had struck out swinging in each of his first four at bats—against opener Hunter Wood in the first and bulk-reliever Ryan Yarborough in the third, fifth, and seventh innings. In the top of the ninth, with the game tied, 6–6, he stepped in the batter's box with two outs and a runner on first to face Diego Castilla, the Rays' third pitcher of the game. On the first pitch, Palka drove a fly ball deep into the center field stands, giving the ChiSox an 8–6 advantage. Although the bullpen surrendered a run in the bottom of the stanza, Chicago still emerged with the 8–7 triumph. The *Chicago Tribune* reported, "Palka's 439-foot bomb came in the ninth, after which he said, 'I just had to forget the first eight-ninths of the game and move on from there."[13]

B. THE DGS PLAYERS WITH BONAFIDE WALK-OFF DOWNTOWNERS
Jim Northrup of the 1971 Detroit Tigers was the first player to manufacture a bonafide walk-off downtown golden sombrero. In the August 1 contest with the visiting Angels, Northrup had gone hitless in his first six trips to the plate—after groundball outs in the first and

third, Northrup struck out swinging in his next four at bats, against Dave LaRoche (sixth), Eddie Fisher (eighth), and Lloyd Allen (10th and 13th). In the bottom of the 16th, with the score knotted at 3–3 and one out, Northrup again squared off against Allen. The *Detroit Free Press* described his rags-to-riches accomplishment thus: "From the sixth inning on, Sunday afternoon, Jim Northrup had one thing on his mind: to hit one out. 'Why not,' he reasoned later. 'We only needed one run so I thought I might as well take a crack at it.' Four times in a row, Northrup struck out. Finally in the 16th he connected, sending a Lloyd Allen fastball for a ride into the right-centerfield seats."[14] Other newspaper accounts corroborate Northrup's swing-for-the-fences strategy: "Of course I was going for it," Northrup said. "I struck out four times in a row. That should tell you something."[15] "I'd been trying to hit a home run all day," Northrup said. "I guess that's why I struck out so many times."[16]

Mike Schmidt was "mired in the most perplexing slump of his marvelous career," reported the *Philadelphia Inquirer*. "And last night [May 28, 1983], it seemed that he had reached the nadir. For when he trudged to the batter's box in the bottom of the ninth inning, with a runner on second in a tie game, he had seen 12 pitches, and all of them had been strikes. His four strikeouts were one short of the one-game major league record. And, as if it had been scripted by Hollywood, Schmidt took one swing and rammed a two-run homer to left field to give the Phils a stranger-than-fiction 5–3 victory over the Montreal Expos."[17] In his first three at-bats Schmidt was fanned by Montreal starter Charlie Lea, leaving five runners on base. In his fourth at bat, Expos reliever Ray Burris sent him back to the dugout with a backward-K. As noted above, 12 pitches, 12 strikes, 4 strikeouts, an "immaculate" golden sombrero! Then the lucky 13th pitch, the 13th strike—the Downtown Golden Sombrero. Schmidt had this to say after the game: "I'm not answering any questions

Table 5. DGS Players with Game-Winning Homers—Bottom of the Last Inning.

DGS #	Game Yr/Mo/D (G)	Player	TM	OPP	HR I (BR)	IS	FS
11	1971–08–01	Jim Northrup	DET*	CAL	16 (0)	4–3	4–3 (16)
24	1983–05–28	Mike Schmidt	PHI*	MON	9 (1)	5–3	5–3
30	1986–07–03	Ray Knight	NYM*	HOU	10 (0)	6–5	6–5 (10)
64	2001–04–22	David Justice	NYY*	BOS	10 (0)	4–3	4–3 (10)
105	2009–08–04	Evan Longoria	TBR*	BOS	13 (1)	4–2	4–2 (13)
113	2013–04–29	Brandon Moss	OAK*	LAA	19 (1)	10–8	10–8 (19)
125	2015–05–29	Derek Norris	SDP*	PIT	9 (3)	6–2	6–2
160	2022–07–04	Victor Caratini	MIL*	CHC	10 (2)	5–2	5–2 (10)
175	2023–09–03	Adolis Garcia	TEX*	MIN	9 (0)	6–5	6–5

tonight. I'll tell you what happened and that's it. I was totally lost, mentally, as a hitter. I was very determined to hit the first pitch. I would have swung wherever it was. It was a fastball down and over the plate and I was concentrating on swinging down and through it. I hit a home run and I'm glad. But there's no way of explaining why I was 0-for-whatever or why I struck out four times tonight. Maybe in a few days."[18]

Ray Knight of the New York Mets had never faced Houston pitcher Jim Deshaies before they squared off on July 3, 1986, for "Fireworks Night" at Shea Stadium. Knight struck out in each of his three at bats against Deshaies. Then, with game tied, 3–3, and two out, he faced Astros reliever Charlie Kerfeld. "'I had a great at bat against Kerfeld in the eighth with the go-ahead run on second,' Knight said. 'I fouled off about eight pitches.' But then Knight struck out for the fourth time on a checked swing."[19] The score remained 3–3 going into the 10th. The Expos pushed a pair a runs across to take a 5–3 lead, and brought in Frank DiPino to close out the game. But the Mets immediately touched him for the equalizers: Lenny Dykstra led off with a walk and Darryl Strawberry belted his second homer of the game. DiPino then set down the next two batters, bringing up Knight. Here's how their fireworks-ending confrontation was described: "'The first pitch he threw me was a slider down and in for a ball,' Knight said. 'Then a changeup away. Then another slider in.' That last slider was the one that never reached catcher Alan Ashby's mitt. 'It was that kind of a game,' Knight said. 'Amazing.'"[20]

David Justice had struck four times swinging during the regulation nine innings of the Yankees-Red Sox game on April 22, 2001, in the Bronx—the first three as a victim of Boston starter Tomo Ohka, the fourth time courtesy of reliever Rod Beck. With the game tied, 2–2, after nine innings, the BoSox took a 3–2 lead in the top of the tenth. The Bronx Bombers answered in Ruthian style. After Derek Jeter was retired to open the bottom half, Paul O'Neill tied the score with a solo homer off Derek Lowe that just made it into the right-field short porch. Then, after Bernie Williams was retired for the second out, Justice stepped to the plate and deposited Lowe's first pitch into the seats for the walk-off. Justice told the *Daily News*, "It wasn't like I was comfortable today, but I was trying to put all that out of my mind. I had thought I don't want to see a curveball with all the shadows coming, so when I got a first-pitch fastball, I swung. The pitch was right there."[21] Lowe had reportedly missed his spot: "Lowe said that he knew Justice loves fastballs but his sinker just stayed up and over the plate."[22] "I'm just glad it turned out that way," Justice said, "because those first four at bats weren't pretty."[23]

Evan Longoria became the first player to go downtown twice in the same golden sombrero game. He achieved this feat with the Tampa Bay Rays on August 4, 2009, in a game against the visiting Red Sox. Boston's starting pitcher, Jon Lester, K'd Longoria in each of their three confrontations, swinging. Then in the eighth, with the BoSox leading, 2–1, Longoria temporarily avoided getting the golden sombrero by leading off the inning with a homer off reliever Daniel Bard, making the score 2–2. Longoria again avoided the golden sombrero in the ninth inning when he was intentionally walked by Ramon Ramirez. In the eleventh, Jonathon Papelbon fanned Longoria to award him the Golden Sombrero, but in the bottom half of the 13th, with Takashi Saito on the mound, the Rays got a runner on with two outs, setting the stage for Longoria. After a first-pitch ball, Longoria went downtown. "It was such a long game, a tough game to stay into mentally," said Longoria. "I was just looking for something to hit."[24] "Longoria came up half-expecting to be given first base. 'It was in the back of my mind,' Longoria said. 'I thought they might walk me and Zobrist to force an out at every base, but I'm happy the way it turned out.' Saito started Longoria with a ball then threw him a 1-and-0 91-miles-per-hour fast ball. 'He just left the ball up in the zone,' Longoria said."[25]

Brandon Moss became the second DGS player to go downtown twice in his golden sombrero game. On April 29, 2013, in a game in Oakland, with the Athletics hosting the Angels, Moss had nine plate appearances, as it took 19 innings to achieve the final verdict. He singled in his first at bat (in the second inning) and struck out swinging in his second at bat (in the fourth). In his third at bat, he slugged a solo homer off starting pitcher Tommy Hanson, which cut the A's deficit to four runs, 6–2. Moss, facing Dane De La Rosa, grounded out in the eighth. In the ninth, he had his second swinging strikeout thanks to Ernesto Frieri, to end the regulation portion of the game with the score knotted, 7–7. In extras, Moss had each of the Three True Outcomes—facing Jerome Williams, he walked in the 12th and struck out swinging in the 14th. Then, after each team scored a run in the 15th, making the score 8–8, Moss put on the Golden Sombrero, courtesy of Michael Kohn. Finally, in the 19th, with one man on and two men out, facing Barry Enright,

Moss connected for the circuit on an 0–1 pitch, giving the Athletics a 10–8 triumph. Moss said afterward, "It was a crazy game and I'm glad it's over. That was exhausting; it really was. You just keep fighting through and keep hoping they throw the ball into your bat. I don't even know how I hit it. I was so late on everything after the 10th inning on. If it was thigh-high or up I couldn't catch it, so I was just trying to get anything down in the zone."[26]

Derek Norris hit the jackpot with his walk-off DGS performance on May 29, 2015. With his Padres hosting the Pirates, Norris struck out swinging in each of his first four at bats—three times on the twirls of starting pitcher Francisco Liriano and once on the offerings of relief hurler Arquimedes Caminero. Then, in the bottom of the ninth, with the score deadlocked, 2–2, with two outs and the bases jammed, he drove a 1–0 pitch from Rob Scahill downtown in deep left-center field, giving San Diego a 10–6 victory—Norris became the first (and still only) DGS player to hit a game-ending game-winning grand slam home run.

Victor Caratini of the Milwaukee Brewers achieved his walk-off DGS clout in the game against the visiting Chicago Cubs on July 4, 2022. He was struck out swinging in each of his first four at bats, three times by starting pitcher Justin Steel and once by reliever David Robertson. Then, in the bottom of the tenth, with the score tied, 2–2, Caratini stepped into the batter's box with runners on second and first and two down. With a 2–1 count, Caratini took Scott Effross downtown, blasting the ball on a line into the center-field seats. Here's what Caratini said afterwards (through a translator): "It's a really hard sport. You know you're going to fail. It's just a matter of staying confident, going to the next at bat, knowing that you've got another at bat and have got to be able to fight it, help the team win, and move on from there."[27]

Adolis Garcia of the Texas Rangers is the most recent player to come through in phoenix fashion in a game against the visiting Minnesota Twins on September 3, 2023. Mired in a horrible slump (batting .153 in his previous 15 games), he was K'd in each of his first four plate appearances—his strike-three swings-and-misses being on "a slider away" (from Kenta Maeda in the first inning with one out and runners on first and second); "a high fastball" (from Maeda in the second inning with two outs and runners on first and third), "another high fastball" (from Maeda leading off in the fifth inning); and "a fastball up-and-away" (from Cole Sands in the sixth inning with two outs and runners on second and third). In his fifth trip to the plate, leading off against Josh Winder, Garcia "belted a 2–2 fastball—one that ran inside and belt-high—430 feet into the second level in left field" for a game-winning homer. "García declined to speak with reporters in the clubhouse afterward. His teammate Mitch Garver nailed the sentiment, though: 'For him to come out there, stay with it and just keep going forward and get the result that he did, couldn't be happier for him.' Rangers manager Bruce Bochy said, 'He's not feeling good about his day at that point. And he got ahold of one. Good for him, good for us.'"[28] "I've got to give a shoutout to Adolis because I've been there, man," Garver said. "I've punched out four times in a game, and you really don't want that fifth at-bat. And for him to come out there and do what he did…it was super impressive." "That's a lot of pressure on you, especially when you're up there with two strikes," Bochy said.[29]

C. THE DGS PLAYERS WHOSE GAME-SAVING DOWNTOWNERS AVERTED IMMINENT DEFEAT

The nine DGS players listed above achieved their bonafide walk-off downtowners with the score tied, and the same goes for the pseudo walk-offs in the section above. None of the 17 game-winning DGS downtowners mentioned so far seized victory from the jaws of defeat. According to my research, there have been just three DGS players whose clutch downtowners were critical in preventing an impending defeat—at least temporarily. (See Table 6.)

Willie Stargell became the first DGS player to come through with a clutch downtowner in a critical do-or-die situation. In the game on July 15, 1971, between the host Pirates and the visiting Padres, Stargell had

Table 6. DGS Players with Homers that Averted Imminent Defeat (at least Temporarily)

DGS #	Game Yr/Mo/D (G)	Player	TM	OPP	HR I (BR)	IS	FS
10	1971–07–15	Willie Stargell	PIT*	SDP	13 (0)	2–2	4–3 (17)
53	1998–08–08	Ray Lankford	SLC*	CHC	11 (2)	7–7	9–8 (13)
61	2000–06–09	Sammy Sosa	CHC	CWS*	9 (1)	5–5	5–6 (14)

been struck out by San Diego's starting pitcher Dave Roberts in each of his first four at bats. After the regulation nine innings, the game was tied, 1–1. Stargell snapped his string of strikeouts in the 11th inning by flying out. The score didn't change until the 13th, when San Diego took a 2–1 lead. In the Pittsburgh half of the frame, after the Padres hurler, Al Severinsen, had struck out the first two batters, Stargell responded to the make-it-or-break-it situation by taking Severinsen downtown to knot the score, 2–2. The Pirates eventually won the game in the 17th, 4–3.

Ray Lankford became the very first player in the NL or AL to achieve a Downtown Platinum Sombrero. Significantly, his downtowner was critical in saving his team from defeat. The game took place on August 8, 1998, between the host St. Louis Cardinals and the guest Chicago Cubs. Lankford struck out the first five times he batted—the first three on the offerings of Cubs starting pitcher Mark Clark (in the second [looking], fourth [swinging], and sixth [swinging]). He also struck out swinging versus Felix Heredia (in the seventh) and Terry Mulholland (in the ninth). At the conclusion of the regulation nine innings, the Cards and Cubs were tied, 5–5. Chicago took the lead, 7–5, in the top of the 11th. Closer Rod Beck was then brought in to save the win for the Cubs. St. Louis proceeded to get a man on with two outs. The next batter, Lankford, was therefore confronted with a do-or-die challenge. Beck's first pitch to Lankford was called a ball. Beck's second offering was sent downtown by Lankford, re-knotting the score, 7–7. Here's what was reported in the newspapers: "Rod Beck threw Lankford a split-fingered fast-ball that Lankford blasted for a game-tying, two-out, two-run homer. 'I'd probably throw it again,' Beck said. 'There's not a lot of secrets between Lankford and me. We've known each other for a long time. It didn't work out for me. I didn't think he hit it that good.'"[30] "I'll tell you what, I was nervous," said Lankford. "I'm not going to lie. But I know what Beck throws me, a lot of off-speed pitches. He got one up and I was able to drive it out of the ballpark. It was a great feeling and it's even greater that we won the ballgame."[31] Lankford also said, "I struck out five times, so I didn't think it could get any worse. I didn't have anything to lose."[32] So, Lankford's downtowner warded off an impending defeat and allowed the game to continue.

The Cubs and Cards then played two more innings, each team plating a run in the 12th, keeping the game tied, 8–8. In the bottom of the 13th, St. Louis emerged victorious as Lankford came through with a bases-loaded single to drive in the game-winning run. "Lankford was down in the count, 1–2, and feared a sixth strikeout, which would have tied a major league record. 'That was kind of scary,' Lankford said. 'With two strikes, I said, Ray, come on now; put the ball in play.'"[33] Speaking about Lankford's early struggles with the bat and his five strikeouts, Cardinals manager Tony LaRussa said, "Lankford told me he was swinging like he had a hole in his bat."[34] Summing up his day, Lankford said, "The first couple of at bats, I was swinging like I was clueless. It was the worst. But no matter what's going on in the game, you still have to be positive. I was able to go out there and fight all those demons off."[35] "I think this was one of the best ballgames I've played in, in a long time."[36]

Sammy Sosa was the second player to "earn" a Downtown Platinum Sombrero. In a crosstown battle in Chicago between the White Sox and the visiting Cubs, Sosa struck out swinging in his first four plate appearances—twice versus starter Kip Wells and once each against Sean Lowe and Bob Howry. In the top of the ninth, the Cubs trailed the Sox, 5–3. The Cubs proceeded to get a man on with two outs, bringing Sosa to the plate, facing Keith Foulke. On an 0–1 pitch, Sosa went downtown to tie the score, 5–5, and prevent an imminent defeat. Unfortunately, these heroics were not enough: the Pale Hose emerged victorious, 6–5, when they pushed across the game-winning run in the bottom of the 14th inning. Meanwhile, Sosa converted his Downtown Golden Sombrero into a Downtown Platinum Sombrero by striking out against Bill Simas in the 12th.

CONCLUSION
Of the 175 regular-season Downtown Golden Sombreros (including the five platinum editions) that have been produced during the 1891–2023 period, 20 featured a key home run—eight pseudo walk-off homers, nine bonafide walk-off homers, and three do-or-die game-saving homers that warded off imminent defeat (at least temporarily). Since the most important objective for every player is helping his team win the game, the seventeen DGS players included in Tables 4 and 5 certainly contributed to the victories their teams achieved—their downtowners provided the actual game-winning runs. Likewise for two of the three DGS players listed in Table 6—their game-saving downtowners warded off impending defeat which allowed their teams to ultimately emerge triumphantly.

As the rate of baseball's Three True Outcomes has steadily risen, so has the number of Downtown

Golden Sombreros (as shown in Table 3), affording more sombrero-wearers the opportunity for phoenix-like performances.[35] During 1969–2023, 17 walk-offs occurred, eight pseudo walk-off homers and nine bonafide walk-offs. Looking down the road, who will be the first DGS player to rise from the ashes of his four strikeouts by hitting a walk-off downtowner that snatches victory from the jaws of defeat? ∎

Acknowledgments

Grateful thanks are extended to Baseball-Reference for its Stathead search engine and PBP details, and to Retrosheet for its PBP narratives. And, as mentioned in note 6, special thanks are gratefully extended to Dave Smith, Pete Palmer, and Jonathan Frankel for their very important contributions to my research effort. I should also like to express my thanks to Jeff Robbins, Gary Stone, and Patrick Todgham for helpful discussions.

Notes

1. The "Three True Outcomes" are the walk, strikeout, and home run. See D. Firstman, "From Usenet Joke to Baseball Flashpoint," *Baseball Research Journal* (Volume 47, Number 1, Spring 2018), 29–37.
2. Baseball-Reference.com: Home –> Seasons –> League Index –> National League –> Batting –> League Year-By-Year Batting—Totals –> 1949; 2019.
3. The 1949–2019 period was chosen for the illustration because it is composed of 70 consecutive fundamentally equivalent seasons. The National League was chosen (rather than the American League or the combined NL and AL) because the NL did not use the designated hitter (which was used in the AL beginning in 1973). The 2019 season was chosen as the "end-season" because the 2020 season was abbreviated to a 60-game schedule. The 1949 season was chosen as the "start-season" (rather than the 1929 or 1939 seasons) because of the World War Two affected seasons of 1942–45.
4. Paul Dickson, *The Dickson Baseball Dictionary*, Third Edition, (New York: W.W. Norton & Company, 2009), 373–74.
5. My interest in players who assembled the combination of striking out four times and slugging a homer in the same game was inspired by Khris "Krush" Davis. I attended the game between the Royals and the Athletics at the Oakland-Alameda County Coliseum on August 16, 2017, in which Davis struck out in his first four plate appearances—first (K), third (K), fifth (backward-K), and seventh (K). In the bottom of the ninth, with Kansas City leading by a 7–6 score, Davis came to bat with one out and nobody on. I hoped that he would atone for his four strikeouts by homering, but alas, he flied out to center field, "FO-8." (Had the drive been caught on the warning track, I would have entered "WT" on my scorecard.) While Davis did not achieve the combo of four strikeouts and one homer, my curiosity was motivated to conduct the research to find out which players did.
6. Special thanks to Dave Smith (Retrosheet) for providing Excel spreadsheets of the ICI sheets for the 1891–1900 National League seasons. Special thanks also to Pete Palmer for his guidance on the strikeout information presented—and missing—in the ICI sheets: "ICI is missing a lot of batter strikeouts, especially 1896–1909 (1912 AL). And of course, there are no ICI sheets for 1876–1890 NL." Thus, for the 1891–1900 period there may be additional players who produced a Downtown Golden Sombrero. Thus, thanks to Jonathan Frankel for providing his independent research results on batter-strikeouts for the 1897-1900 National League seasons. Frankel's in-depth research revealed seven instances of a player having four or more strikeouts in a single game whereas the ICI sheets indicated that there were only five instances of a player having four or more strikeouts in a single game. The two missing instances in the ICI sheets are: (i) Pete Dowling of Louisville on August 15, 1899; the ICI sheets show Dowling with 3 strikeouts. (ii) Noodles Hahn of Cincinnati on July 8, 1900; the ICI sheets show Hahn with no strikeouts (i.e., a blank cell). See also: Jonathan Frankel, "1899 National League Strikeouts," *Baseball Research Journal* (Volume 36, 2007), 46–52.
7. There is also a sub-class of pseudo walk-off homers—those hit by the home team in the bottom of eighth inning, thereby necessitating the closer to shut down the visiting team in the top of the ninth; none of the DGS players had such a pseudo walk-off homer.
8. Willie McCovey had only one other golden sombrero in his 22-year career (1959–80; 2588 games, 521 dingers, 1550 K's). His other golden sombrero came in a 21-inning game in which he had 9 plate appearances. For comparison, Giancarlo Stanton has already had 27 golden sombreros (tied for the most in major-league history with Ryan Howard) in the first 14 years of his career (2010–23; 1535 games, 402 homers, 1820 K's). So far, Stanton has only one downtown golden sombrero.
9. Bill Paschke, "Padres Win in 14 Innings, 2–1, and Grab Share of Fifth Place," *Los Angeles Times*, September 20, 1987, 79.
10. Ted Silary, "Great, Scott, but Phils split," *Philadelphia Daily News*, August 21, 1998, 130; "Dramatic homer lifts team to split," *Tucson Citizen*, August 21, 1998, 50.
11. "Gonzalez gives Jays a win with homer in the tenth," *Alberni Valley* (British Columbia, CN) *Times*, May 2, 2001, 7.
12. Bernie Wilson, "Reynolds saves only hit for last in majors' longest game of year," *Arizona Daily Star*, June 8, 2009, B2.
13. Teddy Greenstein, "Sox's 'Eloy watch' keeps on ticking," *Chicago Tribune*, August 6, 2018, 3–3.
14. Jim Hawkins, "Northrup HR Wins in 16th," *Detroit Free Press*, August 2, 1971, 35.
15. Richard L. Shook, "Tigers win in 16 innings 4–3—Northrup homers to break up another thriller," UPI story, *Battle Creek* (Michigan) *Enquirer*, August 2, 1971, 10.
16. "Northrup Finally Succeeds With Homer In 16th," AP story, *Hillsdale* (Michigan) *Daily News*, August 2, 1971, 8.
17. Peter Pascarelli, "Schmidt ends two slumps on one blow," *Philadelphia Inquirer*, May 29, 1983, 47.
18. Ray Finocchiaro, "Schmidt homer in ninth lifts Phillies," *The* (Wilmington, DE) *Morning News*, May 29, 1983, 43.
19. Jack Lang, "Comeback of the Knight," *Daily News*, July 4, 1986, 46.
20. Jim Naughton, "Extra fireworks," *Daily News*, July 4, 1986, 46.
21. Anthony McCarron, "Yanks flex muscle in 10th," *Daily News*, April 23, 2001, 64.
22. Darren Everson, "Defeat leaves Red Sox closer down in the dumps," *Daily News*, April 23, 2001, 64.
23. David Lennon, "A Rally Good Win," *Newsday*, April 23, 2001, 44.
24. Marc Lancaster, "Longo ends long game," *Tampa Tribune*, August 5, 2009, 17.
25. Adam Kilgore, "Sting Ray," *Boston Globe*, August 5, 2009, C1.
26. "Two games in one: Brandon Moss hits second homer in 19th inning, A's outlast Angels 10–8," *Whitehorse* (Yukon, CN) *Daily Star*, April 30, 2013, 19.
27. Steve Megaree, "Caratini walks off with homer," *Wisconsin State Journal*, July 5, 2022, B1.
28. Shawn McFarland, "What Adolis García's series-salvaging walk-off means as Rangers prepare to host Astros," *Dallas Morning News*, September 3, 2023, https://www.dallasnews.com/sports/rangers/2023/09/03/what-dolis-garcias-series-salvaging-walk-off-means-as-rangers-prepare-to-host-astros/.
29. Kennedi Landry "4 K's? Who cares?! Adolis belts mammoth walk-off homer," September 3, 2023, https://www.mlb.com/news/adolis-garcia-hits-walk-off-home-run-vs-twins.
30. Paul Sullivan, "McGwire's biggest cheerleader? Sosa," *Chicago Tribune*, August 9, 1998, section 3, 4.
31. Joe Ostermeier, "Cards fizzle; Rams fizzle," *Belleville* (Illinois) *News-Democrat*, August 9, 1998, D1.
32. David Wilhelm, "Cardinals find 13th lucky," *Belleville* (Illinois) *News-Democrat*, August 9, 1998, D1.

33. Rick Hummel, "Rallies, homers, spice 13-inning epic,"
    St. Louis Post-Dispatch, August 9, 1998, F1.
34. Jim Salter (Associated Press), "Lankford outshines sluggers as
    Cardinals fight off Cubs," *Lexington* (Kentucky) *Herald-Leader*,
    August 9, 1998, C5.
35. Rick Hummel, "Rallies, homers..."
36. Ostermeier, "Cards fizzle."
37. Jayson Stark and Eno Sarris, "MLB's 'Three True Outcomes' are all
    down for the first time in 17 years. Why?," *The Athletic*, July 21, 2022
    (accessed November 9, 2022).

APPENDICES: Other Interesting Aspects For Players With Dgs Awards

A-1. PLAYERS WITH THE FIRST DGS FOR VARIOUS FRANCHISES

Table A-1 provides, in chronological order, a list of the first DGS achieved by various franchises. Some franchises did not have any of their players achieve a DGS—for example, the Boston Braves, Philadelphia Athletics, Seattle Pilots, or Montreal Expos.

National League				American League			
DGS #	Player	Team	Year	DGS #	Player	Team	Year
001	Jimmy Williams	PIT	1899	002	Bruce Campbell	SLB	1932
003	Frank Robinson	CIN	1956	005	Woodie Held	KCA	1957
004	Joe Adcock	MIL	1957	009	Frank Howard	WAS	1971
006	Duke Snider	LAD	1959	011	Jim Northrup	DET	1971
007	Tommie Agee	NYM	1968	012	George Scott	MIL	1972
008	Willie McCovey	SFG	1970	013	Jerry Moses	CLE	1972
015	Rick Monday	CHC	1974	014	Dick Allen	CWS	1974
024	Mike Schmidt	PHP	1983	017	Tony Solaita	CAL	1976
028	Bob Horner	ATL	1985	020	Jim Rice	BOS	1979
034	Garry Templeton	SDP	1987	033	Gary Ward	NYY	1987
035	Glenn Davis	HOU	1989	037	Harold Baines	TEX	1990
046	Dante Bichette	COL	1995	051	Shane Halter	KCR	1997
050	Ron Gant	SLC	1996	056	John Mabry	SEA	1999
052	Jeromy Burnitz	MIL	1998	065	Alex Gonzalez	TOR	2001
054	Devon White	ARZ	1998	083	Jacque Jones	MIN	2004
072	Andy Fox	FLA	2002	105	Evan Longoria	TBR	2009
107	Adam Dunn	WAS	2010	113	Brandon Moss	OAK	2013
——	————	——	——	117	Matt Wieters	BAL	2013
——	————	——	——	124	Chris Carter	HOU	2014

Table A-1 reveals that it took nearly a century for a St. Louis Cardinals player to achieve a DGS. There had been 89 golden sombreros by players on the Red Birds 1901–96 before Ron Gant earned the DGS in late 1996. That was the longest DGS incubation period for any of the eight franchises comprising the NL at the beginning of the twentieth century. Similarly, the original AL Washington Senators did not have any of their players accomplish a DGS 1901–60. It was not until 44 years after the franchise shifted to Minneapolis and became the Twins, that Jacque Jones collected the first DGS for the Nationals-Senators-Twins in 2004. There were 107 golden sombreros by Nationals-Senators-Twins players before Jones homered for the DGS. Six of the 34 players included in Table A-1 are Hall of Famers—Frank Robinson, Duke Snider, Willie McCovey, Mike Schmidt, Jim Rice, and Harold Baines.

A-2. DGS PLAYERS WITH GRAND SLAM HOMERS

In addition to the jackpot wallop by Derek Norris shown in Table 5, five other players compensated for their four strikeouts with four-run homers. Table A-2 shows the first two jackpot DGSs were slugged by Reggie Jackson when he played for the Angels. He's the only player with a pair of bases-loaded DGSs. Here are some of things Mr. October said about his first jackpot DGS performance: "I know I struck out [four times] but you have to keep plugging. I finally got something good to hit."[1] The *O* had this headline—"One swing wipes out Reggie's four Ks." In the article, Jackson stated, "As much as I strike out, I think I pay for my hits." Seattle manager Rene Lachmann added, "We struck him out four times and he gets four RBIs—four big ones."[2] Since the Angels defeated the Mariners 11–9, Jackson's 4-run downtowner was vital for the victory. Jackson also added, "I was lucky. The kid [Ed Vande Berg] made a mistake. I earned that S.O.B tonight."[3]

DGS #	Game Yr-Mo-D (G)	Player	TM	OPP	HR I (BR)	IS	FS
22	1982-08-06	Reggie Jackson	CAL	SEA*	6 (3)	9-4	11-9
27	1985-06-26	Reggie Jackson	CAL*	CLE	6 (3)	10-5	10-6
31	1987-04-09	Cory Snyder	CLE	TOR*	1 (3)	6-0	14-3
78	2003-05-25	Mark Teixeira	TEX*	BAL	3 (3)	7-6	10-13
125	2015-05-29	Derek Norris	SDP*	PIT	9 (3)	6-2	6-2
129	2017-06-13	Ian Happ	CHC	NYM*	2 (3)	6-1	14-3
140	2019-05-25	Austin Hedges	SDP	TOR*	4 (3)	7-1	19-4

While Reggie was the first (and still the only) player with two bases-loaded DGS performances, he was not the first player to accumulate a pair of DGS awards. That distinction was claimed by Dave Kingman.

A-3. PLAYERS WITH MULTIPLE DGS GAMES

Table A-3a. Players with Two DGS Performances

Table A-3a provides a list of "all" the players who accumulated a pair of DGS awards. In addition to the dozen players with a pair of DGS games, there have been three players with three or more DGS performances; they're listed in Table A-3b. Ryan Howard has the most DGSs—five.

DGS #	Game Yr-Mo-D (G)	Player	TM	OPP	HR I (BR)	IS	FS
16	1975-07-07	Dave Kingman	NYM	ATL*	7 (1)	3-0	3-1
18	1978-04-09		CHC	PIT*	2 (0)	2-0	4-3
22	1982-07-21	Reggie Jackson	CAL	SEA*	6 (3)	9-4	11-9
27	1985-06-26		CAL*	CLE	6 (3)	10-5	10-6
35	1989-04-13	Glenn Davis	HOU	LAD*	8 (0)	2-2	4-2 (15)
36	1989-06-03		HOU*	LAD	4 (0)	1-4	5-4 (22)
32	1987-06-02	Rob Deer	MIL*	KCR	7 (2)	14-1	14-3
38	1990-07-29		MIL	CWS*	8 (1)	6-4	9-8 (11)
43	1995-05-26	Mike Kelly	ATL	HOU*	2 (1)	3-0	8-3
45	1995-06-15		ATL	MON*	5 (0)	1-0	2-0
41	1994-07-20	Jim Thome	CLE*	TEX	1 (1)	2-2	11-13 (14)
57	1999-07-17		CLE	PIT*	6 (2)	5-7	10-13
54	1998-08-20 (2)	Devon White	ARZ	PHP*	11 (2)	12-9	12-9 (11)
60	2000-04-04		LAD	MON*	1 (0)	1-0	10-4
52	1998-06-08	Jeromy Burnitz	MIL	KCR*	5 (1)	4-7	7-8
63	2000-07-22		MIL	CHC*	4 (0)	1-1	2-3 (13)
62	2000-07-20 (1)	Carl Everett	BOS	BAL*	1 (1)	2-0	11-7
69	2001-08-25		BOS	TEX*	2 (0)	1-1	7-8 (18)
70	2002-04-05	Andruw Jones	ATL*	NYM	1 (1)	2-0	3-9
91	2007-07-04		ATL	LAD*	7 (0)	5-2	5-2
114	2013-05-25	Nelson Cruz	TEX	SEA*	5 (0)	4-2	5-2
157	2022-05-07		WAS	LAA*	5 (1)	6-3	7-3
144	2019-09-24	Trevor Story	COL	SFG*	5 (0)	4-3	8-5 (16)
158	2022-05-24		BOS	CWS*	1 (2)	4-0	16-3

Table A-3b. Players with Three or More DGS Performances

DGS #	Game Yr-Mo-D (G)	Player	TM	OPP	HR I (BR)	IS	FS
96	2008-06-11		ARZ	NYM*	9 (2)	3-3	3-5 (13)
101	2009-06-07	Mark Reynolds	ARZ	SDP*	18 (2)	9-6	9-6 (18)
121	2014-04-25		MIL	BOS*	2 (2)	2-0	7-6 (11)
131	2018-04-01		MIN	BAL*	3 (0)	5-0	7-0
141	2019-06-21	Miguel Sano	MIN	KCR*	8 (0)	6-6	8-7
150	2021-05-22		MIN	CLE*	4 (0)	2-3	3-5 (10)
86	2006-07-02		PHP	TOR*	3 (0)	3-3	11-6
89	2007-06-10		PHP	KCR*	5 (1)	5-6	5-17
90	2007-6-26	Ryan Howard	PHP*	CIN	1 (1)	2-1	11-4
100	2009-06-01		PHP	SDP*	5 (0)	4-1	5-3
102	2009-06-12		PHP*	BOS	9 (0)	2-2	2-5 (13)

A-4. PLAYERS WITH MULTIPLE HOMERS IN THEIR DGS GAMES

Four players went downtown twice in their DGS games. As described previously, for two of these players—Evan Longoria and Brandon Moss—their second downtowner was a last-inning, game-winning bonafide walk-off home run.

DGS #	Game Yr-Mo-D (G)	Player	TM	OPP	HR I (BR)	IS	FS
105	2009-0804	Evan Longoria	TBR*	BOS	8 (0) 13 (1)	2-2 4-2	4-2 (13)
113	2013-04-29	Brandon Moss	OAK*	LAA	6 (0) 19 (1)	2-6 10-8	10-8 (19)
136	2018-07-24	Yasmani Grandal	LAD	PHP*	4 (0) 6 (0)	2-0 4-1	4-7 (16)
143	2019-09-23	Austin Hays	BAL	TOR*	3 (2) 5 (0)	3-5 5-6	10-11 (15)

TABLE A-5. DGS PLAYERS WITH GAME-STARTING LEADOFF HOMERS

Seven players started their DGS game with a leadoff home run and then suffered four strikeouts. In fact, two of the players endured five subsequent strikeouts—Brian Dozier and Dexter Fowler—thereby meriting downtown platinum sombrero awards.

DGS #	Game Yr-Mo-D (G)	Player	TM	OPP	HR I (BR)	IS	FS
23	1982-08-18	Chili Davis	SFG	PIT*	1 (0)	1-0	16-9
60	2000-04-04	Devon White	LAD	MON*	1 (0)	1-0	10-4
79	2003-09-10	Ray Durham	SFG	SDP*	1 (0)	1-0	7-1
112	2013-04-20	Alejandro de Aza	CWS*	MIN	1 (0)	1-0	1-2 (10)
130	2017-07-30	Brian Dozier	MIN	OAK*	1 (0)	1-0	5-6 (12)
145	2019-09-24	Dexter Fowler	SLC	ARZ*	1 (0)	1-0	2-3 (19)
171	2023-06-23	Nick Pratto	KCR	TBR*	1 (0)	1-0	3-11

A-6. PLAYERS WHO EARNED THE DOWNTOWN PLATINUM SOMBRERO AWARD

Five players have merited downtown platinum sombrero awards.

DGS #	Game Yr-Mo-D (G)	Player	TM	OPP	HR I (BR)	IS	FS
53	1998-08-08	Ray Lankford	SLC*	CHC	11 (1)	7-7	9-8 (13)
61	2006-06-09	Sammy Sosa	CHC	CWS*	9 (1)	5-5	5-6 (14)
130	2017-07-30	Brian Dozier	MIN	OAK*	1 (0)	1-0	5-6 (12)
145	2019-09-24	Dexter Fowler	SLC	ARZ*	1 (0)	1-0	2-3 (19)
152	2021-06-23	Mike Tauchman	SFG	LAA*	13 (2)	9-2	9-3 (13)

A-7. PLAYERS WHO ACHIEVED A DOWNTOWN GOLDEN SOMBRERO IN THE POSTSEASON

Only four players have merited a DGS award in post-season play. The first one was achieved by Wayne Garrett in the 1973 World Series. It remains the only DGS in the Fall Classic. While there have not yet been any DGSs in the League Championship Series, there have been three DGSs in League Division Series. Of particular interest are the two in the 1996 ALDS—Bobby Bonilla and Rafael Palmeiro achieved their DGSs in the same game. They each went downtown in their first at bat and then struck out four times. Interestingly, they went downtown in back-to-back fashion. Palmeiro, batting clean-up, and Bonilla, batting in the fifth slot, took Cleveland's Charles Nagy downtown in the second inning of the fourth game. Bonilla then struck out in his next four at bats before flying out in his sixth at bat; Palmeiro struck out in his next three at bats before flying out in his fifth at bat and striking out in his sixth at bat.

DGS #	Series (G)	Player	TM	OPP	HR I (BR)	IS	FS
PS-1	1979 WS (2)	Wayne Garrett	NYM	OAK*	3 (0)	2-3	10-7 (12)
PS-2	1996 ALDS (4)	Bobby Bonilla	BAL	CLE*	1 (0)	2-0	4-3 (12)
PS-3	1996 ALDS (4)	Rafael Palmeiro	BAL	CLE*	1 (0)	1-0	4-3 (12)
PS-4	2005 NLDS (4)	Brian McCann	ATL	HOU*	8 (0)	6-1	6-7 (18)

NOTES

1. "Reggie's slam paces Angels," *Tulare* (California) *Advance-Register*, August 7, 1982, 6.
2. "One swing wipes out Reggie's four Ks," *San Francisco Examiner*, August 7, 1982, C3.
3. Mark Wallace, "Jackson, Kelleher key Angels over M's, 11–9," *The* (Tacoma) *News Tribune*, August 7, 1982, B1.

Henry Chadwick and the National League's Performance vs. "Outsiders": 1876–81

Woody Eckard, PhD

At its 1876 founding, the National League presented the nascent professional baseball community with a business model radically different from that of its predecessor: the National Association of 1871–75. The key difference was membership restrictions that were widely criticized as arbitrary and elitist, and were not yet proven to be effective. Perhaps the foremost critic was Henry Chadwick, the leading baseball writer of the era and the only journalist enshrined in the National Baseball Hall of Fame in Cooperstown. He attempted to demonstrate that the league's model was not superior by publicizing the many losses incurred by league clubs in their numerous exhibition games against outsiders. But he often failed to mention the always larger number of wins. This article hopes to set that record straight by summarizing, for the first time, the full results of those games during the key formative period of 1876–81.

The league's successful 1880 and 1881 seasons (as we will discuss) confirmed the efficacy of its business model. In contrast, the National Association, with its erratic model, had failed, as had the minor International/National Association of 1877–80 that had adopted the NA's model. In 1882, the American Association entered the field as a major league, using the league model, and had a generally successful 10-year run. Since then, the league model has been the dominant structure for baseball organizations, major and minor, and most other team sports organizations.

The first section that follows provides relevant background regarding early professional baseball. The second discusses in more detail Chadwick's campaign to undermine the National League's claim of superiority. The third section describes our data-gathering process. The results are then presented, covering more than 900 games between league and non-league clubs during 1876–81. National League teams won more than two-thirds of these games, contrary to Chadwick. The last section provides a summary and conclusions.

BACKGROUND

Professional baseball was first openly accepted for the 1869 season, but the first formal all-professional organization, the National Association, didn't appear until 1871. Its main purpose was to provide structure for the national championship competition. Entry was essentially open, as any club could join simply by paying a nominal fee for a one-year membership. There were no other requirements, i.e., the NA was open to any and all comers. It somewhat resembled an annual tournament rather than a league as the word is now understood.

Mainly for this reason, the NA was highly unstable. Twenty-five different clubs participated over its five-year life, with the number varying annually from eight to 13.[1] Some were relatively sound stock organizations with salaried players, mainly in big cities. Many others, however, often in small towns, were financially weak gate-sharing cooperatives, and still others were hybrids. The turnover was large, with 18 clubs competing in only one or two seasons. Also there were no fewer than 14 midseason failures, mostly co-ops, with at least one in every season. Only three clubs competed in each of the five years: the Athletics of Philadelphia, the Bostons, and the Mutuals of New York. The first season, 1871, began with nine participants. The NA also had a competitive balance problem, with the Boston Red Stockings winning four of five championships.

Dissatisfaction with the NA produced the National League, founded at a meeting in February 1876 whose true purpose was kept secret. It was organized by William Hulbert, president of the NA's Chicago club. As with the NA, a main goal was to determine a national champion. Five other of the NA's top clubs participated, including the mainstay Athletics, Bostons, and Mutuals, causing the NA to fold. The independent Cincinnati and Louisville clubs also were present at the meeting, with all seven attendees having been vetted by Hulbert beforehand. Not invited were any other clubs who might have had an interest in competing for the national championship, including other current and past NA members.

Also excluded from the meeting was Henry Chadwick, likely because he was presumed to favor the

NA's open organizational model over the league's proposed restrictive model.[2] In particular, membership was to be limited to eight stock clubs, only one per city, and only in cities with a minimum population of 75,000, although early exceptions were made to the population minimum. Last, the membership fee was increased substantially to $100 and, while it was still paid annually, membership was presumed to continue indefinitely until resignation or expulsion.[3] The restrictions were designed to achieve league stability by promoting the financial success of clubs and minimizing midseason failures.

But the exclusion of other interested contestants for the national championship was criticized as arbitrary and elitist by many in the professional baseball community. For example, as business of baseball historian Michael Haupert notes, "Several newspapers spoke out against the league."[4] As Tom Melville observed in *Early Baseball and the Rise of the National League*: "The main criticism of the National League was its closed circuit format, the self-appointed right…to designate [the clubs] entitled to compete for the national championship."[5] Additionally, Chadwick accused Hulbert of having an unstated goal of usurping control of the professional game, which may indeed have been true. Many historians feel that he also took umbrage at his personal exclusion from the meeting, an affront to his image as America's preeminent baseball writer.[6]

With the benefit of hindsight from a century and a half, the superiority of the league model seems obvious. But that was by no means clear at the time. While its performance during 1876–81 was an improvement over the NA, by modern standards it was still very much a work in progress. Table 1 summarizes league membership during this six-year period. It included 19 different clubs, with 11 competing in only one or two seasons. The 1877 Cincinnatis failed in June, but were quickly replaced with another Cincinnati club.[7] And in 1879, Syracuse failed a few weeks before the season's end, but with no replacement. By 1878, only two of the charter members remained: the Bostons and Chicagos, who participated in all six seasons.

But toward the end of the period, membership stabilized. In 1880, six of the eight clubs from the prior season returned, with a new club in Cincinnati, and in 1881 seven of eight returned. And in 1882, for the first time, league membership remained unchanged.

The economic depression that began in 1873 and lasted until March 1879 no doubt contributed to the league's problems in its first few years.[8] It was not a propitious time to initiate a major new business undertaking. For example, according to an official league statement published in August 1878, the "business depression has so far affected the receipts [of league clubs] that a loss is already assured."[9]

The league also suffered from a balance problem. Table 2 shows the cumulative standings of the 17 clubs for 1876–81. Only six had a winning average above .500, and 45% of total wins were accounted for by just

Table 1. National League Membership: 1876–81

Club	Years	1876	1877	1878	1879	1880	1881
Athletic	1	X					
Boston	6	X	X	X	X	X	X
Buffalo	3				X	X	X
Chicago	6	X	X	X	X	X	X
Cincinnati	5	X	X	X	X	X	
Cleveland	3				X	X	X
Detroit	1						X
Hartford	2	X	X				
Indianapolis	1			X			
Louisville	2	X	X				
Milwaukee	1			X			
Mutual	1	X					
Providence	4			X	X	X	X
St. Louis	2	X	X				
Syracuse	1				X		
Troy City	3				X	X	X
Worcester	2					X	X
Total		**8**	**6**	**6**	**8**	**8**	**8**

Table 2. National League Cumulative Standings: 1876–81 (Tie Games Omitted)

Club	Yrs	G	W	L	PCT
Chicago	6	432	277	155	.641
Hartford	2	126	78	48	.619
Providence	4	312	191	121	.612
St. Louis	2	124	73	51	.589
Boston	6	441	254	187	.576
Louisville	2	126	65	61	.516
Detroit	1	84	41	43	.488
Buffalo	3	243	115	128	.473
Cleveland	3	250	110	140	.440
Worcester	2	165	72	93	.436
Troy	3	242	99	143	.409
Indianapolis	1	60	24	36	.400
Mutual	1	56	21	35	.375
Cincinnati	5	342	125	217	.365
Syracuse	1	70	22	48	.314
Milwaukee	1	60	15	45	.250
Athletic	1	59	14	45	.237
Totals	**6**		**1,596**	**1,596**	**.500**

NOTE: The records of the three Cincinnati clubs of 1876–80 are combined.

three clubs: Chicago, Boston, and Providence. And only two—Chicago and Boston—won five of the six championships.

Thus, during most of this formative period the jury was still out on the league and its unique business model.

CHADWICK'S CAMPAIGN

The league's founding meeting occurred at a New York City hotel on February 2, 1876. On February 12, a lengthy article describing the meeting and its outcome appeared in the weekly *New York Clipper*, the leading national baseball newspaper at that time.[10] It was the first mention of the meeting in the *Clipper*.[11] Henry Chadwick was the *Clipper*'s baseball editor and, while the article had no byline, there can be little doubt that he was the author.

The article took a strong editorial position critical of the league. In fact, in *The League That Lasted*, Neil W. Macdonald describes Chadwick as "the leader of the reportorial minority who opposed Hulbert's creation."[12] The *Clipper* article's title referred to the league's formation as "a startling coup d'état," implying a hidden intent to displace the NA. The February 2 meeting was described as a "sad blunder," "anti-American," and "a star-chamber method of attaining the ostensible [objectives]."[13]

Chadwick, an ardent moral reformer, considered the main (and related) problems confronting professional baseball to be alcohol abuse and dishonesty, i.e., "the 'selling' or 'throwing' of games for betting purposes." However, the league's focus was on its organization and operation. Chadwick regarded business matters such as "confining the contests…to those [clubs] who are capable of carrying out the season's programme" as merely a "supplement" to the more important moral issues needing attention.[14] Furthermore, he believed that all these matters could be adequately addressed at the planned March convention of the still existing National Association. A new organization was unnecessary.

Chadwick's antipathy towards the league did not fade quickly. One manifestation was his attempt to undermine the league's position that its restrictive business model produced higher quality ballplaying, and he wasn't the only such critic. For example, historian David Quentin Voigt notes that "in these years newspapers often ridiculed the league's claim of major league status."[15] To this end, Chadwick periodically used the *Clipper* to point out that league clubs lost many of their numerous exhibition games against non-league opponents. These articles summarized losses,

but league victories usually were not reported, a fact that revealed Chadwick's agenda.

The first such article appeared in early September 1876, titled "Outside Club Victories." It was self-described as "a record of *victories* won by 'outside clubs' against league-club nines from May to August" (emphasis added), followed by a list of 17 such games including club names and scores. It noted that "All but the Chicago and Louisville teams have had to succumb to outsiders, and the New Havens have defeated league nines eight times."[16] The New Haven Club had been a NA member that sought and was denied admission to the league. The article did not mention league victories.

The 1876 record was completed in another *Clipper* article in late February 1877 titled "League Club Defeats." It was self-described as "a record of the outside defeats sustained by league clubs at the hands of non-league nines in 1876."[17] The list included 37 games with club names and scores. The article title implied all were defeats, but by my count there were 33 defeats plus four ties. As Macdonald notes, quoting an 1876 *Chicago Tribune* article: "they probably won far more; 'but Chadwick, demonstrating his prejudice against the League's claim of superiority, never tabulated their wins.'"[18] David Nemec makes the same point in *The Great Encyclopedia of Nineteenth Century Major League Baseball* regarding Chadwick's tabulations.[19]

Figure 1 shows the *Clipper*'s 1877 midseason reckoning of league outsider defeats, published on June 30.[20] It reports 23 such defeats by that date, including eight in which the league club was "Chicagoed," i.e., shut out. Once more, no league victories were mentioned. The *Clipper* summarized the league's complete 1877 experience with outsider clubs in late December as follows:

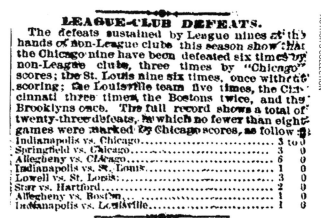

Figure 1. *New York Clipper* article from June 30, 1877, summarizing National League club defeats by outside clubs.

> Last season it was plainly evident that too many outside games were played by League nines. What with the frequency of such contests, and the number of defeats League clubs sustained at the hands of outside teams—*seventy-two* in all during the season—the prestige of League nines was so weakened as to materially lessen the power to draw paying crowds. (Emphasis added.[21])

The claimed financial impact was not otherwise supported. Eight months later, the *Clipper* published the abovementioned league statement attributing financial difficulties at that time to the ongoing economic depression and made no mention of outsider losses affecting profits. Also, 1877 was the second season in which league losses against outsiders were presented with no mention of wins.

After 1877, Chadwick switched his focus from all outside clubs to members of the minor International Association. It operated from 1877 to 1880 and included some of the strongest non-league clubs.[22] Figure 2 shows the *Clipper*'s detailed 1878 summary titled "League vs. International," although the two tables actually include a few clubs not involved in the International championship competition.[23] The article was published at the end of September, a month before the season concluded. Other clubs belonged to the International, but played no games against the league. The tables show that the league lost 21 games against these significant outsiders, but also won 33. League victories were included for the first time.[24] Note that the accompanying text repeats 1877's loss record against (all) outsiders: "no fewer than seventy-two games," again with no mention of wins.[25]

Figure 3 presents the text from the *Clipper*'s November summary of 1879 league results against the minor National Association, a continuation of the International.[26] First, it updates the 1878 league outsider loss record to include all games that year (see above), with losses increasing from 21 to 34.[27] However, 1878 wins were not updated (or mentioned). Second, the 1877 record of (all) league outsider losses is again repeated; now stated as 73 and again with no mention of wins; and it is erroneously attributed to International Association clubs only. The 1879 article also contained separate lists of 1879 games won and games lost against six National Association clubs, with scores, which are excluded from Figure 3 to save space.[28] The text states that "the record of defeats is but twenty," but my count for the "League Defeats" list is 19.[29] The "League Victories" list contained 26 wins, plus four draws.[30]

LEAGUE vs. INTERNATIONAL.

Our files show a record of twenty-one victories by International nines over League teams this season, and of thirty-two victories by League nines over International teams. The record thus far is not up to the standard of 1877 as far as outside club triumphs are concerned, for in 1877 the League clubs lost no fewer than seventy-two games to "outside" club nines. This season the League nines have done better. The record of International club victories as recorded in THE CLIPPER is as follows:

	Boston...	Cincinnati.	Chicago...	Indianapolis.	Milwaukee.	Prov'd'nce	Total....
Buffalo	0	1	1	1	1	1	5
Forest City	0	1	2	2	0	0	5
Lowell	0	1	0	1	0	0	2
New Bedford	0	0	1	1	0	0	2
Peoria Reds	1	0	0	0	1	0	2
Worcester	1	0	0	0	0	0	1
Utica	1	0	0	0	0	0	1
National	0	0	0	0	0	1	1
Star	0	0	0	1	0	0	1
Rochester	0	0	0	1	0	0	1
Games lost	3	3	4	7	2	2	21

LEAGUE VICTORIES.

	Spring'd	Manche'r	Utica	Star	Hayma'r	N. Bed'd	Lowell..	Daven't.	Roches'r.	P. Reds..	National	Buffalo..	F. City..	Total....
Boston	0	0	0	0	0	1	0	1	1	0	0	1	0	4
Cincinnati	0	0	0	1	0	0	0	0	1	0	0	1	1	4
Providence	0	0	0	0	1	0	0	0	0	0	2	2	2	7
Chicago	0	0	1	0	0	0	0	1	0	1	0	1	0	4
Indianapolis	0	0	0	0	0	1	1	0	1	2	0	0	1	6
Milwaukee	1	1	0	0	0	0	1	0	0	1	2	0	2	8
Totals	1	1	1	1	1	2	2	2	3	4	4	5	6	33

On Aug. 20 four of the six League clubs were defeated by outside club teams. If there are any games that have been played which are not recorded in the above tables, we shall be obliged by the scores being sent in.

AUTHOR'S COLLECTION

Figure 2. ***New York Clipper* article from September 28, 1878, summarizing National League club records against International Association clubs.**

LEAGUE vs. NATIONAL CLUBS.

In 1877 the largest number of games yet played between the League clubs and those of the rival association took place. In 1878 there was a falling-off in the number, and in 1879 there were still fewer such games played. In 1877 the League clubs sustained no fewer than *seventy-three defeats* at the hands of International club-teams, Chicago losing 16, Louisville 15, Boston 14, St. Louis 14, Cincinnati 11, and Hartford but 3. In 1878 the League nines were defeated by International teams thirty-four times, Chicago being defeated 9 times, Indianapolis 7, Providence 7, Boston 5, Cincinnati 4, and Milwaukee 2. This season the record of defeats is but twenty, as follows:

Figure 3. ***New York Clipper* article from November 15, 1879, summarizing National League club losses against all outsider clubs in 1877 and 1878, and against National Association clubs in 1879.**

The 1880 summary was titled "League vs. National" and contained a single sentence of text: "The following is the record of the games played up to the 9th of August between the League and National club teams."[31] The National Association that summer was a rump organization with only four clubs and, in fact, had folded at the end of July. The summary included a list of 53 games with scores, but a count of losses or wins was not provided. By my count, this small group had an 18–33–2 record against the National League.[32]

The wording of the September 1881 summary suggests that Chadwick may have mellowed somewhat toward the league. While its title—"League Club Defeats"—retains the emphasis on losses, the text reads: "Apart from the [New York] Metropolitan Club victories, there have been but five defeats of League nines this season by other clubs, the smallest number on record."[33] A postseason *Clipper* article presented a detailed review of the Metropolitans' games against the league, reporting an 18–42 record.[34]

To my knowledge there has been no complete enumeration of the National League record against non-league clubs during this formative period. The selective and biased reporting of the *Clipper* summarized above, covering an incomplete sample of such games, appears to be the best existing source.

Reliance on the *Clipper* data, however, can adversely impact historical analysis, inadvertently incorporating similar biases. For example, Tom Melville, in discussing the 1876 season, concluded: "Though the [National League] claimed to represent baseball's highest competitive echelon, their competitive record against non-National League clubs over the 1876 season raised serious doubts about this. [The league] lost no less than 37 times [sic] to outside clubs that year."[35] Similarly, the 72 (or 73) league loss figure for 1877 noted in the abovementioned *Clipper* article covering that year, then repeated in 1878 and 1879 articles, has been accepted in several modern histories as a reliable indication of league club vulnerability vis-à-vis non-league clubs.[36]

DATA COLLECTION

Our objective is to obtain a list of game results for National League clubs against non-league clubs during the period 1876–81, as complete and accurate as possible. All League clubs were fully professional stock companies with salaried players. Outside clubs, however, were organized in a variety of ways, on a continuum from fully professional to fully amateur. And the extent of press coverage declined moving toward the amateur end of the continuum.

Some outside clubs, usually the strongest, were organized like league clubs, although these were a minority. Many others were gate-sharing cooperatives, with players splitting the net proceeds after covering costs like playing field rental, equipment, and travel expenses. And hybrid forms existed where some players

were salaried, such as the pitcher and catcher, and the remainder shared gate money. Semiprofessional teams had a mix of paid and amateur players. And some were purely amateur, although these were scarce by the late 1870s. Apparently a significant proportion of those claiming amateur status at this time secretly paid at least a few team members. For example, in 1876 the *Clipper* reported that "Mr. Chadwick has resigned his position as Chairman of the Committee of Rules of the Amateur Association, nearly all the clubs having become semi-professional organizations."[37]

While an "apples-to-apples" comparison in terms of club professional status would be desirable, as a practical matter this can only rarely be determined for individual clubs. We therefore include all non-league clubs, except "picked-nines," in our enumeration of outsiders without attempting to distinguish among them by professional status.[38] To partly deal with this issue, we report separate results for league clubs against the minor International/National Association of 1877–80, whose members were mostly, if not entirely, fully professional.

The primary source for individual game results was the weekly *New York Clipper*, which, as noted above, was the main national baseball newspaper of the period.[39] Each issue during the season contained extensive coverage of game results and various additional news items covering a wide variety of clubs. All league championship games were reported along with league games with outsider clubs and outsider vs. outsider games. Usually an individual game report included a box score and a brief game synopsis, although the latter could sometimes be extensive. If box scores were not available, line scores were reported or sometimes simply the final game outcome.[40]

The first step in the collection process was a review of every issue of the *Clipper* during the seasons of 1876 through 1881, identifying games between league clubs and outsiders and entering the results in a spreadsheet.[41] For various reasons, the *Clipper* reports could be erroneous and some games may have been overlooked. For example, the last sentence in the *Clipper* article of Figure 2 specifically requests readers to send in the scores of "any games that have been played which are not recorded in the above tables."

The second step was to confirm the *Clipper*-reported results with a report in another newspaper via searches on newspapers.com. A variety of papers were used, although the *Boston Globe*, *Chicago Tribune*, and *Cincinnati Enquirer* were most common, as they were the main baseball-reporting papers for the three principal league cities over our full study period.

Reviewing all games reported in the papers used for confirmation also provided an opportunity to identify those missed by the *Clipper*. These were then confirmed by locating a second game report in an another newspaper via newspapers.com. If, say, the number of runs reported for the teams differed between two papers, a third was consulted to resolve the "dispute."

The resulting enumeration yielded over 900 games during the six years. While, of course, care was taken in the process, errors of both commission and omission may remain, despite the double checking of each game result.

Before presenting the results of these exhibition games, however, some caveats are in order. First, player motivation was likely lower in these non-championship contests, although league clubs needed to be careful lest losses to weak outsiders damage their "brand," including raising suspicions of "hippodroming," as game-fixing was called. Second, one must keep in mind that league clubs often did not have their "A" team on the field. Exhibitions were an opportunity to, e.g., provide the "change" pitcher and/or catcher some practice, as well as any reserve players. Another factor was that league rules meant that these games were usually on the opposing team's home field, often meaning a home team umpire. And the outsider's players may have had added motivation, perceiving the game as a "tryout" for the league visitors. Thus, the Outsider's overall performance in these exhibitions must be viewed as, at most, only an upper bound on their quality relative to the National League.

THE LEAGUE RECORD AGAINST OUTSIDERS

Table 3 summarizes the overall league won-lost record against non-league clubs for each of the six years of our study period. The appendix provides the yearly results for individual league clubs. We identified a total of 921 outsider games, of which league clubs won more than 70 percent. In individual years, the winning averages are similar, varying from .659 (1878) to .812 (1881). Certainly the league was doing very well against outsiders, despite Chadwick's insinuations.

We can conduct a formal statistical test of the implicit Chadwick hypothesis that league and non-league clubs were of equal quality. If true, then over our six-year study period, the league winning average against outsiders should average close to .500. In fact, the mean of the six yearly averages was .720. We can perform a t-test to determine the likelihood of observing our average (or a larger one) in a six-year sample if the underlying true average is .500.[43] The resulting t-test statistic is 8.63 with a p-value of 0.00034, indicating the

chance that the hypothesis is true is less than one in 1,000. Thus, we can be very confident that the league clubs were, on average, superior to non-league clubs.

Chadwick's reports of league losses to all outsiders in 1876 and 1877 can now be put into perspective. He reported 33 losses in 1876, plus four ties, although our search yielded 44 losses and six ties. But he failed to mention that 215 games were played and that the league won 165, well over three times the losses. Similarly, in 1877 Chadwick tabulated 72 (or 73) losses, while we found 77, plus seven ties. Again, he fails to mention the much larger number of games played, 255, of which the League won 171, over twice the number of losses. With the losses "scaled" correctly, it appears that the league was doing very well against outsiders. And recall that, as noted above, these comparisons most likely underestimate the league's superiority.

Table 4 provides additional analysis of outsider games. First, the total number varied significantly, from 255 in 1877 to only 81 in 1879. Notable is the fact that just over half of all games—470, or 51%, occurred in the first two years. The annual average per club increased from 26.9 games in 1876 to a high of 42.5 in 1877. This may have been due partly to more open schedule slots caused by a drop in the membership from eight clubs to six and a reduction in the number of championship games per team by 10 from 70 in 1876 to 60 in 1877.

Table 3. Summary of National League Club Game Results Against Non-league Clubs: 1876–81.

Year	Games	W	L	T	PCT
1876	215	165	44	6	.781
1877	255	171	77	7	.684
1878	116	74	37	5	.659
1879	81	52	24	5	.673
1880	116	81	32	3	.711
1881	138	112	26	0	.812
Total	921	655	240	26	.725

Table 4. Summary of National League Outsider Games: 1876–81

Year	League Clubs	Outsider Games	Games Per Club	No. of Outsiders	CR5
1876	8	215	26.9	61	.40
1877	6	255	42.5	43	.49
1878	6	116	19.3	24	.53
1879	8	81	10.1	22	.65
1880	8	116	14.5	21	.68
1881	8	138	17.3	18	.80

But after 1877, the per-club average dropped by more than half to 19.3 in 1878, followed by a further drop in 1879, again almost by half, to only 10.1. The large 1878 drop was likely due to new league regulations that significantly limited the number of outsider games. Games were pushed to the postseason, by which time many outside clubs had failed. For example, the December 1877 league convention ruled that "no league club can play a game with any organized club prior to the commencement of the League season, nor can any club play on its grounds a game with any club outside of the League during the League season."[44] The additional 1879 drop was likely caused by an increase in the number of championship games per team from 60 to 84 as the league returned to an eight club format and also increased the championship games required with each other team from 10 to 12. The average number of outsider games then rose in 1880 and again in 1881, perhaps due to the general economic recovery beginning in the Spring of 1879 (see above), which may have made such games more profitable.

Column 5 of Table 4 shows the annual number of *different* outsider clubs involved in games with the league. There were 61 in 1876, but two years later there were only 24. After that, the number decreased gradually to 18 in 1881. The large drop from 1876 to 1878 may have been caused in part by the economic depression and its impact on the number of outsider clubs available as opponents. The last column addresses the distribution of games among the outsiders, i.e., whether the games were concentrated mainly among a few clubs. The data shown are the averages of all outsider games accounted for by the top five clubs in terms of games played, called the "five-club concentration ratio" or CR5.[45] The distribution was far from even, as the top five outsiders had 40 percent of league games in 1876, increasing to 65 percent in 1879 and finally to 80 percent in 1881.

Table 5 shows the main outsider opponents by year, defined as those with at least 10 league games, a total of 21 such teams during the study period. New York's Metropolitan Club of 1881 led with 59 games, followed by Indianapolis with 43 in 1877, and New Haven at 38 in 1876. Six other clubs had at least 20 games in one season. The only clubs among those with 10-plus games that broke even or better against the league were the Lowells, at 12–6 in 1877; the Worcesters, at 7–5 in 1879; the Buffalos, at 10–8 in 1878; and the Stars of Syracuse in 1877, at 12–12–1.[46]

Six of these primary outside opponents subsequently were "promoted" to the National League. At the December 1876 annual meeting, the league added a constitutional provision describing the circumstances

Table 5. Leading Non-League Opponents (With At Least 10 League Games): 1876–81

Year	Opponent	G	W	L	T	PCT	League
1876	New Haven	38	11	26	1	.303	
1876	Indianapolis	20	3	17	0	.150	
1876	Buckeye	11	4	5	2	.455	
1877	Indianapolis	43	16	24	3	.407	
1877	Star	25	12	12	1	.500	
1877	Allegheny	20	9	11	0	.450	IA
1877	Lowell	18	12	6	0	.667	
1877	Athletic	18	2	16	0	.111	
1877	Memphis Reds	12	1	11	0	.083	
1877	Rhode Island	10	4	6	0	.400	
1878	Buffalo	18	10	8	0	.556	IA
1878	Forest City	17	5	11	1	.324	
1879	Albany	16	4	10	2	.313	NA
1879	Worcester	12	7	5	0	.583	NA
1879	Capital City	11	4	7	0	.364	NA
1880	National	29	12	15	2	.448	NA
1880	Albany	22	7	15	0	.318	NA
1880	Metropolitan	16	5	10	1	.344	
1881	Metropolitan	59	18	41	0	.305	ECA
1881	Athletic	27	3	24	0	.111	ECA
1881	Akron	10	2	8	0	.200	

NOTES: **IA** = International Association; **NA** = National Association **ECA** = Eastern Championship Association; **Buckeye**: Columbus OH **Star**: Syracuse; **Allegheny**: Allegheny City (Pittsburgh); **Athletic**: Philadelphia **Forest City**: Cleveland; **Capital City**: Albany/Rochester; **National**: Washington **Metropolitan**: New York

under which an outside club would be "eligible to membership in this League." The door was opened for admitting outside clubs.[47]

First, the Indianapolis club, with 20 games in 1876 and 43 in 1877, joined the league in 1878 along with their pitching phenom "The Only" Nolan. The Rhode Islands, with 10 games in 1877, also were admitted in 1878 as the Providence Club, winning the National League championship the next year. The Star Club, after 25 games as an independent in 1877 and another seven in 1878 as a member of the International Association, was admitted to the league in 1879 as the Syracuse club.[48] The Buffalos, with 18 games in 1878, also were admitted in 1879 and finished third. Another 1879 promotion was Forest Cities, with 17 games in 1878, admitted as the Cleveland club. Last, the Worcesters, with 12 games in 1879, joined in 1880. Indianapolis and Syracuse lasted only one season, but the other four continued through to 1881.

Thus, by 1881, half of the eight league members were former significant outsider opponents. While, on average, non-league clubs were certainly below National League quality, the league itself evidently considered at least this small group of clubs to be major league.[49]

73

In addition, the league's top two opponents by games played in 1881 later joined the new American Association. The Athletics of Philadelphia, with 27 league games in 1881, became a charter member in 1882. And the Metropolitans of New York, with 16 league games in 1880 and 59 in 1881, joined the AA in 1883 after a year as an independent.

Table 6 shows the cumulative record of National League clubs against outsiders. Notable is the fact that only one club, Indianapolis, has a sub-.500 winning percentage, and that only for one year. Consistent with our statistical test results above, this would be very unlikely if the league and outsider clubs were of equal quality, per Chadwick.

Table 6. National League Club Cumulative Records Against Non-League Clubs

Club	Years	G	W	L	T	PCT	Games per Year
Syracuse	1	1	1	0	0	1.000	1
Mutual	1	18	15	3	0	.833	18
Milwaukee	1	15	12	2	1	.833	15
Hartford	2	76	61	11	4	.829	38
Worcester	2	35	27	7	1	.786	17.5
Cleveland	3	25	19	5	1	.780	8.3
Boston	6	184	139	42	3	.764	3.7
Detroit	1	24	18	6	0	.750	24
Providence	4	79	57	18	4	.747	19.8
Louisville	2	70	51	17	2	.743	35
Troy City	3	63	45	16	2	.730	21
Athletic	1	18	13	5	0	.722	18
Chicago	6	140	95	40	5	.696	23.3
St. Louis	2	60	39	19	2	.667	30
Cincinnati	5	70	42	27	1	.607	14
Buffalo	3	30	16	14	0	.533	10
Indianapolis	1	13	5	8	0	.385	13

Table 6 also reports the average number of outsider games played per year by each club, although the results are distorted by the above-mentioned concentration of such games in the first two years. Five of the first six clubs ranked by average games were active in both 1876 and 1877. While the Bostons and Chicagos alone accounted for more than one-third of all outsider games, they ranked only seventh and 14th in winning percentage. Syracuse's single outsider game in its only year of league membership could indicate some missing games, or it could have resulted from the club's disbanding on September 10, three weeks before the championship season ended, i.e., before league rules permitted significant outside play.

As noted above, a comparison of National League clubs to non-league clubs that also were fully profes-

sional would be desirable. While we can't make this determination for all outside clubs, the International/National Association of 1877–80 had a membership that, for the most part, was fully professional. Table 7 presents the league's record against the IA/NA, an average of six clubs per year. While few in number, during 1878–80 they nevertheless accounted for more than half of the league's outside games.[50] The annual winning averages varied from .575 to .673. The overall average of .621 was lower than the league's overall average of .725 against all outsiders reported in Table 3. Thus, this group apparently had higher quality clubs than other outsiders.

Table 7. National League Club Game Results Against International/National Association Clubs: 1877–80

Year	No. of NA/ IL foes	G	W	L	T	PCT
1877	6	55	37	18	0	.673
1878	8	60	33	24	3	.575
1879	6	54	31	19	4	.611
1880	4	63	38	23	2	.619
		228	137	82	9	.621

NOTE: In 1877, 1878, and 1879, additional clubs were IA/NA members but played no games against the league.

Nevertheless, by the same statistical test conducted earlier, the league is superior by a statistically significant amount. Again, the null hypothesis is equal quality, i.e., an expected league winning average of .500. The significance test yields a t-test statistic of 5.92 and a p-value of 0.010. Thus, there is a chance of only about one in 100 that the equal-quality hypothesis is true.

SUMMARY AND CONCLUSIONS

The National League's 1876 founding created controversy in professional baseball circles. Chief among critics was premier baseball journalist Henry Chadwick, who used his position as baseball editor of the *New York Clipper* to conduct a campaign aimed at undermining the league's prestige. In particular, he publicized the many losses of league clubs in exhibition games against outsiders, generally ignoring the fact that there were many more victories. His presumed intent was to create the impression that there was little quality difference.

To correct this impression, the present article summarizes the results of *all* National League games against outsider clubs, losses and wins, for the formative period of 1876–81. To my knowledge, this is the first such enumeration. Our online search of contemporary newspapers yields 921 outsider games, an average of

SABR / THE RUCKER ARCHIVE

The Indianapolis club of 1877, which would join the National League in 1878. Their pitching phenom Edward "The Only" Nolan is standing, third from left.

154 per year. National League clubs won over 70 percent against all outsiders during the full period and over 80 percent in the final year. Also, they won almost two-thirds of their 228 games with International/ National Association clubs, most fully professional, during 1877–80. Certainly, they did very well against non-league clubs and formal statistical tests leave little doubt that league clubs were superior.

Nevertheless, some outsiders were competitive with the National League. In fact, during 1878–80 six such clubs were admitted, all having been significant opponents prior to joining. One finished third in its initial league year and another won the championship in its second year, although two others lasted but one season. Also, three outsiders that played at least a dozen league games sported winning records. Thus, Chadwick might have been partially correct: While National League clubs were clearly superior to the great majority of outsiders, there was no bright line separating league and non-league clubs circa 1880 such as exists today between the major and minor leagues. ∎

Acknowledgments

I'd like to thank two reviewers for helpful comments.

Notes

1. David Nemec, *The Great Encyclopedia of Nineteenth Century Major League Baseball*, 2nd edition (Tuscaloosa: University of Alabama Press, 2006); William J. Ryczek, *Blackguards and Red Stockings: A History of Baseball's National Association, 1871–1875*, Revised Edition (Jefferson, NC: McFarland & Company, (2006); Baseball Reference, https://baseballreference.com.
2. Michael Haupert, "Pulling Baseball from a Slough of Corruption and Disgrace: The Origin of the National League, the 1875 Winter Meetings," *Baseball's 19th Century"Winter" Meetings: 1857–1900*, Jeremy K. Hodges and Bill Nowlin, eds. (Phoenix: Society for American Baseball Research, 2018). The only member of the press invited to the meeting was Lewis Meacham of the *Chicago Tribune*, a Hulbert supporter.
3. Adjusting for inflation, $100 in the mid-1870s would be worth roughly $2,700 today, per the Federal Reserve Bank of Minneapolis, https://www.minneapolisfed.org/about-us/monetary-policy/inflation-calculator/consumer-price-index-1800-.
4. Haupert, "Pulling Baseball": 137.
5. Tom Melville, *Early Baseball and the Rise of the National League* (Jefferson, NC: McFarland & Company, 2001), 81.
6. See, e.g., Neil W. Macdonald, *The League That Lasted: 1876 and the Founding of the National League of Professional Base Ball Clubs* (Jefferson, NC: McFarland & Company, 2004), 61; John Thorn, *Baseball in the Garden of Eden: The Secret History of the Early Game* (New York: Simon & Schuster Paperbacks, 2011), 163.
7. Woody Eckard, "The 1877 National League's Two Cincinnati Clubs: Were They In or Out, and Why the Confusion?" *Baseball Research Journal* 52, no. 1 (2023). The second club began play a few weeks after the first club failed, with the same name but different ownership, and completed the original club's league schedule. Today, MLB combines the records of the two clubs, showing them as a single league member, although after the 1877 season the league excluded both clubs from its final standings.
8. "US Business Cycle Expansions and Contractions," *National Bureau of Economic Research*, https://www.nber.org/research/data/us-business-cycle-expansions-and-contractions, accessed September 12, 2023.
9. "The League Meeting," *New York Clipper*, August 17, 1878, 162.
10. "National League of Professional Clubs [*sic*]: A Startling Coup d'Etat," *New York Clipper*, February 12, 1876, 362. The *Clipper* billed itself as "The Oldest American Sporting and Theatrical Journal."
11. "The Centennial Campaign," *New York Clipper*, February 5, 1876, 357. The *Clipper* of February 5 contained a lengthy article on the upcoming 1876 season, but made no mention of the February 2 meeting or the National League.
12. Macdonald, *The League That Lasted*, 61.
13. "National League of Professional Clubs [*sic*]: A Startling Coup d'Etat," *New York Clipper*.
14. "National League of Professional Clubs [*sic*].
15. David Quentin Voigt, American Baseball, Vol. 1, *From the Gentleman's Sport to the Commissioner System* (University Park, PA: Pennsylvania State University Press, 1983), 77.
16. "Outside Club Victories," *New York Clipper*, September 2, 1876, 181.
17. "League Club Defeats," *New York Clipper*, February 24, 1877, 378.
18. Macdonald, *The League That Lasted*, 207.
19. Nemec, *The Great Encyclopedia*, 115.
20. "League-Club Defeats," *New York Clipper*, June 30, 1877, 107.
21. "The Work of the League," *New York Clipper*, December 22, 1877, 309.
22. See David Pietrusza, *Major Leagues: The Formation, Sometimes Absorption and Mostly Inevitable Demise of 18 Professional Baseball Organizations, 1871 to Present* (Lemur Press, 2020 [1991], Chapter 3, https://lemurpress.com. Chadwick became a "cheerleader" for the newly formed International Association, which had aspirations to challenge the National League, providing supportive coverage in the *Clipper*.
23. "League vs. International," *New York Clipper*, September 28, 1878, 210.
24. The Star Club listed in the upper table was from Syracuse.
25. "League vs. International," *New York Clipper*.
26. "League vs. National Clubs," *New York Clipper*, November 15, 1879, 269. The International Association changed its name after its two Canadian members had withdrawn.
27. *Beadle's Dime Base-Ball Player 1879*, edited by Chadwick, lists the 34 1878 lost games on page 52.
28. Three other clubs were involved in the National Association's championship competition, but played no games against the league.
29. "League vs. National Clubs," *New York Clipper*.
30. Our reckoning of the National League's 1879 record against the National Association is 31–19–4, i.e., identical losses and ties but five more wins (see Table 7).
31. "League vs. National," *New York Clipper*, August 21, 1880, 170.
32. Our reckoning of the National Association's 1880 record against the National League is 23–38–2, i.e, adding five wins and five losses. After August 9, only two former NA clubs were still active.

33. "League Club Defeats," *New York Clipper*, September 10, 1881, 397.

34. "The Metropolitan Club Season: Their League Club Record," *New York Clipper*, October 22, 1881, 498. The author's research finds an 18–41 record for the 1881 Metropolitans (Table 5).

35. Melville, *Early Baseball and the Rise of the National League*, 83

36. For example, see Harold Seymour, *Baseball: The Early Years* (New York: Oxford University Press, 1960), 94; Melville, *Early Baseball and the Rise of the National League*, 83; and Thorn, *Baseball in the Garden of Eden*, 170.

37. "Short Stops," *New York Clipper*, October 7, 1876, 219.

38. One suspects that even the few top college teams that played National League clubs were subsidizing, i.e., paying, at least some of their players.

39. For 1877, the *Beadle's Dime Base-Ball Player 1878* guidebook was also used. It contains an incomplete list of 1877 game results (single-figure scores only) for 38 non-league clubs, including games against league clubs (33–57).

40. Retrosheet lists 618 NL exhibitions 1876-81, whereas I found 921.

41. *New York Clipper* issues can be accessed via the Illinois Digital Newspaper Collections, University of Illinois Library: https://idnc.library.illinois.edu/?a=cl&cl=CL1&sp=NYC&e=-------en-20--1--txt-txIN----------

42. Throughout, we calculate winning percentages counting ties as a half game won and a half game lost.

43. The sample of six years is small, but the student-t distribution, in effect, adjusts for this.

44. "League Association Convention," *New York Clipper*, December 15, 1877, 298. For more discussion of these regulations, see also "League Nine [*sic*] vs. Non-League Teams," *New York Clipper*, May 10, 1879, 50.

45. The concentration ratio is a statistic often used in the economic analysis of markets, e.g., to measure the concentration of sales among firms in a particular market.

46. In fact, the Lowell Club of 1877 was likely as good, and perhaps better, than the National League champion Bostons. See Eckard, "Lowell Base Ball Club of 1877: National Champions?" *Nineteenth Century Notes* (SABR), Bob Bailey and Peter Mancuso, eds. (Summer 2022).

47. Haupert, "Pulling Baseball": 144.

48. The league required its members to bear the name of the cities they represented.

49. Of these four cities, only Worcester's 1880 population of 58,291 was less than the league's avowed minimum of 75,000.

50. See Tables 3 and 7.

APPENDIX: Individual NL Club Records Against Outsiders: 1876–81

NL Club	G	W	L	T	PCT	League Position
			1876			**League**
Chicago	31	30	1	0	.968	1
Louisville	37	34	1	2	.946	5
Mutual	18	15	3	0	.833	6
Boston	42	32	9	1	.774	4
St. Louis	22	16	6	0	.727	2
Athletic	18	13	5	0	.722	7
Hartford	27	18	7	2	.704	3
Cincinnati	20	7	12	1	.375	8
	215	**165**	**44**	**6**	**.781**	

NL Club	G	W	L	T	PCT	League Position
			1877			**League**
Hartford	49	43	4	2	.898	3
Boston	62	44	17	1	.718	1
Cincinnati	28	18	10	0	.643	6
St. Louis	38	23	13	2	.632	4
Chicago	45	26	17	2	.600	5
Louisville*	33	17	16	0	.515	2
	255	**171**	**77**	**7**	**.684**	

*Louisville was known to have thrown some of these games.

NL Club	G	W	L	T	PCT	League Position
			1878			**League**
Milwaukee	15	12	2	1	.833	6
Boston	29	21	7	1	.741	1
Cincinnati	13	9	4	0	.692	2
Providence	28	18	8	2	.679	3
Chicago	18	9	8	1	.528	4
Indianapolis	13	5	8	0	.385	5
	116	**74**	**37**	**5**	**.659**	

NL Club	G	W	L	T	PCT	League Position
			1879			**League**
Cincinnati	3	3	0	0	1.000	5
Syracuse	1	1	0	0	1.000	7
Boston	19	14	5	0	.737	2
Providence	19	13	5	1	.711	1
Troy City	17	10	5	2	.647	8
Buffalo	7	4	3	0	.571	3
Chicago	14	7	5	2	.571	4
Cleveland	1	0	1	0	.000	6
	81	**52**	**24**	**5**	**.673**	

NL Club	G	W	L	T	PCT	League Position
			1880			**League**
Cincinnati	6	5	1	0	.833	8
Boston	11	9	2	0	.818	6
Cleveland	18	14	3	1	.806	3
Providence	12	9	2	1	.792	2
Worcester	21	15	5	1	.738	5
Chicago	21	14	7	0	.667	1
Troy City	17	11	6	0	.647	4
Buffalo	10	4	6	0	.400	7
	116	**81**	**32**	**3**	**.711**	

NL Club	G	W	L	T	PCT	League Position
			1881			**League**
Boston	21	19	2	0	.905	6
Worcester	14	12	2	0	.857	8
Providence	20	17	3	0	.850	2
Cleveland	6	5	1	0	.833	7
Troy City	29	24	5	0	.828	5
Chicago	11	9	2	0	.818	1
Detroit	24	18	6	0	.750	4
Buffalo	13	8	5	0	.615	3
	138	**112**	**26**	**0**	**.812**	

The History of the Manchester Yankees

Christopher Chavis

The Boston Red Sox and New York Yankees have one of the fiercest rivalries in American sports. It is a rivalry borne out of regional differences that date back to Colonial America. The rivalry goes beyond sports—New York and Boston were early economic rivals, eventually becoming a cultural rivalry between New York and New England. While the Yankees-Red Sox rivalry was birthed by history, it was raised on the baseball diamond. The Red Sox were the dominant team in the first two decades of the twentieth century, winning five World Series before 1919.

However, that dominance ended abruptly after the 1919 season when owner Harry Frazee sold Babe Ruth (and other pieces) to the Yankees, which helped form the nucleus of a Yankees team that went on to dominate the 1920s and 1930s. As the Yankees' fortunes climbed, the Red Sox sank. Not until Tom Yawkey purchased the team in 1933 did the Red Sox see a reversal of fortune that saw them compete directly with the Yankees during the 1930s and 1940s. It was during the height of this competitive era between the two teams that the Manchester Yankees were born.

MANCHESTER, NEW HAMPSHIRE

Manchester sits along the Merrimack River in southern New Hampshire, around 50 miles northwest of Boston. While Manchester never developed into a manufacturing powerhouse at the level of its namesake in England, it became an important economic hub in northern New England. Its mills lined the river and provided employment for migrants from across rural New England and immigrants from French Canada. Today, Manchester sits as the most populous city in northern New England.

Professional baseball has been played in Manchester, albeit not on a continuous basis, since 1877, when the city hosted a founding member of the New England Association.[1] The city was granted a team in the New England League (a successor league to the New England Association) in 1887.[2] Manchester's fortunes as a baseball city were inconsistent and the team saw numerous entries and exits from the New England League, which had numerous unsuccessful incarnations between its founding in 1886 and its ultimate demise in 1949. The last iteration of the New England League began play in 1946, with Manchester hosting the Giants, the Class B affiliate of the New York Giants.[3] The 1940s iteration of the Manchester franchise played at Athletic Field.[4] The team was an on-field success in its first two seasons, making the playoffs (but losing in the first round) in 1946 and losing to their downstate rival, the Nashua Dodgers, in the Governor's Cup the next year.

Like much of New England, Manchester has a symbiotic relationship with Boston. In 1837, a group of businessmen from Boston founded Amoskeag Manufacturing Mills, which owned and operated the textile mills that dominated Manchester over the next century.[5] In the modern day, Manchester sits firmly in the Boston media market and its residents get most of their television stations from Boston. In fact, there is only one television station licensed to New Hampshire, Manchester's WMUR-TV. At the time of the founding of the Manchester Yankees, the hometown papers across New Hampshire covered the Red Sox and Boston Braves as the home teams, and the *Boston Globe* even regularly offered original reporting on news events in New Hampshire. New Englanders also take pride in their regional identity, and that extends to any regional rivalry with New York. Against this backdrop, it might seem unusual that the Yankees would set up shop in Manchester.

THE YANKEES TAKE THE FIELD

In February 1948, it was announced that the Manchester franchise in the Class B New England League had both been sold and signed a working agreement with the Newark Bears, a Triple-A affiliate of the New York Yankees.[6] The Manchester franchise was to be renamed the Manchester Yankees. The new ownership group was led by Edward C. Bourassa, who had led the group that founded the franchise in 1946. Bourassa had been forced out of his management role by the Giants after just one season over his desire to fire

Quebec native Josaphat T. Benoit served nine consecutive terms as mayor of Manchester, from 1944 to 1961.

manager Hal Gruber. Bourassa left after 1946, but the withdrawal of the Giants from their agreement with Manchester opened the door for him to purchase the team again before the 1948 season.[7] The new ownership group committed to making the team a community project, selling shares to members of the public for $100 each.[8] The team also announced that Manchester native Tom Padden would be the manager.[9]

The Manchester Yankees' original roster mainly consisted of players pulled from the Sunbury, Pennsylvania, franchise after the New York Yankees withdrew their minor league affiliation after the 1947 season.[10] In April, the team reported to Edenton, North Carolina, for three weeks of spring training in preparation for their May 5 opener at home against Nashua.[11] The Dodgers had beaten Manchester the previous year to win the Governor's Cup, the championship for the New England League, and the two cities were eager to resume the rivalry.[12]

The arrival of the Yankees to Manchester was met with much fanfare. On Opening Day, the team paraded down Elm Street, and Mayor Josaphat Benoit threw out the first pitch in front of a sellout crowd.[13] However, the Yankees fell short in their first game in Manchester, 9–3.[14] The Yankees were plagued by poor fielding, making six errors, including two in the second inning, which helped the Dodgers get the lead they never gave up.[15] The Yankees turned the tables the next night when they traveled to Nashua to defeat the Dodgers, 4–1, in a game that saw them commit no errors.[16]

The Yankees were never able to gain much traction in their inaugural season, playing much of the season below .500. In the eight-team league, the Yankees were consistently in the middle of the pack, and by July, it was clear that the Portland Pilots, Nashua Dodgers, and Lynn Red Sox were the best teams in the New England League. However, four teams made the playoffs, and the Yankees spent much of the year in contention for the fourth playoff spot. A hot streak at the end of June and the beginning of July solidified their claim. On July 2, the Yankees defeated the Providence Chiefs to move into a tie for the final playoff spot. It was their eighth victory in 10 games.[17] They defeated the Springfield Cubs the next night to win their fifth straight game and take sole possession of the final playoff spot.[18] The Yankees were still below .500, but in contention to take Manchester back to the postseason.

On July 12, the Yankees dropped a 1–0 game to the Red Sox, which started a cold streak that saw them lose fourth place to the Pawtucket Slaters.[19] On July 15, the Portland Pilots swept the Yankees in a doubleheader, which handed fourth place to the Slaters.[20] On July 19, the Slaters solidified their claim by handing the Yankees their seventh straight loss.[21] The Yankees, however, showed some signs of life the following day by sweeping the last-place Fall River Indians in a doubleheader.[22] While the Pilots, Red Sox, and Dodgers had an insurmountable advantage in the standings, fourth place was still up for grabs. The Slaters were hot, but the Yankees had started to rally and were not yet out of contention.[23] A doubleheader sweep of the Pilots on July 29 moved the Yankees back into fourth place.[24] The next day, a second doubleheader sweep of the Pilots gave the Yankees a two and a half-game lead over the Slaters for the final playoff spot.[25]

The Yankees held the final playoff spot for much of August, with the Slaters hot on their tail. On August 19, the two teams met for a pivotal doubleheader in Manchester. The Yankees entered with a two and a half-game lead over the Slaters, which dwindled to just a half-game after the Slaters swept.[26] The Slaters moved back into fourth place after their own victory over Springfield on August 22.[27] The Yankees never again held the playoff spot and concluded their season on September 6 with a doubleheader sweep by the Dodgers.[28] A fitting end to a disappointing season that saw the Manchester franchise fail to reach the heights it had achieved the previous season.

The 1948 Manchester Yankees finished 58–68, good enough for fifth place. The team was also a loser on the balance sheet, posting an $18,000 loss, much of which was attributed to the high cost of spring training.[29] The media questioned the team's ability to even return in 1949.[30] The New York Yankees attempted to make up for the losses by funding the team's spring training expenses.[31] The Manchester team reported to Dillon, South Carolina, for a joint spring training with the Yankees' Class B affiliate in the Piedmont League, the Norfolk Tars.[32] This move may have only delayed the inevitable closure of the team, which came just months into the 1949 season.

1948 was the only full season that the Yankees played in the New England League. By July 1949, the Yankees were dissolved, and the New England League itself voted to dissolve in December of that year.

THE DEATH OF THE NEW ENGLAND LEAGUE

Nineteen-forty-eight was a great year for New England baseball. The Braves and Red Sox were fighting for the pennants in their respective leagues, and fans saw the potential for the World Series trophy landing in Boston for the first time in 30 years. Beyond that, they saw the potential for an all-Boston World Series. However, it was the excitement generated in Boston that was partially to blame for the death of the final minor league dedicated solely to New England baseball.

One major factor in the failure of the Manchester Yankees was the proximity of the Braves and Red Sox, in addition to televised night games that came out of Boston.[33] The other major factor was Manchester's economic conditions. Manchester was a working-class mill town, and people could not afford to attend multiple games a week, especially if the choices were the local minor league team or an excursion to watch the major league teams in Boston.[34]

Other New England cities saw their teams die for similar reasons, and the teams that saw the highest attendance (and thus were two of the last three teams alive when the league folded) were the teams in Portland, Maine, and Springfield, Massachusetts, the two cities farthest from Boston.[35] Pawtucket, Rhode Island, hosted the third and final New England League team, though their lifeline may have been the folding of the team in Providence earlier in the season.

THE YANKEES RETURN TO MANCHESTER

But the story of the Manchester Yankees does not quite end there. The name was revived in January 1969 when the New York Yankees decided to move their Double-A Eastern League franchise from Binghamton, New York, to Manchester. The failure of the Binghamton club to secure a playing site and the New York-Pennsylvania League's decision to block the franchise's move to

Oneonta, New York, just 60 miles from Binghamton, necessitated the move.[36] The Yankees still had a few logistics to work out. They didn't even have an owner for the team or a stadium in which to play. The Yankees kept open the possibility of operating the team directly. Johnny Johnson, the vice president in charge of minor league operations, arrived in Manchester in early February to confer with the city about the logistics of the team arriving there, including its use of city-owned Gill Stadium (which had been known as Athletic Field during the Manchester Yankees' prior tenure).[37]

But the question remained as to whether this team could succeed. A February article in the *Union Leader* in Manchester asked this question and cautioned the Eastern League to avoid scheduling games at the same time as televised Boston Red Sox games in order to avoid the fate of the last iteration of the Manchester Yankees and the New England League as a whole.[38] The article also stated another potential barrier to success for the Manchester Yankees and one of the reasons for the failure of its last iteration: Manchester's proximity to Boston. Would fans turn out for a minor league team when they could drive an hour to Fenway Park? There was also the valid question of whether Red Sox fans in New Hampshire would even support a Yankees farm team.[39]

The details of the team's usage of Gill Stadium were also subject to scrutiny by Manchester Alderman Peter Psaledas, who questioned whether it was appropriate for a minor league team to use a stadium that was under the city's ownership and introduced a motion to block the Yankees' usage of Gill Stadium. Psaledas reasoned that any such use would take away from local organizations such as the American Legion or youth leagues. The City Council did not recognize Psaledas' motion and overwhelmingly supported the team's usage of Gill Stadium.[40]

A NEW OWNER EMERGES

After two weeks of speculation and negotiation, John Alevizos, a Boston University professor, ultimately purchased the team.[41] Alevizos immediately set out to address the issues raised by Psaledas and find a way to ensure that the Yankees' use of the stadium did not interfere with local concerns. They arrived at a compromise, including the American Legion team often playing games on the same day as Yankees games.[42] Psaledas seemed satisfied with the arrangements.

On February 28, the Manchester Yankees announced that they had hired 30-year-old Jerry Walker as manager. Walker had pitched for Baltimore, Kansas City, and Cleveland between 1957 and 1964 and managed the Yankees' New York-Pennsylvania League team in Oneonta to a league championship in 1968.[43] On March 9, Alevizos announced more staff additions, which consisted entirely of New Hampshire natives. Alevizos drew attention to the fact that the staff was entirely made up of local people except for his manager. While he did not follow in his predecessor's footsteps and directly sell shares of the team, he did announce that the Yankees offices in Manchester would be open to the public.[44] He spent March speaking to local groups, including the Lions Club and Chamber of Commerce.

In his first month as owner, Alevizos had gone the extra mile to endear himself to the people of Manchester, which the local press noted.[45]

He also addressed concerns about competing with the Red Sox and the opportunity to keep fans in New Hampshire. In a Lions Club speech, Alevizos noted that people in the Manchester, Concord, and Nashua areas spent $800,000 annually at Fenway Park. He said that he hoped to keep a third of that in Manchester. He also said that he needed 100,000 spectators to show up to Gill Stadium for the team to break even.[46]

Governor Walter Peterson accepted the team's invitation to attend Opening Day on April 22. In accepting the invitation, he encouraged all residents of New Hampshire to support the Yankees.[47] He even declared the day "Manchester Yankees Day" throughout the state.[48] The *Union Leader* framed the success of the Manchester Yankees as a success for all of New Hampshire.[49]

THE NEW YANKEES HEAD NORTH FOR THE FIRST TIME

This iteration of the Manchester Yankees wrapped up spring training in Hollywood, Florida, and headed north to Waterbury, Connecticut, for their debut on April 19.[50] However, Mother Nature had other plans for the Yankees, and their debut would have to wait another day. Rain rolled into Waterbury and postponed Opening Day.[51] The Yankees lost their first game to the Waterbury Indians, 5–3, after the home team rallied in the seventh inning.[52]

The Yankees picked up a 7–6 victory over Waterbury the next night, scoring the winning run in the seventh inning. The Yankees were able to capitalize on the fielding miscues of the Indians, who allowed five unearned runs on four errors.[53] After splitting their initial series, the two teams headed north to Manchester for Opening Day at Gill Stadium on April 22.

The Yankees planned to take the field with much fanfare, with "colorful, elaborate, pre-game ceremonies"

and dignitaries like Governor Walter Peterson and Mayor John Mongan in attendance.[54] Governor Peterson was even set to throw out the ceremonial first pitch.[55] However, Mother Nature again had other plans, and the home opener was postponed.[56]

The rain did not let up the next night and the game was postponed again.[57] But it was still a big night for New England baseball. Anyone who wanted their baseball fix could have driven down to Boston or turned on the radio to listen to Ted Williams make his return to Fenway Park as manager of the Washington Senators and defeat the Red Sox, 9–3.[58] Cold weather and the continued threat of rain forced another postponement the following night, closing the door for an April home Opening Day.[59]

Baseball officially returned to Manchester, New Hampshire, on May 2 as the Yankees finally took the field and defeated the Pioneers of Elmira, New York, 9–2.[60] Because of the rescheduled date, Governor Peterson could not attend and was represented by New Hampshire State Senate President Arthur Tufts. Much like his predecessor two decades prior, Mayor Mongan threw out the first pitch to start the festivities.[61] Four thousand fans were on hand for the return of the Yankees.[62]

The Yankees were also able to announce that they would have a couple of games broadcast on WMUR-TV on a test basis to expose more of New Hampshire to the team and get residents' support.[63] The first planned broadcast was the May 5 game against the York Pirates.[64] Fans across New Hampshire watched as the Yankees defeated the Pirates, 8–3, for their third win in their first four home games.[65]

On May 13, the Yankees were a party to one of the rarest events in baseball as they were no-hit by the Pittsfield Red Sox—but they were able to win the road game because of fielding errors by the Red Sox.[66] The Yankees ultimately swept the Red Sox in their first series.[67] The sweep also put the Yankees at .500 for the first time in their short existence.

The Yankees and Red Sox took the field for the first time in Manchester on May 19.[68] With the help of a home run by Charlestown, New Hampshire, resident Carlton Fisk, the Red Sox defeated the Yankees, 4–2.[69]

JOHN ALEVIZOS' RELATIONSHIP WITH THE CITY BEGINS TO DECLINE

Much like their predecessors in Manchester, the Yankees started with much support, but that tapered off as the season went along. A June article in the *Union Leader* lamented that only 325 fans showed up to a Sunday afternoon game.[70] A similar point had been made just a couple of days earlier after fans did not

Gill Stadium sits on land previously owned by the Amoskeag Manufacturing Company, who built the concrete-and-steel stadium in 1913 with a gently curving grandstand, making it usable for other sports, such as football, as well as baseball.

turn out during the previous homestand.[71] In June, the *Union Leader* called out Alevizos for referring to Manchester's "negativism" in multiple public speeches to local groups.[72] By August, rumors had emerged that Alevizos might relocate the team for the 1970 season. He called a press conference to dispel them.[73]

Alevizos soon entered into a dispute with the city regarding his lease at Gill Stadium, even resorting to placing his rent payment in escrow until the issue could get resolved.[74] In his letter to the city's Parks and Recreation Department, he alleged several violations, including failing to install a batting cage, water fountains, and other facilities.[75] The city responded by saying that it had lived up to the obligations of the lease and accused Alevizos of looking for an out so he could relocate the team.[76] In a meeting with the department, Alevizos' attorney, Thomas Tessier, claimed that the team had lost $10,000 in 1969.[77]

On August 21, the *Union Leader* reported that Alevizos had failed to pay a $5,500 bond that the city required to secure Gill Stadium for the 1970 season and that the city had informed him that the team would not be able to play at the stadium unless he paid within 30 days.[78] Alevizos quickly paid the $5,500 bond, assured fans that the Yankees would remain in Manchester, and cited support from the fans in his decision to do so.[79]

On the field, this iteration of the Yankees spent much of their inaugural season at around .500. As the season wound down in late August, the *Union Leader* published an editorial criticizing Alevizos' approach to running the Yankees and saying that his battles with the city were a distraction to his team on the field and

drew correlations between major events, such as his speeches on "negativism" and his dispute over the lease, and the team's poor performance.[80]

Any goodwill Alevizos built with his preseason charm offensive had run out.

SEASON ENDINGS AND ALMOST EVICTIONS

The season ended on August 29 with a doubleheader against the Waterbury Indians. The team honored two players, Gary Washington and Ron Blomberg, who were slated to be called up to New York at the end of the season.[81] The Yankees and Indians split the final doubleheader, which featured a sportswriter getting an at-bat.[82] George Sullivan was a reporter for the *Boston Herald Traveler* who was working on a firsthand story about playing in the minor leagues.[83] The Yankees finished their first season back in Manchester with a 64–75 record, in fifth place in the six-team Eastern League. Despite their on-field struggles and the reported decline in attendance throughout the season, the Yankees led the Eastern League in attendance, with 91,116 fans.[84]

On September 3, Alevizos met with the Manchester Parks and Recreation Commission regarding issues at Gill Stadium. The first reports indicated that the two sides agreed on addressing any outstanding issues before the 1970 season.[85]

With the team firmly in place in Manchester, Alevizos sought to rehabilitate his image, even hosting a public ceremony where new Manchester Mayor Henry Pariseau purchased 1970 season tickets and Alevizos promised to give the 92,116th fan to enter Gill Stadium in 1970 two all-expense-paid trips to Florida. He also announced the creation of a local "board of directors" that would oversee policies for ensuring "maximum service to the public."[86] Alevizos promised that professional baseball would remain in Manchester and that the only change fans should expect would be for Manchester to become a Triple-A city in the future. Neither of those promises would be fulfilled.

THE DEPARTURE OF JOHN ALEVIZOS

Before the first fan entered Gill Stadium, Alevizos already had one foot out the door. By early May, Alevizos had accepted a position with the Boston Red Sox. In fact, he attended the Manchester Yankees' home opener as a representative of the Red Sox.[87] He had even spent his spring in Winter Haven, Florida, helping the Red Sox negotiate their expanded presence there.[88] There was even ambiguity around Alevizos' role with the Yankees. On May 6, Alevizos spoke at New Hampshire College's Athletic Awards Banquet in a dual role as Boston Red Sox vice president and Manchester Yankees owner.[89] By June, Alevizos insisted that he had no formal role with the Yankees, and his uncle, George Alevizos, served as team president.[90]

In late May, a nonprofit called Baseball Inc. was chartered by local interests who wanted to purchase the franchise to get Alevizos to divest his shares in the Yankees.[91] Alevizos and Baseball Inc. were unable to come to terms on a sale. Despite this, Alevizos said he would consider donating the team to a civic-minded organization or individual.[92] That proclamation attracted the attention of the future buyers of the team.[93]

Despite his reduced role, Alevizos' battles with the city of Manchester continued. He missed rent payments for the season's first two months, almost prompting the city to lock the Yankees out of their home stadium.[94] Much as he had in the past, Alevizos made the payments necessary to avoid trouble, but only after pushing the team to the brink.

On July 1, the Yankees announced the team's sale to businessmen Ronald C. Duke, Kenneth E. Cail, James Fary, and Henry Fary. Duke and Cail were residents of Massachusetts, while the Fary brothers were residents of Salem, New Hampshire.[95]

At long last, the John Alevizos experience was over for Manchester.

THE YANKEES BEGIN THE SEASON

In February 1970, the Yankees confirmed that they would return to Hollywood, Florida, for spring training. Then they would play the newly relocated Pawtucket Red Sox in Rhode Island on April 24. Their home opener, also against the Red Sox, was scheduled for May 5.[96]

Yankees leadership had also been revamped for the coming season. The Yankees had hired 24-year-old Suffolk University law school student Jimmy Brent to serve as general manager and Gene Hassell to serve as manager.[97]

The Yankees headed north from Hollywood with an 18–3 record in spring training.[98] However, their momentum did not carry into the season, and they posted a 4–7 record in their opening 11-game road trip. For the second straight year, New Hampshire Governor Walter Peterson was scheduled to throw out the first ball, and he was once again relieved by a Manchester mayor.[99] The Yankees dropped their home opener, 8–1. It was unclear how John Alevizos felt about the outcome.

Their initial stumble aside, the Yankees got off to a good start and were second in the Eastern League by the end of May.[100] On June 8, they moved into a tie for first in the Eastern League with a victory over the Elmira Pioneers.[101] Unfortunately for the Yankees, this was the peak of their season. By the end of the month—and when the new owners took over—the Yankees were hovering around .500, third in the Eastern League. However, it was a tight battle at the top of the league, and the Yankees were only four and a half games out of first place.[102]

THE NEW OWNERS ARRIVE—AND THE STRUGGLES CONTINUE

In early July, Brent was relieved of his duties as GM, with the new owners citing a desire to assume the role themselves.[103] They also scheduled a Get Acquainted Night for the team's July 10 game against the Waterbury Pirates so they could meet the fans.[104] The Yankees announced that new Manchester Mayor Charles R. Stanton would throw out the first pitch to mark the festivities.[105]

Despite the Yankees contending on the field, they were not attracting people to the games, a fact that concerned New York Yankees management.[106] The decision by the new owners to host a special night did not help attendance, and the Get Acquainted Night on July 10 drew only 568 fans.[107] To make matters worse, the Yankees lost, 2–0, to the Pirates. The Yankees were also once again the subject of relocation rumors, with reports emerging that the team may seek a move to the west to Keene, New Hampshire, in 1971, a rumor that was boosted by the Yankees' decision to play a July home game in Keene. On August 5, the *Union Leader* reported that the owners denied any plans to move the team and reiterated their commitment (and the New York Yankees' commitment) to Manchester.[108]

By the end of August, the Yankees had sunk to 62–69, 12 games out of the lead, and well out of contention for a playoff spot. The team had been plagued by injuries, with most of its players, including key contributors, missing time.[109] The off-the-field chaos also plagued the Yankees. They played for two owners, with almost half the season spent waiting for a new owner to arrive. On September 7, the 1970 Manchester Yankees lost their final game, 8–0, to the Pawtucket Red Sox.

The *Union Leader* did not provide attendance figures, but attendance had sunk to 36,928. The team's lack of success at the box office was the topic of a talk given by co-owner Ronald Duke to the Kiwanis Club in Manchester in February 1971. In his remarks, Duke cited competition from the Boston Red Sox, lack of support from the business community because of Alevizos' "hard sell" style, and the team's losing record.[111] The owners reported early successes in selling season ticket packages. By March, they had sold 160, compared to 129 the year prior. The owners indicated that they would need to sell 75,000 tickets throughout the season to break even.[112]

THE FINAL SEASON

The Manchester Yankees prepared to take the field in 1971 by naming former Washington Senators manager and American League batting average champion Mickey Vernon as their new manager. Vernon had managed the Richmond Braves in the International League in 1970. The Yankees reassigned Hassell to their affiliate in Kinston, North Carolina, where Hassell had worked in 1969.[113] The Yankees headed north in mid-April from their spring training site in Hollywood, Florida, to begin their season at home against the Pawtucket Red Sox.[114] To get the local fans excited for the season, the team hosted its first annual Meet the Yankees Dinner, where season ticket holders and the news media could meet the team.[115]

As it turned out, however, there was little on the field to excite the home fans. On April 19, the season began with a first pitch from Manchester Mayor Stanton and a one-run loss by the home team.[116] The Yankees dropped five of the six games of their opening homestand.[117] Cold and rainy weather also besieged the team, which was a precursor for things to come.[118]

Going on the road did not help. Overall, the Yankees dropped 10 of their first 11 games.[119] Given the situation, the team needed help drumming up interest among the local fans. The owners attempted to remedy the situation by offering free tickets to their June 7 game against the Waterbury Pirates.[120] That game was even preceded by a hot streak that temporarily pulled the Yankees out of last place in the American Division of

the Eastern League.[121] Despite giving away free tickets, the Yankees only managed to fill a third of the seats.[122] Unfortunately for the fans who showed up to the free game, the Yankees lost, 8–6.[123]

The ownership attempted to spur interest by lowering ticket prices for the June 20–24 homestand.[124] By July, they indicated that they would decide whether to remain in Manchester in 1972 by the end of the regular season.[125] The New York Yankees made it clear that the decision to move would be left to the Manchester ownership, and the parent club would defer to them in the matter.[126] The Eastern League's president made the same declaration.[127]

A LONG GOODBYE

The Yankees spent the rest of the season in the cellar, with fans not showing up to the ballpark to offer their support. They concluded their home schedule on August 26 with a 7–2 loss to the Elmira Royals in front of just 326 fans at Gill Stadium.[128] The Yankees finished in last place, and the few fans were left to wonder whether the team would remain in Manchester in 1972.

The owners did not quickly announce a decision on the matter. In November, the Eastern League owners unanimously approved a Yankees relocation.[129] The owners were looking at West Haven and Waterbury, Connecticut, as potential relocation sites. The latter was set to lose its Eastern League team, and New York Yankees management preferred it because of the big club's fan base in the area.[130] Despite the parent club's preference, Waterbury could not match the offer made by West Haven, and the Manchester Yankees owners began to zero in on West Haven as a relocation site.[131]

But by December, the Yankees had yet to officially move, and the owners had not ruled out remaining in Manchester for the 1972 season. The delay in a final decision was partially caused by the city of West Haven's inability to finalize its incentives package, which the outgoing mayor had vetoed.[132]

However, if they did decide to stay, the Yankees would be without a home. The Manchester Parks and Recreation Commission had voted unanimously not to renew the team's lease at Gill Stadium.[133] This vote had essentially put the nail in the coffin of the Manchester Yankees.

On January 26, 1972, the Eastern League announced its approval of the team's move to West Haven, officially ending its tenure in Manchester.[134]

The Manchester Yankees were dead, and Manchester would not see a minor league team again until 2004, when the New Hampshire Fisher Cats began playing in the Eastern League.

CONCLUSION

The overarching narrative of the Manchester Yankees was on-field futility and fan apathy. While the team's first iteration fell victim to the greater forces that sunk the New England League, instability and turmoil besieged the team's second iteration. John Alevizos had fostered a hostile relationship with the city and its fan base. By the time Alevizos sold the team, the damage had been done, and the team never fully recovered.

It would be difficult to categorize the Yankees' foray into New England as a success on either occasion. In the 1940s, they failed because of economic forces beyond their control and two hot teams down in Boston. In the 1970s, they failed because of a chaotic team ownership situation, fights with the city, and a bad on-field product. ■

Notes

1. Charles Bevis, *The New England League: A Baseball History 1885–1949* (Jefferson, NC: McFarland Books, 2008), 14.
2. Bevis, 49.
3. Bevis, 268.
4. "Dodgers in Manchester Tonight," *Nashua Telegraph*, June 17, 1947: 11.
5. Bevis, *The New England League*, 22.
6. "Manchester Franchise In New Hands," *Portland Press Herald*, February 7, 1948: 7.
7. "Manchester Franchise In New Hands": 7.
8. "Selling Stock in Manchester's Baseball Team," *Nashua Telegraph*, March 8, 1948: 10.
9. "Tom Padden Named Manchester Manager," *Boston Globe*, February 28, 1948: 4.
10. "Manchester Club Set," *Nashua Telegraph*, February 9, 1948: 9.
11. "Manchester Yankees On Way to Camp," *Nashua Telegraph*, April 7, 1948: 10.
12. "Bankhead on Mound for Locals," *Nashua Telegraph*, May 5, 1948: 13.
13. "Bankhead on Mound. for Locals": 13.
14. "Nashua Dodgers 9 to 3 Victors over Yankees," *Rutland Daily Herald*, May 6, 1948: 16.
15. "Nashua Dodgers 9 to 3 Victors over Yankees": 16.
16. "Locals Bow, 4–1, to Manchester Yanks," *Nashua Telegraph*, May 7, 1948: 15.
17. "Yanks Defeat Chiefs, 6–4," *Kennebec Journal*, July 3, 1948: 2.
18. "Manchester Tips Springfield, 7–2," *Portland Press Herald*, July 5, 1948: 13.
19. "Red Sox Take Full Game NE Lead League," *Nashua Telegraph*, July 13, 1948: 9.
20. "Portland Takes Two From Yanks, Lynn Divides," *Biddeford-Saco Journal*, July 16, 1948: 6.
21. "Twarkins Chains Cubs for Pilots," *Portland Evening Express*, July 19, 1948: 23.
22. "Pilots Climb in NE League," *Concord Monitor*, July 20, 1948: 9.
23. Bud Cornish, "Providence Chiefs Play Here Sunday," *Portland Evening Express*, July 24, 1948: 9.
24. "Manchester Takes Twin-Bill From Portland Pilots," *Biddeford-Saco Journal*, July 29, 1948: 6.
25. "Red Sox Take Over NE Loop First Place," *Nashua Telegraph*, July 30, 1948: 9.
26. "Manchester Fights for Playoff Spot," *Portsmouth Herald*, August 20, 1948: 6.
27. "Dodgers Smack Pilots to Gain Lead in League," *Biddeford-Saco Journal*, August 23, 1948: 6.
28. "Lynn Red Sox Top N.E. Loop for Third Year," *Portsmouth Herald*, September 7, 1948: 9 .
29. "New England League Notes," *Nashua Telegraph*, February 7, 1949: 9.
30. Bevis, *The New England League*, 279.
31. "New England League Notes": 9.
32. "Baseball Breezes," *Nashua Telegraph*, February 17, 1949: 17.
33. Bevis, *The New England League*, 8.
34. Bevis, 8.
35. Bevis, 8–10.
36. Roger O'Gara, "Manchester, N.H. will Become Sixth Member of Eastern League," *Berkshire Eagle*, January 29, 1969: 35.
37. Ray Valliere, "Johnny Johnson in Manchester on Thursday," *Manchester Union Leader*, February 2, 1969: 39.
38. Joe Barnea, "Barnstorming with Barnea," *Manchester Union Leader*, February 4, 1969: 18.
39. Barnea, "Barnstorming with Barnea," *Manchester Union Leader*, February 12, 1969: 30.
40. J. Leo Dery, "Alderman Ask Contract Check," *Manchester Union Leader*, February 5, 1969: 1.
41. Al Nettel, "BU Prof. Buys Yanks' Control," *Manchester Union Leader*, February 21, 1969: 1.
42. Valliere, "Alevizos Works Hard for Harmony," *Manchester Union Leader*, February 24, 1969: 13.
43. Nettel, "Jerry Walker Named to Manage Manchester Yankees," *Manchester Union Leader*, February 28, 1969: 18.
44. "Yankee Office Open to Public Says Alevizos," *Manchester Union Leader*, March 13, 1969: 28.
45. "Alevizos Unveils Yankee Staff," *Manchester Union Leader*, March 9, 1969: 33.
46. Nettel, "Manchester Yankee Impact to Be Felt," *Manchester Union Leader*, March 21, 1969: 20.
47. "Gov. Peterson Accepts Invite to Yank Openers," *Manchester Union Leader*, March 21, 1969: 20.
48. Joe McQuaid, "Yankee Day Set for Tuesday," *Manchester Union Leader*, April 20, 1969: 42.
49. Don Anderson, "As I See It," *Manchester Union Leader*, April 19, 1969: 11.
50. Anderson, "Yankee Infield Pleases Jerry Walker, *Manchester Union Leader*, April 16, 1969: 40.
51. "Rain Postpones Yankee Clash at Waterbury," *Manchester Union Leader*, April 20, 1969: 67.
52. "Yanks Look for First Win," *Manchester Union Leader*, April 21, 1969: 22.
53. "Yankees Return Home After Nipping Indians, 7–6," *Manchester Union Leader*, April 22, 1969: 19.
54. Nettel, "Yanks in Gala Home Opener This Evening," *Manchester Union Leader*, April 22, 1969: 1.
55. "List Schedule of Governor," *Manchester Union Leader*, April 22, 1969: 3.
56. Nettel, "Rain KO's Yankee Opener," *Manchester Union Leader*, April 22, 1969: 1.
57. McQuaid, "Rain Stalls Yank Opener Again," *Manchester Union Leader*, April 24, 1969: 24.
58. "Hose Beaten By Nats, 9–3," *Manchester Union Leader*, April 24, 1969: 24.
59. "Weather Postpones Yank-Indian Game," *Manchester Union Leader*, April 24, 1969: 1.
60. Bob Donahue, "Yankees vs. York to Be Telecast," *Manchester Union Leader*, May 3, 1969: 12.
61. "Fans Pour Out for the Yankees," *Manchester Union Leader*, May 3, 1969: 14
62. "Fans Pour Out For the Yankees": 14.
63. Donahue, "Yankees vs. York To Be Telecast": 12.
64. Donahue, "Yankees vs. York To Be Telecast": 12.
65. McQuaid, "Yankees Belt York Pirates," *Manchester Union Leader*, May 6, 1969: 37.
66. "Hitless Yanks Blank Pittsfield," *Manchester Union Leader*, May 14, 1969: 43.
67. "Yankees Sweep Pittsfield, 9–0," *Manchester Union Leader*, May 16, 1969: 22.

68. "Yanks, Sox Open 5-Game Set," *Manchester Union Leader*, May 19, 1969: 24.
69. "Pittsfield Tops Yanks, 4–2; Fisk, Blomberg Hit Homers," *Manchester Union Leader*, May 20, 1969: 20.
70. Bob Hilliard, "The Sports Desk," *Manchester Union Leader*, June 1, 1969: 78.
71. Barnea, "Barnstorming with Barnea," *Manchester Union Leader*, May 29, 1969: 22.
72. "Advice from the Bleachers," *Manchester Union Leader*, June 6, 1969: 9.
73. Nettel, "Manchester Yanks Will Remain Here," *Manchester Union Leader*, August 7, 1969: 1, 15.
74. Nettel, "Alevizos Puts Rental On Stadium in Escrow," *Manchester Union Leader*, August 13, 1969: 1.
75. Nettel: 1.
76. Nettel, "Soucy Charges Yankees Owner Looking for Out," *Manchester Union Leader*, August 15, 1969: 10.
77. John R. Hussey, "Yankees, P&R Meet September 3," *Manchester Union Leader*, August 20, 1969: 39.
78. Nettel, "Alevizos Told Contract Hinges on Paying Bond," *Manchester Union Leader*, August 22, 1969: 19.
79. "Alevizos Will Pay Bond of $5,500," *Manchester Union Leader*, August 23, 1969: 13.
80. "Bull in a China Shop," *Manchester Union Leader*, August 20, 1969: 15.
81. In the end Washington was added to the 40-man roster, but not called up. Nettel, "Final 'Curtain' for Yankees," *Manchester Union Leader*, August 29, 1969: 18.
82. C.J. McCarthy, "Yanks, Waterbury Indians Split," *Manchester Union Leader*, August 30, 1969: 12.
83. Marvin Pave, "George Sullivan, 83, a sportswriter, author, and professor," *Boston Globe*, June 18, 2017: B13.
84. Barnea, "Barnstorming With Barnea," *Manchester Union Leader*, November 19, 1969: 47.
85. "Yanks, P-R Body Settle Difficulties," *Manchester Union Leader*, September 4, 1969: 22.
86. "Mayor Buys First Yankee Ducat," *Manchester Union Leader*, January 26, 1970: 22.
87. "Red Sox Brass to See Opener," *Manchester Union Leader*, May 3, 1970: 57.
88. "Rain Hurt Pitching Routine of Red Sox," *Morning Sentinel*, March 26, 1970: 13.
89. Russ Pelletier, "Veteran Guard Sam Lewis NHC Athlete of the Year," *Manchester Union Leader*, May 6, 1970: 49.
90. Nettel, "Yankees Transfer Talks End—No Sale," *Manchester Union Leader*, June 10, 1970: 12.
91. Nettel: 12.
92. Nettel: 12.
93. Ken Cail, "Barnstorming with Barnea," *Manchester Union Leader*, July 15, 1970: 38.
94. Phil Chase, "Many Queen Cityians Would Prefer New Yankee Management," *New Hampshire Sunday News*, June 14, 1970: 51.
95. "Manchester Yankees Sold," *Manchester Union Leader*, July 1, 1970: 37.
96. Anderson, "As I See It," *Manchester Union Leader*, February 7, 1970: 14.
97. "Yankee GM Brent Eager for Opener," *Manchester Union Leader*, April 17, 1970: 24, 28.
98. Valliere, "Yankees Break Camp—Head North for Manchester," *Manchester Union Leader*, April 20, 1970: 25.
99. "Mayor Pariseau Tosses Strike," *Manchester Union Leader*, May 6, 1970: 47.
100. McCarthy, "Yanks Send Gowell Against Senators," *Manchester Union Leader*, May 28, 1970: 22.
101. "Yanks Gain Tie for the Lead, Host Waterbury Tonight," *Manchester Union Leader*, June 9, 1970: 23.
102. "Manchester Yankees Sold," *Manchester Union Leader*, July 1, 1970: 37.
103. "Yankees Relieve Brent of GM Duties," *Manchester Union Leader*, July 8, 1970: 39.
104. Nettel, "Get Acquainted Night Scheduled," *Manchester Union Leader*, July 8, 1970: 37.
105. Stanton was elected mayor after the death of the previous mayor.
106. Chase, "Many Queen Cityians Would Prefer New Yankee Management:" 51.
107. McCarthy, "Pirates Blank Yankees, 2–0," *Manchester Union Leader*, July 11, 1970: 13.
108. "Yankees Not Moving," *Manchester Union Leader*, August 5, 1970: 42.
109. McCarthy, "Injuries Key to Yankees Woes," *Manchester Union Leader*, August 26, 1970: 47.
110. McCarthy, "Yankees Drop Finale to Pawtucket 8–0," *Manchester Union Leader*, September 8, 1970: 22.
111. "New Owners Tell of Acquiring Yankees," *Manchester Union Leader*, February 17, 1971: 6.
112. Barnea, "Barnstorming with Barnea," *Manchester Union Leader*, March 4, 1971: 22.
113. "Yanks Name Vernon Pilot," *Manchester Union Leader*, January 13, 1971: 37, 42.
114. Guy Nadeau, "Yank Roster Set; Opener Monday," *Manchester Union Leader*, April 14, 1971: 51.
115. "Vernon, Gore to Headline 'Meet the Yankees' Dinner," *Manchester Union Leader*, April 16, 1971: 23.
116. Nadeau, "Yankees Return 'Warmed' Fans," *Manchester Union Leader*, April 20, 1971: 25.
117. Jim Heath, "Disastrous Stand Ends for Yankees," *Manchester Union Leader*, April 30, 1971: 47.
118. "Yanks Rained out Again, *Manchester Union Leader*, April 30, 1971: 23.
119. Anderson, "As I See It," *Manchester Union Leader*, May 8, 1971: 17.
120. "Free Yank Ducats," *Manchester Union Leader*, May 25, 1971: 23.
121. "Yankees Climb out of Eastern League Cellar," *Manchester Union Leader*, June 2, 1971: 45.
122. Nettel, "View from the Press Box," *Manchester Union Leader*, July 4, 1971: 39.
123. "Eastern Hurler Tosses 2-Hitter," *Manchester Union Leader*, June 8, 1971: 20.
124. "Yankees Reduce Ticket Prices," *Manchester Union Leader*, June 18, 1971: 30.
125. Nettel, "View From the Press Box," *Manchester Union Leader*, July 4, 1971: 39.
126. McCarthy, "MacPhail Denies Move from N.Y.," *Manchester Union Leader*, July 31, 1971: 15.
127. Bob Dobens, "Move 'Up To Owners' – Jackson," *Manchester Union Leader*: August 27, 1971: 23.
128. Phil Denis, "Royals Spoil Yankees Finale," *Manchester Union Leader*: August 27, 1971: 19.
129. McCarthy, "Manchester Yankees May Move," *Manchester Union Leader*: November 2, 1971: 21.
130. McCarthy: 21.
131. McCarthy, "Yankees 48 Hours Away from Leaving Queen City," *Manchester Union Leader*, November 9, 1971: 21.
132. Nettel, "View from the Press Box," *Manchester Union Leader*, December 12, 1971: 64
133. Nettel and Dery, "Yanks Without Stadium—if Team's Stays," *Manchester Union Leader*, December 15, 1971: 51.
134. "West Haven New Home for Yankee Farm Team," *Hartford Courant*, January 27, 1972: 64.

Examining Dusty Baker's Hope

Is Help on the Way?

David C. Ogden, PhD

Had Michael Brantley stayed healthy, the 2022 World Series could have avoided becoming the first Fall Classic since 1950 to have no African American players. As it was, the Astros outfielder and lone African American on either team's roster suffered a season-ending shoulder injury that kept him out of postseason play.[1] The only other African American in the dugout was Astros manager Dusty Baker, who gave a dour assessment on the absence of African American players: "[It] looks bad...I am ashamed of the game," he said. "It lets us know there's obviously a lot of work to be done to create opportunities for Black kids to pursue their dream at the highest level."[2]

But Baker also offered optimism. He forecast brighter days ahead for African Americans in baseball: "The [baseball] academies are producing players.... [T]here is help on the way. You can tell by the number of African-American No. 1 draft choices."[3]

Baker's comments refer to two measures of success in increasing the proportion of African Americans in the minor leagues and Major League Baseball: the number of African Americans in the most competitive levels of youth travel baseball and in the MLB amateur draft. The 2022 draft, in which four of the first five selections were African American, gave credence to his prediction that "help is on the way." So do the almost 19 percent of first- and second-round picks who are African American from the last 10 drafts.[4] With systemically low numbers of African Americans at every level of baseball, those percentages and Baker's comments merit further exploration into the draft and the extent to which youth baseball organizations are helping Black players to get drafted (or be recruited by a college). The following research questions will drive this exploration:

RQ 1: How many African Americans are being selected in the first five rounds of the draft?

RQ 2: To what extent are African Americans, in proportion to other races, coming down the talent pipeline (beginning with youth travel ball)?

RQ 3: Through what types of youth baseball programs are African Americans entering college baseball and/or the draft?

Baker's comments imply that youth travel baseball will boost the percentage of players who are African American in the MLB amateur draft. By examining MLB draftees' playing histories, we can clarify the link between youth travel baseball and higher leagues—both college and professional ball. Their histories reveal the types of baseball "academies" from which African American draftees come and whether there are racial differences in the number of draftees "graduating" from those "academies"—a moniker that many youth travel teams began applying to themselves in the 2000s.[5] To put Baker's comments in perspective requires understanding the changes in youth travel baseball over the past two decades. Looking at the number of African Americans who have played for such academies and who were subsequently drafted by a major league team can be used to test Baker's assertion. Do these academies serve as portals for African Americans?

THE TRANSFORMATION OF ELITE YOUTH BASEBALL

In his 2009 book, *Perfect Game USA and the Future of Baseball: How the Remaking of Youth Scouting Affects the National Pastime*, Les Edgerton argued that travel team baseball was superseding high school baseball as a more auspicious path to college and professional baseball.[6] Travel ball has encroached on the two mainstays of high-level competitive baseball for mid- and late-teen males: high school baseball and American Legion Baseball.

Over the past few years, both state high school associations and American Legion chapters reported fewer male teens playing baseball. The number of North Carolina high school players dropped by more than 500 between 2016 and 2022, and a 2019 national survey also showed a decrease in high school baseball players, along with other scholastic sports.[7] Even the *Huffington Post* sounded the alarm that "high schools are struggling to recruit enough players."[8] Although part of the decrease is due to the COVID-19 pandemic, the effect of travel ball is also contributing.

HIGH SCHOOL BASEBALL

Travel ball has not only taken players away from high school ball, it has also tipped the balance in high school competition. Muskegon, Michigan, high school and travel baseball coach Red Pastor has said that travel ball has rendered high school baseball into the "have's" and "have not's." Those teams that have travel-ball players have a significant advantage over teams with few or no travel-ball players. The competition becomes diluted as a handful of teams raise the bar that other teams can't reach.[9] According to Pastor, "You're just not going to be successful anymore if your program doesn't have at least four or five kids that played all year round and your pitcher better be one of them."[10]

Benson High School in Omaha, Nebraska, serves as another example. Even with an enrollment of 1,400 students, the school did not have enough players to field a baseball team for three years. Those who wanted to play did so on a co-op team with another Omaha high school. In 2022, two Benson teachers were able to assemble a roster of 25 players, but only four had played baseball previously. *Omaha World-Herald* reporter Marjie Ducey wrote that none had even played Little League, nor had anyone on Benson's roster played "select baseball through junior high like many of the other Metro Conference and Class A schools." As a result, the Benson team did not fare well against those schools, and "sometimes the players get frustrated, especially when every game ends early because of the mercy rule."[11] Pastor observed many "mercy rule" games and attributed those lopsided losses to the winning team having "a ton of travel kids" and the losing team having few or none.[12]

Ohio high school officials in 2016 codified their concerns about travel ball's interference with their baseball programs. The Ohio High School Athletic Association banned players and coaches from participating in any travel ball activities during the high school season.[13]

AMERICAN LEGION BASEBALL

Even more than high school ball, the other decades-long staple of teenage baseball, American Legion Baseball, has been hurt by travel teams. Because the seasons of American Legion and travel ball overlap, players are forced to choose. The best players opt for travel ball, where "[e]verybody's going to these showcase base-ball things where you go play in front of college coaches on the weekend," explained Ryan Redeker, an Emporia, Kansas, baseball coach. "All the elite players have gone to that, so your Legion has gone down to your smaller type schools."[14]

Between 2007 and 2017, 25 percent of American Legion baseball teams folded, and the number continues to dwindle. Some states lost up to 80 percent of their teams.[15] From just 2016 to 2018, American Legion Baseball lost more than 300 teams.[16] Maine typifies what's happening to American Legion Baseball around the nation. Between 2016 and 2018 Maine lost 15 of its 33 teams. At its peak in 2007, the state had 48 teams.[17] Galesburg, Illinois, is another microcosm of American Legion ball. After 60 years of fielding a team, the town's American Legion Baseball shut down in 2017. Four years later, the Legion post revived the team, although Coach Jeremy Kleine conceded he had trouble maintaining his initial roster of 18 players, with several missing games at times. "Last night (Tuesday) we were missing five players. Saturday (at Crawfordsville, Indiana) we'll be missing five players," said Kleine. "These days the players don't put everything aside for baseball."[18] While some cite organizational problems within the American Legion and others cite changes in cultural attitudes, most agree that travel baseball siphons off the most talented players, leaving less serious players to populate high school and American Legion teams.[19]

THE PROMINENCE OF ELITE TRAVEL BASEBALL

"The travel or as some call them, the 'showcase' teams, have taken over," proclaimed Pro Baseball Insider (PBI) in 2014.[20] PBI echoes other youth baseball coaches and officials regarding reasons for the travel ball "takeover": Players know that travel baseball offers the greatest chance of being scouted by a university or major league team, and the scouts know that travel ball tournaments save time and offer the greatest convenience in observing some of the best teen players in the nation. Former Southern New Hampshire University coach Ryan Copp questioned why he or any other scout would go to an American Legion game on a solitary field, when "I could go to one site with five fields and they would roll out a game every two hours."[21]

Copp was referencing how tournaments have become the center stage for elite youth baseball teams. Regional tournaments sprang up in the early 1990s as the number of travel teams grew. Before that time, travel teams were sparse, but in that decade groups of parents and local businesses began forming private baseball teams for youngsters. Those often comprised the best players in the local grade schools, junior high, and high schools.[22] Regional tournaments have since led to national tournaments. Youth sport entrepreneurs cashed in on the phenomenon and have built youth "baseball destinations," such as Cooperstown All-Star Village. That facility in Oneonta, New York, about 10 miles south of Cooperstown, offers elaborate baseball camps and facilities, including lodging, a restaurant, a heated swimming pool, and other family-appealing amenities.[23] The Village hosts week-long tournaments, as does another nearby destination, Cooperstown Dreams Park. Just south of Cooperstown, Dreams Park hosts week-long tournaments from June through August. Before the COVID-19 pandemic, approximately 100 teams from throughout the nation played there each week.[24]

The College World Series each June in Omaha is another baseball destination, but not just for college baseball teams and their fans. Claiming to be the "world's largest youth baseball tournament," the Slumpbuster Tournament is held concurrently with the College World Series. The 2023 tournament drew 630 teams from 40 states during the two weeks of the CWS and its festivities.[25] But even though it may be the largest, even the Slumpbuster is not necessarily the most prestigious travel ball or showcase tournament. Several organizations, including the USSSA (United States Specialty Sports Association) and the AAU (Amateur Athletic Union), sponsor and sanction travel ball tournaments around the country. But according to *Sports Business Journal*, the organization most associated with "showcase" tournaments that draw the best teen talent in baseball—and therefore the college and professional scouts to watch them—is Perfect Game. Based in Cedar Rapids, Iowa, Perfect Game "has helped to remake the landscape of youth baseball."[26] Calling itself the "world's largest" youth baseball scouting organization, Perfect Game not only holds national travel ball tournaments and talent showcases, but it has "built an entire culture around them," according to *SBJ*. "The idea of an American baseball player getting to the major leagues, or even the minors, without having played at a Perfect Game event or generating a Perfect Game profile has become almost inconceivable," the *Journal*'s Bruce Shoenfeld wrote.[27]

Since starting as an indoor baseball facility and youth select baseball sponsor 30 years ago, Perfect Game has grown into a $30-million-per-year business with more than 60 full-time employees and dozens of part-time scouts. "Tournaments that we started with 32 teams are now 400 teams," said founder Jerry Ford.[28] Perfect Game has built an information network of some of the most prominent national travel teams, and in doing so has provided information to college coaches and MLB scouts on teams and prospects. According to Perfect Game, 14,465 players who have played in one of their events were drafted by MLB teams, with 1,847 making it to the major leagues.[29] Perfect Game epitomizes Klein, Macauley, and Cooper's description of travel-team baseball: "a strong intersection with financial capital and summer travel coaches, college coaches, and major league scouts."[30]

Perfect Game developed alongside the growth of large-scale youth elite baseball organizations. By 2005, Canes Baseball, Marucci Elite, and other programs had begun organizing teams and recruiting from coast to coast. The "nationalization" of travel teams was underway, and their "expansion and influence move[d] forward almost entirely unchecked."[31]

But to what extent, if any, has the expansion and influence of elite travel ball helped African Americans to be drafted? We must identify the types of academies most likely to propel African Americans to the upper echelons of baseball and investigate differences between the types of teams that launch players into their post-high-school baseball careers.

METHODOLOGY

This study covered all players who were drafted by MLB teams in the first five rounds of the MLB Draft during the last 10 years (2013–22). The study was restricted to those rounds because of time and resource limitations. In addition, we looked at the highest-ranked prospects who, according to scouts and baseball prognosticators, have the greatest chance of joining the major league ranks. To explore one of Baker's comments—that the number of African Americans being drafted by MLB teams bodes well— and to answer RQ1, the players from those first five rounds were categorized by race (White, African American, Latino or Hispanic American, Asian American, or Pacific Islander). To evaluate the statement that "academies," or youth baseball programs, were producing African American players of high caliber, draftees were also categorized by the type of baseball team on which they played right before being drafted or playing college baseball.

Each player's race was determined by skin color, hair type, and facial features. When in doubt, the primary coder researched surnames, particularly for Hispanic or Latino name origins using searches on the websites Forebears and House of Names.[32,33] As a precaution against personal bias, a second coder (in addition to the primary coder) viewed a sample of

MLB draftee photos (printed mostly from Perfect Game and college baseball websites) and also categorized the players by race. Cohen's Kappa for inter-coder reliability was .90 for African American players, .86 for Hispanic and Latino players, and .94 for White players. (Asian and Pacific Islander players were so few that inter-coder reliability was not calculated.) All the Kappa values indicate strong agreement between the coders and thus the results of the racial categorization are acceptable.[34]

The next step in the methodology addressed RQ2 by comparing the results of RQ1 (the number of African Americans in the draft) with the percentages of players who are African American in youth travel baseball and college baseball. Results from studies on the racial composition of youth travel teams (for players, ages 9 to 18[35]) and the University of Central Florida's *Racial and Gender Report Card* on college sports provided those percentages.[36]

While RQ2 deals tangentially with the role of baseball academies, RQ3 was designed to delve more deeply into Baker's acknowledgment of that role. This meant determining the extent to which African American draftees, compared with draftees of other races, played travel ball in the year or years before being drafted or entering a college program. Previous research shows that the wider a geographic area a showcase or travel team's participants represent, the greater the team's prominence or stature.[37] That stature also depends on the travel team's connections to college coaches and major league scouts, an aspect that will be discussed below.

To address RQ3 and Baker's assertion, draftees' travel teams were categorized based on the sizes of the geographic areas which the team roster reflected:

- **Urban**—players came from one city or its suburbs

- **Statewide**—players came from different areas of the same state

- **Regional**—players came from different states, but within the same geographic region

- **Multi-regional**—players came from two or three geographic regions

- **National**—players represented all four geographic US regions

This study used US Census Bureau guidelines to define the four regions—West, Midwest, Northeast, and South—and the states included in them.[38]

If a high school team was a player's last stop before entering college or the draft, that team was considered as one city, since those high school players usually live in the same metropolitan or suburban area. The exceptions were national secondary education schools, like IMG Academy in Florida.

For a region to be counted as being represented on a team, at least two players had to come from a state or states within that region. This requirement was meant to avoid circumstances in which a team accepted a player solely because of a friendship or family relationship with another player or coach on the team. This study is designed to focus on players who were recruited solely because of their talent level or selected via tryout, and the two-player guideline increases the likelihood of that.

In looking at a travel team's role in creating paths for their players to college and professional baseball, semi-structured interviews were conducted via telephone with two coaches and a former coach who now coordinates travel team tournaments. Those interviews allowed coaches to elucidate aspects of their participation in and their teams' impact on their young charges' futures. Their responses also add perspective to the scant research literature on travel team coaches.

RESULTS

Between 2013 and 2022, 1,646 players were selected in the first five rounds of the MLB amateur draft, 1,631 of whom were included in the study. (15 Canadian players were excepted.) African Americans constituted 12.3 percent of the included draftees, while White players comprised 79.4 percent, Hispanic/Latinos 7.8 percent, and Asian American and Pacific Islanders less than 1 percent. These percentages address RQ1, but mean little without putting them in context. Nationally, African Americans comprise 14.2 percent of 18–24-year-old males, the age group covering the vast majority of those taken in the amateur draft.[39] Trailing the national average by less than 2 percent may not seem encouraging, but the percentage of draftees who are African American has outpaced the proportion of players who are African American at elite levels of competition during the past decade, from youth travel ball to MLB.

That lends credence to Baker's assertion that more African Americans are being drafted. However, tracking that percentage annually from 2013–22 tempers that finding. During that time span, the annual percentages have fluctuated.[40] In the 2013 draft, African Americans comprised 15.8 percent of the first five rounds of players, while in 2022 it was 14 percent. In between, the percentage has ranged between 8.5 percent (2017) and 16.7 percent (2015).

Regardless of their inconsistency, those percentages still remain well above the proportion of African Americans coming down baseball's talent pipeline, the focus of RQ2. A 20-year study covering 1,064 youth travel teams (more than 12,000 players, ages 9–18) in 40 states shows that only 3 percent of those rosters were African Americans.[41] Another study of photographs of 3,263 teams (more than 38,500 players, mostly 12 years old) that played at tournaments at the Cooperstown All-Star Village and Cooperstown Dreams Park from 2014 through 2022 showed that 5.4 percent of those players were African American.[42] The percentage remains in the single digits in the college ranks. In NCAA Division I baseball, African Americans made up 4.2 percent of the players in 2022.[43] And in Major League Baseball, 6.3 percent of the 2023 26-man rosters are African American.[44]

Evidence to support Baker's faith in youth baseball academies, however, appears justified, despite the low percentage of African Americans in travel ball. At least 90 percent of the draftees in this study played youth travel ball, with no significant difference between races. The other 10 percent played high school baseball and may have also played travel ball, but the scant information about their playing histories didn't include that experience.

While the findings show travel baseball to be a steady influence in the draft over the past 10 years,

Figure 1. Trends in Player Sourcing 2013–22

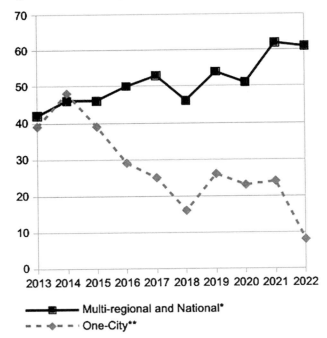

NOTE: A Pearson correlation shows the trends to be significant.
*r(10) = .871, p < .01; **r(10) = -.715, p < .05

elite youth competition continues to evolve, as demonstrated by the preponderance of multi-regional and national teams. Figure 1 illustrates that those teams are growing as sources of players, particularly African Americans, for college and eventually the MLB Draft. That trend provides detail in answering RQ 3 and adds substance to Baker's point. African American draftees were significantly more likely than Hispanic/Latino and White draftees to have played on a regional, multi-regional, or national team before being drafted. (See Table 1.) More than 70 percent of African American draftees played on one of those teams as their "last stop" before college or the pros. Approximately 50 percent of White draftees and 46 percent of Hispanic/Latino draftees played on regional, multi-regional, or national teams. (Note that although Asian Americans and Pacific Islander draftees are included in the total number of players (1,631), they did not constitute a separate racial category, because their low number—less than 1 percent—could confound overall results in a Chi square calculation.)

Table 1. Race and Type of Travel Team (2013–22)

Type of Team	African American*	Hispanic/ Latino	White
One City	15 (7.5%)	25 (19.7%)	255 (19.9%)
Statewide	38 (19%)	43 (33.9%)	381 (29.4%)
Regional	53 (26.5%)	22 (17.3%)	282 (21.8%)
Multi-regional	71 (35.5%)	32 (25.2%)	302 (23.3%)
National	23 (11.5%)	5 (3.9%)	75 (5.79%)
Total**	200	127	1,295

* X^2 (8, N=1,631)=45.898, p<.001
** All percentages were calculated using the total per each group.
  Not included in the totals are four Asian Americans and five Pacific Islanders.

Examining the individual categories of regional, multi-regional, and national teams adds more detail. Of the 357 draftees from regional teams, 66 percent played on southern teams. Approximately 13 percent played on teams from the West, 12 percent on Midwestern teams, and 9 percent on Northeastern teams. But there were no significant racial differences in which region draftees played. White and Hispanic players were as likely to play on Southern teams as African Americans were, and the same was true for all other regions.

Multi-regional and national teams are a different matter. Their influence as sources of African American talent has grown in the last five years of the decade. From 2018–22, more than half of African American draftees, compared with 31 percent of White and 33 percent of Hispanic/Latino draftees, came from multi-regional and national teams. Those teams produced 50

African American draftees during that period, compared with 44 from 2013–17. National teams also grew as a source of White players, with the number of those players doubling during the second half of the decade. (See Table 2.)

Conversely, teams from one city or urban area produced few African American draftees, with just over 7 percent playing their last travel ball on urban categorized teams. (See Table 1.) Almost 20 percent of White draftees played on single-city teams, as did the same percentage of Hispanic/Latinos. But these teams are losing their influence as sources of MLB draftees. While numbers for multi-regional and national teams as sources of MLB draftees are increasing, the number of teams whose rosters represent only one urban area is decreasing. (See Figure 1.) So has the number of draftees who played on those teams. In 2013, five of the 26 African American players (19 percent) in the first five rounds of that year's draft came from an urban team and eight (31 percent) came from national and multi-regional teams. The percentage of African Americans from urban teams could be even higher in MLB drafts before 2013, when rules for compensatory picks were changed and competitive balance picks were added. A preliminary analysis of the first five rounds of the 2012 draft showed that urban teams (consisting mostly of high school and American Legion teams) were the last known stops before college or professional baseball for almost 70 percent of African Americans drafted that year. Only 9 percent came from multi-regional and national teams.

More than 10 years later, few African American draftees come from urban teams. Those teams accounted for only three of the 23 African American draftees (13 percent) in the 2022 draft, while national and multi-regional teams accounted for 13 (57 percent). As such, some of the teams with the largest geographic scope have emerged as leaders in getting African Americans to the next level of competition, be it college or pro baseball. In the last 10 years, Canes Baseball,

a national travel team organization, had 11 African American players taken in the first five rounds of the MLB amateur draft, more than any other national or multi-regional program. Marucci Elite and The Royals Scout Team each had five African American alumni make the draft, while the Ohio Warhawks contributed four such players. The IMG Academy, MLB Breakthrough Series, and Blackhawks National each contributed several African American alumni to the draft. As previously noted, national, multi-regional, and regional teams accounted for the majority of African Americans in the first five rounds. To attract top talent, some travel teams offer incentives, especially financial assistance. Researchers, journalists, youth baseball, officials, and MLB players and officials have cited the expense of travel baseball as a major obstacle to African American participation. Some multi-regional and national travel teams not only remove that obstacle, but also cover living expenses, and in some cases, educational costs for players.

DISCUSSION

Results from this research justify Baker's hope that larger numbers of African Americans are poised to join the rosters of Major League Baseball teams. Although the year-to-year percentage of major league draftees who are African American is uneven, a trend toward more multi-regional and national teams as sources of draftees bodes well, since a greater percentage of African Americans, compared with other races, come from those teams. The diminishment of travel teams from single urban areas or cities adds perspective to the growth of multi-regional and national teams. Rick Goff, founder of the Michigan Sports Academy and now director of The Travel Ball Select National Championship, noted that in the late 1990s and early years of the next decade, travel teams were localized and most played regionally "within 3 or 4 hours from home... There were very few of what we would call national [teams] that were willing to travel anywhere

Table 2. Race and Type of Travel Team 2013–17 and 2018–22

Type of Travel Team	African American*		Hispanic/Latino		White	
	2013–17	2018–22	2013–17	2018–22	2013–17	2018–22
One City	9 (8.6%)*	6 (7%)	16 (25%)	9 (14.3%)	153 (23.8%)	102 (15.6%)
Statewide	21 (20%)	7 (8.2%)	21 (32.8%)	22 (34.9%)	188 (29.2%)	193 (29.6%)
Regional	31 (29.5%)*	22 (25.8%)	11 (17.2%)	11 (17.5%)	27 (19.7%)	155 (23.8%)
Multi-regional	34 (32.4%)*	37 (43.5%)**	14 (21.9%)	18 (28.6%)	151 (23.4%)	151 (23.2%)
National	10 (9.5%)*	13 (15.3%)**	2 (3.1%)	3 (4.8%)	24 (3.7%)	51 (7.8%)**
Total	105 (100%)	85 (100%)	64 (100%)	63 (100%)	643 (100%)	652 (100%)

*$X2$ (8, N=812)=27.661, p<.001
**$X2$ (8, N=810)=23.623, p=.003

in the country, and we were one of those national teams."[45]

Goff, who primarily coached travel teams for 14-year-olds and younger, built his rosters partly through scouting by his own players. His players would tip him off to talented players on other teams at tournaments: "A player would talk to one of my kids and my kids are like, 'Hey, we're always looking for players. Come play with us.'"[46] Goff would then watch the player at some point during the tournament before extending an invitation for the following season. "One time I had kids who came out of Pittsburgh, Pennsylvania, Chicago, Fort Wayne, Madison. They would come and play with me full-time in Michigan; and they just traveled wherever we traveled to play."[47]

While those programs have eroded high school and American Legion baseball, they have created wider portals for entry into high-level youth competition. Bob Herold, an IMG Academy coach, said those portals have benefited African American players. His organization often takes its cues from MLB, which shows "a lot of interest in getting those guys [African Americans] to the Big Leagues."[48]

Herold, a former minor league manager and coach with the Kansas City Royals and Pittsburgh Pirates, said MLB is giving African American players extra scrutiny. "MLB is going to make sure that if they get an African American that's a good athlete, they're going to give him every opportunity to play at higher levels," he said. "Baseball doesn't want to be out of line with society."[49]

Herold points to IMG alumnus Elijah Green, the fifth overall pick in the 2022 MLB amateur draft, and one of four African Americans in the first five selections. Herold said IMG coaches recruited Green after they saw him play on an opposing team. "IMG pulled him off to the side and said, 'We'll pay everything here for the school year. We know you're going to be drafted,'" Herold said. "He would have been drafted whether he stayed in Orlando or here."[50]

Green also serves as an example of how IMG and other national programs compete for the best young baseball talent in the nation. Herold said IMG baseball prospects know that they "don't pay a dime" to attend the academy, an attraction for those who can't afford the usual expenses of travel ball.[51] The Ohio Warhawks follow the same strategy. The Warhawks website proclaims they "have never, and never will charge any player fees."[52] The Warhawks give players, "regardless of their financial background, a free and equal opportunity to improve their baseball skills and increase their chances of advancing to higher levels of baseball." The Warhawks also own a 4,000-square-foot facility that contains lodging for coaches and players, training and shower facilities, and a laundry and a recreation area.[53]

The MLB Breakthrough Series, in which several first-round African American draftees played (i.e. KeBryan Hayes and Addison Russell, among others), also covers expenses for players. The Breakthrough Series, co-sponsored with USA Baseball, not only supports players throughout the season, but also offers players "additional development and instructional opportunities throughout the year."[54] Brooks, Knudson, and Smith note that the intentions of such programs are not entirely altruistic: "[T]he recruitment of talented youth athletes of color by predominantly White high schools [and youth sports institutions] is an exchange that presumably benefits the youth of color," but the institutions also benefit.[55] The researchers say that recruiting the best Black baseball talent gives a team "bragging rights" and "a perception of inclusion, and revenues." Indeed, national programs hone that image and tout their "bragging rights."[56] The Motor City Hit Dogs, for example, calls itself "one of the top 5 programs nationally,"[57] and Marucci Elite (sponsored by the Marucci baseball equipment company) claims to be "one of the nation's most prolific amateur baseball organizations."[58]

Some organizations imply their national prominence by stressing the high standards they set for their players and the stringent process for players trying to make a team. To be considered for a tryout for Canes Baseball, players must file an application form which asks for information such as pitch velocity, "pop time" (for catchers), 60-yard dash time, current travel team, talent showcases attended, and college coaches or pro scouts who have contacted them. The application cautions: "Please understand that talent of only the highest level will be considered a potential prospect and not all submissions will receive a response."[59]

Canes coach Donald Murray said high-profile travel programs can afford to be picky. "I'm in competition for players," Murray said, but "I don't have to accept guys who don't want to compete and who aren't respectful."[60]

National programs can maintain such stringency in both talent and character because of their constant recruiting and roster building. "These top level travel teams in today's world will recruit kids all year long from other teams, other states," Goff said, and the teams "don't care if you're White, Black, Hispanic or if you're something else. If you can play baseball, you're in."[61] Herold agreed, but with a caveat: "Particular organizations really make it a point of getting African Americans."[62]

To be sure, the Canes, Marucci Elite, and other national and multi-regional programs are creating more opportunities and entry points for African Americans and other players. The programs are throwing a wider net to get talent and expanding their base of players by creating more teams. Marucci Elite fielded 50 travel teams in 2022.[63] In 2020, Canes Baseball fortified its regional network of teams by establishing "Canes of the Great Plains" and calling it "a true national pipeline running throughout the region."[64] The region includes Oklahoma, Kansas, Nebraska, Iowa, and Missouri. As a result, Canes Baseball absorbed the Wichita (KS) Vipers and another travel team organization, SWAT Academy, in Oklahoma City.[65] In that same year, Canes Baseball also assumed management of the Carrollton City (GA) Recreation Baseball League.[66]

Blackhawks National has also built its own pipeline to stock talent. Blackhawks National sponsors teams for grade-school-aged and junior high school players.[67] Canes Baseball even looks for prodigies in preschool, offering baseball activities for children as young as three. Those children can then graduate to T-ball, then to leagues with pitching machines, before moving on by age 11 to "live" pitching.[68] As regional, multi-regional, and national travel team organizations expand, so does the symbiosis between the best young baseball talent and the "gatekeepers" to the college and professional ranks (i.e. college coaches and MLB scouts). The "go-between" is the travel coach. The coach brings that talent and the gatekeepers together. His team attracts talent because of its connections to colleges and major league scouts, and that attraction becomes self-perpetuating, since those coaches and scouts will go where the talent is. To expose its players to a wide swath of post-secondary coaches, Marucci Elite "partners" with 77 university and college baseball programs, including 39 in Division I.[69]

These relationships have created what Klein and colleagues call the "professionalization" of travel baseball through "the presence of heavy professional scouting and collegiate recruiting during summer travel baseball."[70] Those researchers contend that this professionalization gives travel team coaches considerable influence and leverage in the fate of their players. The players and their families depend on the coaches' connections and counsel in navigating through the college or MLB recruitment process. "Thus, the travel coach becomes an important figure in the youth and high school baseball socialization process."[71]

As they have evolved, travel teams with a broad geographic base have concentrated the talent pool and made it less likely for players on single city teams to be

Dusty Baker followed a 19-year major league playing career with 26 years as a manager, and has won the Manager of the Year award three times.

scouted by colleges or pro teams. That goes especially for African Americans. As noted previously, research shows that approximately 3 percent of those on youth select teams in the Slumpbuster Tournament were African American.[72] The majority of those teams were single-city teams, and such teams tend to be rooted in the suburbs. Thus, it should not be surprising that so few African American players came to college or the pros from single-city teams. That may also explain why the diminishment of high school and American Legion Baseball has had little, if any, impact on the number of African Americans being selected in the first five rounds of the draft. Simply put, there aren't many African Americans on those local teams to be drafted.

CONCLUSION

What Klein refers to as the "professionalization" of youth baseball has happened alongside the nationalization of youth baseball. An amalgamation of wide-scale travel team "brands" and a complex network of information centers, travel team organizations, college coaches, and MLB organizations are exposing more African American prospects than their numbers show in youth elite-level baseball.

In 2013 and 2015, the percentage of African American draftees in the first five rounds exceeded the national percentage of 18–24-year-old males who are African American, but that has not happened in the last seven years (although 14 percent in 2022 was closest since 2015). A long-term trend in growth has not materialized thus far. Perhaps Baker's comments about more African Americans in the draft should be approached with cautious optimism, as should his hope that travel baseball will provide a consistent and lasting source of African American prospects.

While this study determined the types of baseball academies from which African American draftees came, it does not identify what influenced those draftees to prevail as among the top talent, as assessed by MLB teams. Previous research has described factors related to African American youths' sports and recreational choices, but framing them in the context of the MLB draft requires further research. That research should explore more deeply the nuances of how elite youth baseball programs form allegiances and work closely with college and university baseball teams and professional leagues to identify talent. What can be identified in this study are the characteristics shared by those programs that are most successful in contributing African American players to the highest rounds of the MLB draft. There are four such similarities:

One is the broadening of their player base, both in numbers and geographically. The Canes, Marucci Elite, and The Blackhawks have developed extensive "feeder" programs by sponsoring teams for grade-school-aged players or by franchising teams in different areas of the country. These programs also have extensive coaching and administrative staffs, as well as their own practice and training facilities. A second characteristic is the aggressive recruitment of talent. As Goff, Herold, and Murray noted, travel team programs compete for talent in various ways. Social media apps and websites have facilitated regional and national recruitment by allowing coaches and far-flung teammates to communicate easily. Third, coaches in the programs forge relationships with college coaches and pro scouts and provide player access to them. As such, the travel coaches are the link between travel ball and baseball beyond high school. They serve as the linchpins to a players' baseball future.

The fourth characteristic, although not shared by all national programs, is defraying costs to provide African American players with baseball experiences "that they might not otherwise afford, that would not be open to them socially, if they were not elite athletes."[73] The MLB Breakthrough Series has made financial aid a cornerstone of its related programs, like the Dream Series showcase, that gives African American players in high school a chance to perform in front of MLB scouts.

The extent to which other large-scale travel ball programs share these characteristics or contribute to the number of African American draftees is unknown because of the limited number of players in this study. At the very least, coaches, family members, and mentors of talented, motivated and young African American baseball players can use these characteristics as guideposts in directing their players to ever higher levels of baseball. This could be particularly useful for parents in finding youth baseball organizations that tap into larger organizations, offer financial assistance, and offer the eventual likelihood of exposure to coaches and scouts. Some researchers say that too often parents cede control of their sons' futures to travel and college coaches, instead of taking a proactive role in their sons' baseball career decisions.[74]

Expanding this research beyond the first five rounds of the MLB amateur draft and analyzing drafts years, if not decades, before 2013 might uncover other characteristics common to teams on which African Americans played before college or the draft. The ideal would be to determine the races and playing histories of the MLB draftees in all 40 rounds from 2013–19 (5 rounds in 2020, and 20 rounds since). Extending the time span to include more MLB drafts of the past would add historical perspective and might provide definitive evidence to support Baker's opinion that more African Americans are reaching the highest rungs of youth travel baseball and the MLB Draft.

Despite this study's limitations, the qualitative nature of the draft (i.e. the best are taken first) gives heft and purpose to examining the first few rounds. Those rounds might indicate how African Americans figure in the draft strategies and interests of MLB teams. As Coach Bob Herold said, MLB is paying attention to African American players, who "are going to get a shot to play" upon reaching the threshold to college and pro baseball.[75] Initiatives like the MLB Breakthrough Series and high draft picks by MLB teams seem to support Herold's observations. If so, that attention could explain why the percentage of MLB draftees who are African American exceeds the percentage in travel ball, college ball, and the major leagues. So far, that high percentage of draftees has not yet translated into an increase in African Americans on major league rosters. Herold thinks it will: "You heard Dusty Baker say it. Help is on the way."[76] ∎

Notes

1. Jalen Brown and Justin Gamble, "Major League Baseball Has a Diversity Problem, Experts Say. This Year's World Series is Proof ," CNN, November 2, 2022, as broadcast by WLFI, Lafayette, IN, https://www.wlfi.com/news/national/major-league-baseball-has-a-diversity-problem-experts-say-this-years-world-series-is-proof/article, accessed February 15, 2023.
2. Ron Wynn, "World Series Lack African American Participation," *Tennessee Tribune*, November 3, 2022, https://tntribune.com/world-series-lack-african-american-participation/, accessed February 15, 2023.
3. Wynn, "World Series Lack African American Participation."
4. David Waldstein, "MLB Works to Build a New Generation of Black American Players," *The New York Times*, January 17, 2023, https://www.nytimes.com/2023/01/17/sports/baseball/mlb-dream-series.html, accessed February 20, 2023.

5. David C. Ogden, "Specialization in Youth Baseball: Channeling Players to Higher Competition or Choking Youthful Desire?" Paper presented at the 22nd annual Cooperstown Symposium on Baseball and American Culture, June 2-4, 2010, Cooperstown, NY.

6. Les Edgerton, *Perfect Game USA and the Future of Baseball: How the Remaking of Youth Scouting Affects the National Pastime* (Jefferson, N.C.: McFarland & Company, Inc., 2009).

7. Nick Stevens, "NC High School Sports Participation Declined In All But 5 Sports After Pandemic" *High School OT*, September 22, 2022, https://www.highschoolot.com/nc-high-school-sports-participation-declined-in-all-but-5-sports-after-pandemic/20487621/, accessed January 15, 2023.

8. Laura Handby Hudgens, "The Decline of Baseball and Why It Matters," *The Huffington Post*, December 6, 2017, accessed January 15, 2023.

9. Josh VanDyke, "How Michigan Travel League Programs Have Created Competitive Gap in High School Baseball, Softball," MichiganLive, September 22, 2021, https://www.mlive.com/highschoolsports/2021/05/how-travel-league-programs-have-created-seismic-talent-gap-in-prep-baseball-softball.html, accessed February 20, 2023.

10. VanDyke, "How Michigan Travel League Programs."

11. Marjie Ducey, "Benson Baseball is Reborn," *Omaha World-Herald*, January 19, 2023, https://omaha.com/sports/high-school/benson-baseball-is-reborn-with-the-help-of-two-teachers-and-players-determination/article, accessed February 20, 2023.

12. VanDyke, "How Michigan Travel League Programs."

13. Jerry Snodgrass, "This Week in Baseball—2016," The Ohio High School Athletic Association, https://www.ohsaa.org/sports/bb/boys/TWIBAdviceforSummerTeamCoaches.pdf, accessed January 10, 2023.

14. Christopher Adams, "What Has Happened to Legion Baseball?" *Emporia* (KS) *Gazette*, July 28, 2022, http://www.emporiagazette.com/sports/article_3999e6f4-0ea4-11ed-a3e2-03b7182e40fc.html, accessed January 15, 2023.

15. Adams, "What Has Happened to Legion Baseball?"

16. Adam Feiner, "Sad Demise of Legion Ball," Shaw Local News Network (IL), August 3, 2018, https://www.shawlocal.com/2018/08/03/sad-demise-of-legion-ball/a3v0ony/, accessed February 20, 2023.

17. Steve Craig, "American Legion Baseball Is on the Decline in Maine," *Portland* (ME) *Press Herald*, June 21, 2018. https://www.pressherald.com/2018/06/21/american-legion-baseball-is-on-the-decline-in-maine/, accessed February 21, 2023.

18. Mike Trueblood, "They're Back! What to Know as American Legion Returns to Galesburg After 4-year Hiatus," *Galesburg* (IL) *Register-Mail*, July 9, 2022, https://www.galesburg.com/story/sports/2022/06/09/galesburg-american-legion-baseball-returns-2022-after-4-year-hiatus/7566873001/, accessed February 20, 2023.

19. Frank Fitzpatrick, "American Legion Baseball: The Summer Tradition Slowly Fading Away," *Philadelphia Inquirer*, July 27, 2019, https://www.inquirer.com/high-school-sports/american-legion-baseball-decline-military-aau-showcases-20190727.html, accessed January 15, 2023.

20. "Travel Baseball vs. American Legion Baseball—What's the Difference?", Pro Baseball Insider, 2014, https://probaseballinsider.com/travel-baseball-vs-american-legion-baseball-whats-the-difference/, accessed July 19, 2020.

21. Craig, "American Legion Baseball Is on the Decline in Maine."

22. David C. Ogden, "The Welcome Theory: An Approach to Studying African-American Youth Interest and Involvement in Baseball." *Nine: A Journal of Baseball History and Culture* 12, no. 2 (Spring 2004): 114–22. Also see David C. Ogden, "It's Suburban and Serious: The State of Youth Select Baseball in the U.S." Paper presented at the 10th Annual Indiana State University Conference on Baseball in Literature and Culture, Terre Haute, IN, April 15, 2005; Edgerton, *Perfect Game USA and the Future of Baseball*.

23. Cooperstown All Star Village, https://cooperstown.com/, accessed March 1, 2023.

24. Cooperstown Dreams Park, https://www.cooperstowndreamspark.com/home/, accessed March 1, 2023.

25. Omaha Slumpbuster, https://www.omahaslumpbuster.com/, accessed August 19, 2023.

26. Bruce Shoenfeld, "Remaking the Landscape of Youth Baseball," *Sports Business Journal*, August 5, 2019, https://www.sportsbusinessjournal.com/Journal/Issues/2019/08/05/Leagues-and-Governing-Bodies/Youth-baseball.aspx, accessed February 20, 2023.

27. Shoenfeld, "Remaking the Landscape of Youth Baseball."

28. Shoenfeld, "Remaking the Landscape of Youth Baseball."

29. These numbers are given on the Perfect Game website (https://www.perfectgame.org/articles/View.aspx?article=21814#:~:text=To%20date%2C%20more%20than%201%2C847,First%2DYear%20Amateur%20Player%20Draft., accessed August 31, 2023). See also Shoenfeld, "Remaking the Landscape of Youth Baseball," who cites 12,000 draftees via Perfect Game.

30. Max Klein, Charles Macaulay, and Joseph Cooper, " The Perfect Game: An Ecological Systems Approach to the Influences of Elite Youth and High School Baseball Socialization," *Journal of Athlete Development and Experience* 2, no. 1 (March 2020): 14-35 (quote on 22).

31. Robert Nicholas Itri, "Understanding the Impact of Travel Sports on High School Athletes' Perception of High School Sports" (doctoral dissertation, Graduate School of Troy University, Troy, AL, 2021), 2.

32. Forebears, https://forebears.io/surnames/.

33. House of Names, https://www.houseofnames.com/.

34. Mary L. McHugh, "Interrater Reliability: The Kappa Statistic," *Biochemia Medica*, (October 22, 2012): 276–82.

35. David C. Ogden, "Tracking the Decline: Results of a Two-Decade Study of African Americans in Youth Select Baseball." Paper presented at the 28th annual Nine Spring Training Conference, March 13, 2021, Tempe, AZ.

36. Richard Lapchick, 2022 *Racial and Gender Report Card: College Sport*, The Institute for Diversity and Ethics in Sport (Orlando: University of Central Florida, March 22, 2023), https://www.tidesport.org/_files/ugd/c01324_d0d17cf9f4c7469fbe410704a056db35.pdf, accessed March 22, 2023.

37. See Shoenfeld, "Remaking the Landscape of Youth Baseball"; Adams, "What Has Happened to Legion Baseball?", and Edgerton, *Perfect Game USA and the Future of Baseball*.

38. "Census Regions and Divisions of the United States," U.S. Census Bureau, https://www2.census.gov/geo/pdfs/maps-data/maps/reference/us_regdiv.pdf, accessed January 7, 2023.

39. "Sex by Age," U.S. Census Bureau, https://data.census.gov/table?g=0100000US,$0400000&d=ACS+5-Year+Estimates+Detailed+Tables&tid=ACSDT5Y2021.B01001B, accessed January 7, 2023.

40. Percentages based on MLB Draft Tracker, https://www.mlb.com/draft/tracker, and photos and information from Perfect Game, https://www.perfectgame.org/, and various college Web sites.

41. Ogden, "Tracking the Decline." Results of the survey of 213 teams at the 2021 and 2022 Slumpbuster Tournaments were added to the results presented at the Nine Spring Training Conference.

42. The results of this study have not been published. Team photographs from the Cooperstown Dreams Park Web site (https://www.cooperstowndreamspark.com/home/) and Cooperstown All Star Village, (https://cooperstown.com/) were analyzed for racial composition June to September 2022. A second coder analyzed a sample of the photographs and a Cohen's Kappa for intercoder reliability was .88 for African Americans.

43. Lapchick, *2022 Racial and Gender Report Card: College Sport*, 70.

44. Richard Lapchick, *2023 Racial and Gender Report Card: Major League Baseball*, 40, https://www.tidesport.org/_files/ugd/ac4087_3801e61a4fd04fbda329c9af387ca948.pdf, August 19, 2023. This percentage lags far behind that of other major league team sports. "Blacks or African Americans," according to Lapchick, constitute more than 70 percent of players in the National Basketball Association, *2023 Racial and Gender Report Card: National Basketball Association*, 59,

https://www.tidesport.org/_files/ugd/c01324_abb94cf8275d49499e89fa14f0777901.pdf, August 19, 2023. In 2022 Blacks or African Americans comprised more than 56 percent of players in the National Football League and almost 25 percent of Major League Soccer players, *The Complete 2022 Racial and Gender Report Card*, 20, 16, https://www.tidesport.org/_files/ugd/ac4087_31b60a6a51574cbe9b552831c0fcbd3f.pdf, August 19, 2023.

45. Rick Goff, telephone interview, January 21, 2023.
46. Goff, telephone interview.
47. Goff, telephone interview.
48. Bob Herold, telephone interview, January 16, 2023.
49. Herold, telephone interview.
50. Herold, telephone interview.
51. Herold, telephone interview.
52. Ohio Warhawks Baseball, "History," https://ohiowarhawks.net/Pages/1-column.htm, accessed March 1, 2023.
53. Ohio Warhawks Baseball, "History."
54. MLB Breakthrough Series, "What Is the Breakthrough Series?", https://www.mlb.com/breakthrough-series, accessed March 1, 2023.
55. Scott N. Brooks, Matt Knudtson, and Isais Smith, "Some Kids Are Left Behind: The Failure of a Perspective, Using Critical Race Theory to Expand the Coverage in the Sociology of Youth Sports, *Sociology Compass* 11, no. 2 (October 31, 2016): 1–14 (quote on 9).
56. Brooks, Knudtson, and Smith, "Some Kids Are Left Behind," 7.
57. Motor City Hit Dogs, "Our Mission," https://motorcityhitdogs.com/about-us/our-mission/, March 1, 2023.
58. Marucci Elite, "Marucci Elite," https://maruccisports.com/elite/, accessed January 16, 2023.
59. The Canes Baseball Club, "Prospect Form," https://canesbaseball.net/prospect-form/, February 20, 2023.
60. Donald Murray, telephone interview, February 3, 2023.
61. Goff, telephone interview.
62. Herold, telephone interview.
63. Marucci Elite Baseball, "Our Franchise Club Teams," https://maruccisports.com/organizations/, January 16, 2023.
64. The Canes Baseball Club, "Canes Baseball Announces Addition of Canes of the Great Plains," https://canesbaseball.net/canes-baseball-announces-addition-of-canes-of-the-great-plains/, accessed February 20, 2023.
65. The Canes Baseball Club, "Canes Baseball Announces Addition of Canes Oklahoma," https://canesbaseball.net/canes-baseball-announces-addition-of-canes-oklahoma/, accessed February 20, 2023.
66. The Canes Baseball Club, "Canes Southeast," https://www.canessoutheast.com/, accessed February 20, 2023.
67. Blackhawks National Baseball, https://blackhawksnational.com/, January 21, 2023.
68. The Canes Baseball Club, "Canes Southeast."
69. Marucci Elite Baseball, "Marucci College Partners," https://maruccisports.com/colleges/, February 20, 2023.
70. Klein, Macaulay and Cooper, "The Perfect Game: An Ecological Systems Approach," 28.
71. Klein, Macaulay and Cooper, "The Perfect Game: An Ecological Systems Approach," 25.
72. Ogden, "Tracking the Decline."
73. Brooks, Knudtson, and Smith, "Some Kids Are Left Behind," 6.
74. Klein, Macaulay and Cooper, "The Perfect Game: An Ecological Systems Approach," 24.
75. Herold, telephone interview.
76. Herold, telephone interview.

Keith Hernandez and Cooperstown

A Data Synthesis and Visualization Project

Stephen D. Dertinger, PhD

There is no shortage of arguments either for or against Keith Hernandez's enshrinement in the Hall of Fame. I have no horse in this race. I am not a rabid Mets fan, and I did not know much about Hernandez prior to this project. I was aware he played an important role for the 1986 World Series champion Mets, appeared in two *Seinfeld* episodes, and served as a well-regarded color commentator for Mets baseball games. That's about it. However, I was intrigued by Chris Bodig's well-researched article at Cooperstown Cred, which stated the complex case for and against Hernandez's enshrinement.[1] Articles about Hall of Fame controversies often construct an argument by piling one statistic on top of another. I wondered whether a data synthesis and visualization tool described in a previous *BRJ* article might shed some light on the case.[2]

This approach analyzes the performance of MLB players using software originally intended for use in toxicology.[3] The initial reports demonstrated that the program and its output are particularly useful for ranking, categorizing, and generally comparing the performance of multiple players. The Hernandez controversy encouraged me to investigate whether this flexible data analysis tool might help the baseball community consider Hall of Fame candidates objectively. The current project involves comparing Hernandez to his contemporaries, as well several Hall of Fame first basemen who did not overlap with him, in order to provide additional benchmarking opportunities. To my knowledge, Keith Hernandez is the first such player to be evaluated in this way and for this purpose.

METHODS

Software Overview. The Toxicological Prioritization Index, or ToxPi for short, is an analytical software package that transforms multiple sources of evidence into integrated visual profiles. It was developed by Professor David Reif and colleagues at the North Carolina State University. They have made the Java-executable script freely available at the Toxicological Prioritization Index website.[4]

Visually, ToxPi profiles are represented as circles that have been divided into a user-defined number of slices.

Keith Hernandez

For the analyses described here, each circle represents a different MLB player, and each slice within a circle represents a particular performance metric. The distance each slice protrudes from the center of a circle is proportional to a player's performance. The lowest value found for any particular statistic within a dataset under consideration is given a value of zero, and the highest value is given a value of one. All intermediate values are scaled proportionally. The worst performer for any particular statistic will show a slice with no protrusion, and the best performer for any particular statistic will show a protrusion that extends all the way to the circle's perimeter. The program also calculates an overall ToxPi Score. This is the sum of the slice scores, and is also rescaled to a value between zero and one.

It is possible to give different "weights" to each slice, but this feature was not utilized for the analyses described here.

Figure 1 shows two player profiles and is provided to familiarize readers with the basic ToxPi structure. Besides the software's ability to distill complex statistics into informative summary graphics, it provides quantitative results in the form of Slice Scores, which correspond to individual performance metrics, as well as an aggregate performance metric, the ToxPi Score.

The analyses presented here use FanGraphs data. Analyses focused on first basemen who played at least five seasons in a similar timeframe to Hernandez (between 1970 and 1995). To qualify as a season, the player needed to appear in a minimum of 100 games. Several Hall of Fame first basemen who came before or after Hernandez were also included. In total, 30 first basemen were evaluated, seven of whom are in Cooperstown: Harmon Killebrew, Orlando Cepeda, Tony Perez, Willie McCovey, Eddie Murray, Jeff Bagwell, and Frank Thomas.

Traditional Statistics. Two types of ToxPi-based analyses were conducted. The first relied on what we'll refer to here as traditional statistics. This analysis considered the slash line statistics AVG, OBP, and SLG. Additionally, All-Star selections, Gold Gloves, and MVPs were tabulated and considered at the career level. Since many of the seasons considered pre-date the beginning of the Silver Slugger Award in 1980, it was not factored into the analysis.

Advanced Statistics. The second type of analysis is referred to here as advanced statistics. This analysis considered Def, Off, and WAR. As explained at FanGraphs, Def is Defensive Runs Above Average, which measures a player's defensive value relative to league average.[5] Unlike some other advanced statistics that provide information about a player's value relative to league average, Def adds a positional adjustment to facilitate comparisons across positions. Off is Offensive Runs Above Average, which combines FanGraphs' park-adjusted Batting Runs with Weighted Stolen Base Runs, Weighted Double Play Runs, and Ultimate Base Running in order to give players credit for the quality and quantity of their offensive performance.[6] WAR is Wins Above Replacement, a widely utilized statistic that attempts to summarize a player's total contribution to their team in one metric.[7]

RESULTS AND DISCUSSION

Traditional Statistics. The traditional statistics were evaluated for 30 MLB first basemen using ToxPi. The resulting ToxPi Profiles for every player are shown in Figure 2. Slice Scores and aggregate ToxPi Scores accompany each image. These images are arranged from highest to lowest ToxPi Score as one would read a page of a book—from left to right, top to bottom. Figure 3 (page 100) plots the ToxPi Scores in ascending order. From these graphics, it is apparent that Hernandez has the second-highest aggregate ToxPi Score. Only Frank Thomas has a higher value. It is also noteworthy that Hernandez has a higher ToxPi Score than six of the Hall of Famers in this group.

ToxPi has a hierarchical clustering module that automatically groups similar ToxPi Profiles. This module can be useful for evaluating similarity in performance

Figure 1. Anatomy of a ToxPi profile; The key on the left indicates which slice represents each statistic. The middle and right profiles show the career-level statistics of Keith Hernandez and Willie McCovey. Hernandez exhibits the highest Def rating, whereas McCovey's Off and WAR statistics are superior. The ToxPi Score shows Hernandez above McCovey, 0.7449 to 0.6163.

Key

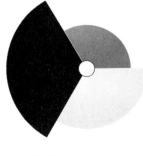

Keith Hernandez
ToxPi Score = 0.7449
Off = 0.5003
Def = 1.0000
WAR = 0.7344

Willie McCovey
ToxPi Score = 0.6163
Off = 0.7852
Def = 0.2271
WAR = 0.8365

Figure 2. ToxPi Profiles using traditional statistics AVG, OBP, and SLG, as well as Gold Gloves (GG), All-Star appearances (AS), and MVP awards. Disregard the "Rank" values which, confusingly rank the best performer as 30 and the worst as 1.

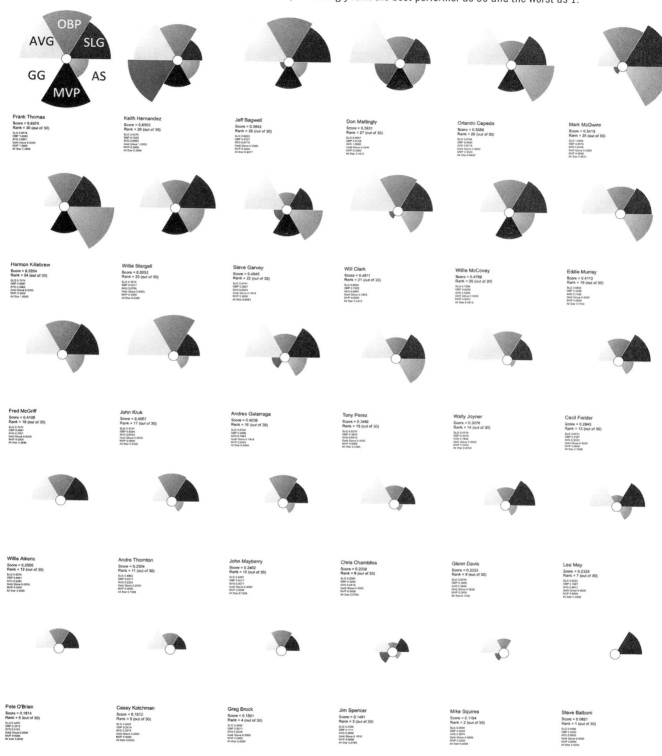

Figure 3. Keith Hernandez exhibits the second-highest aggregate ToxPi Score using traditional statistics and accolades. Only Frank Thomas ranks higher.

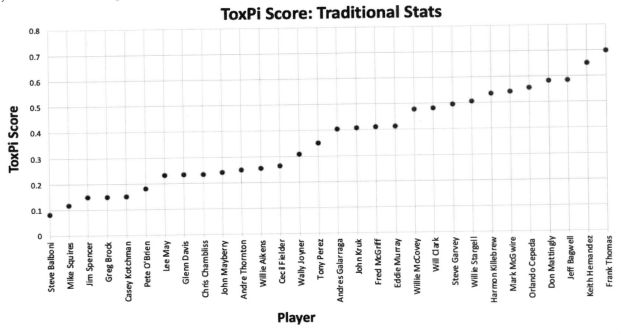

characteristics. Hierarchical clustering results are provided in Figure 4. Keith Hernandez clusters next to Hall of Fame first basemen such as Harmon Killebrew and Frank Thomas. Interestingly, according to this analysis, Hernandez is most similar to Don Mattingly, another well-rounded first baseman who is currently experiencing a contentious Hall of Fame candidacy.

Advanced Statistics. The ToxPi Profiles for advanced statistics are shown in Figure 5 (page 102). Slice Scores and aggregate ToxPi Scores accompany each image. Figure 6 (page 103) plots the ToxPi Scores in ascending order. Some rankings changed significantly when using advanced statistics rather than traditional statistics. For instance, Jeff Bagwell replaced Frank Thomas in first place, while Thomas fell to seventh. Although Thomas's prodigious offensive contributions are still apparent, these ToxPi Profiles make it clear that his defensive skills were the weakest of the group. Interestingly, Hernandez's ranking stayed the same. In both cases, he exhibited the second-highest ToxPi Score.

Prior to the publication of this article, a thorough review of the Advanced Statistics-based ToxPi profiles was conducted by a subject matter expert. This reviewer drew attention to the cases of Willie Aikens and Steve Balboni, both of whom possess reputations for stronger offensive capabilities compared to defensive skills. The reviewer highlighted the counter-intuitiveness of these players' ToxPi profiles, specifically, the way the graphics show shorter projections for the Off slices and

longer projections for the Def slices. Addressing this concern presents a valuable opportunity to discuss a key feature of this platform. That is, the focus of these analyses is inter-player comparisons, not intra-player. A related point to keep in mind is that we are comparing first basemen (historically, where weak defenders have been positioned), and Hall of Fame caliber players are highly represented. Thus, in light of this dataset's composition, it is in fact accurate and insightful to represent these players as exhibiting *relatively* high defensive performance (Def values for Aikens, Balboni, and the average for all 30 players are -61.5, -84.6, and -107.6, respectively). Conversely, while they may have had reputations for good offense, that is not the case when compared to the 28 other players in this dataset. (Off values for Aikens, Balboni, and the average for all 30 first basemen are 69.5, -1.6, and 228.9, respectively.) I hope this discussion of Aikens' and Balboni's results reinforce key aspects of the information being conveyed by ToxPi-based analyses—the focus is on inter-player comparisons, and the performance assessments are highly dependent on the range of player performances under consideration.

ToxPi's hierarchical clustering results are provided in Figure 7 (page 103). As with the traditional statistics, Hernandez clusters alongside Hall of Fame first basemen. This analysis places Hernandez in a subgroup that includes Tony Perez and Orlando Cepeda, though Hernandez's profile is somewhat offset, owing to his remarkable defense.

Figure 4. The hierarchical clustering module shows that Keith Hernandez belongs alongside high-performing first basemen, including current Hall of Famers.

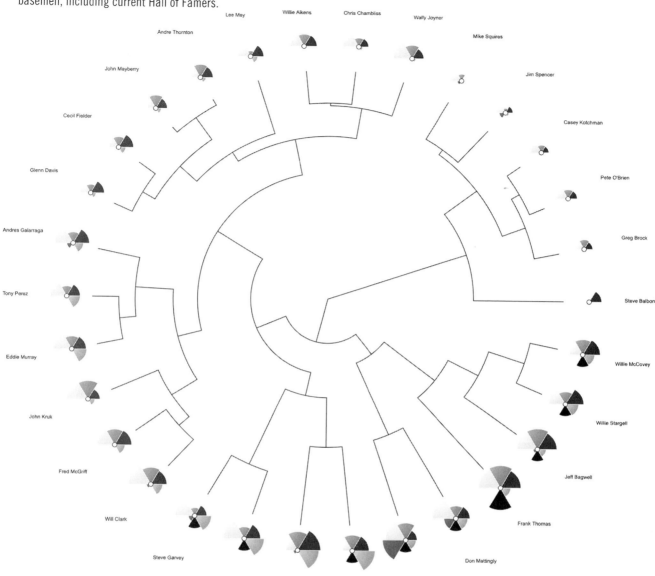

CONCLUSIONS

ToxPi-based player performance analyses provided interesting insights into Keith Hernandez's Hall of Fame case. A key component of this methodology involved synthesizing carefully chosen performance metrics into composite scores. While player performances were distilled into single values, the associated ToxPi visuals provided a clear indication of where they excelled and where they did not.

Hernandez's ToxPi Profiles revealed defensive excellence both compared to his contemporaries and compared to Hall of Fame first basemen. This supports the conclusions of the many knowledgeable fans who consider Hernandez one of the best defensive first basemen in the history of the sport. ToxPi analyses make it clear that his offense also contributes to his Hall of Fame case.

Whether considering traditional or advanced statistics, ToxPi-based integrated analyses support the contention that Keith Hernandez belongs in Cooperstown. This is clearly something that should be addressed and corrected by the Veterans Committee. Lastly, while the ToxPi-based assessments made no attempt to address sportsmanship, leadership, and other intangibles, general consensus indicates that Hernandez possessed these qualities, further supporting the argument for his enshrinement. ∎

Figure 5. ToxPi Profiles using advanced statistics.

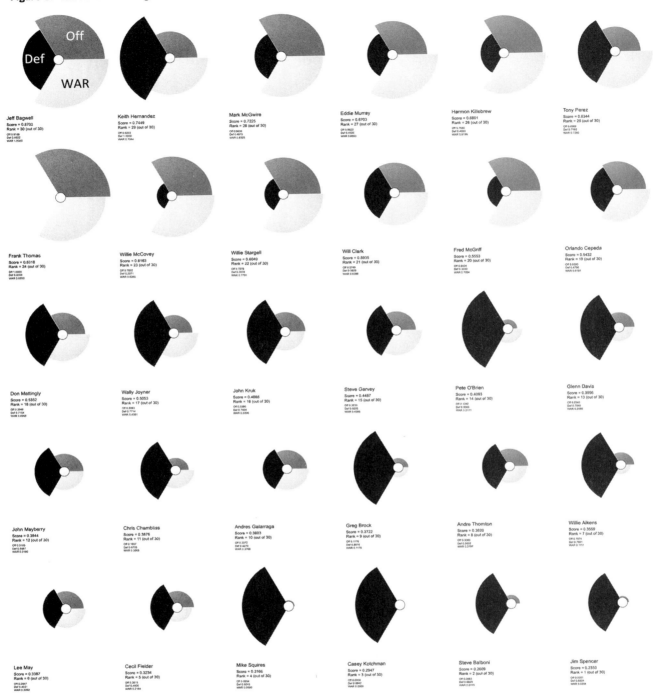

Figure 6. Aggregate ToxPi Scores using advanced statistics. Hernandez once again ranks second, this time to Jeff Bagwell.

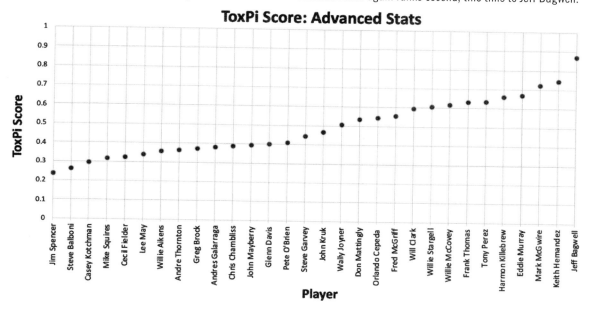

Figure 7. Using advanced statistics, the hierarchical clustering module shows Keith Hernandez alongside high-performing first basemen, including current Hall of Famers.

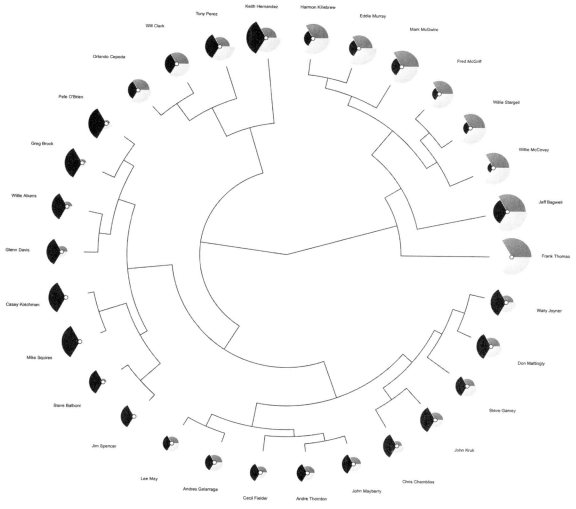

Notes

1. Chris Bodig, "Why Keith Hernandez Belongs in the Hall of Fame," July 9, 2022, accessed August, 2023. https://www.cooperstowncred.com/keith-hernandez-belongs-hall-fame/.

2. Benjamin J. Dertinger, Stephen D. Dertinger, "Baseball, Hot Dogs, and ToxPi: An Approach for Visualizing Player Performer Metrics," *Baseball Research Journal*, Spring, 2022, accessed March 3, 2023. https://sabr.org/journal/article/baseball-hot-dogs-and-toxpi-an-approach-for-visualizing-player-performance-metrics/.

3. Skylar W. Marvel, Kimberly To, Fabian A. Grimm, Fred A. Wright, Ivan Rusyn, David M. Reif, "ToxPi Graphical User Interface 2.0: Dynamic Exploration, Visualization, and Sharing of Integrated Data Models," *BMC Bioinformatics* 19 (2018) 80, accessed August 5, 2023. https://bmcbioinformatics.biomedcentral.com/articles/10.1186/s12859-018-2089-2/.

4. ToxPi: Toxicological Prioritization Index, accessed March 3, 2023, https://toxpi.org/.

5. Neil Weinberg, "Def," FanGraphs, September 4, 2014. https://library.fangraphs.com/defense/def/.

6. Neil Weinberg, "Off," FanGraphs, August 28, 2014. https://library.fangraphs.com/offense/off/.

7. Piper Slowinski, "WAR for Position Players," FanGraphs, April 2, 2012. https://library.fangraphs.com/war/war-position-players/.

Balancing Starter and Bullpen Workloads in a Seven-Game Postseason Series

David J. Gordon, MD, PhD

One of major league baseball's most enduring trends over its one and a half centuries has been the distribution of the innings workload among an ever-increasing number of pitchers. When the National League opened for business in 1876, only 34 pitchers (just over four per team) were needed to navigate the 26-week season, in which eight teams played a total of 260 games (about 2.5 games per team per week).[1] Only 23 pitchers started games (fewer than three per team), and they completed 472 of their 520 starts, 91%.[2] In 2022, with 30 teams playing nearly every day, 871 pitchers saw action (29 per team!), and less than one percent of starts (0.75%) resulted in a complete game.[3]

Although the early expansion of the number of pitchers per team was dictated by the demands of throwing overhand with high velocity and the greater frequency of games, this trend has persisted even after the schedule stabilized at 162 games in 1962 (Figure 1). After 20 years of stability at 15 pitchers per team, this number began to creep upward at a rate of one extra pitcher every four years from 1983 to 2012 (as shown by the dashed trend lines, which ignore the pandemic-shortened 2020 season). From 2013–22, this rate of increase accelerated threefold, as the number of pitchers per team climbed from 22.6 to 29 over a nine-year period. During this same period, the percentage of complete games, already in decline, fell by more than two-thirds from 2.55% to 0.75% (Figure 2, page 106).

The mainstreaming of analytics—a novelty when Michael Lewis wrote *Moneyball* in 2003—to a standard department of every major-league front office has undoubtedly played a prominent role in the acceleration of the trend toward expansion of major-league pitching staffs and the advancing extinction of complete games.[4] Specifically, the observation that starting pitchers, on average, lose effectiveness after two turns through the batting order has transformed how the workloads of major-league pitching staffs are managed. Although this concept dates as far back as 1996, the "times through the order penalty (TTOP)" was first formally elucidated and quantified in late 2013.[5]

Quantitatively, opposing hitters gain roughly 10 to 15 points in weighted on-base average (wOBA) each time a pitcher cycles through the lineup.[6] Studies have suggested that the TTOP is larger in pitchers who rely heavily on fastballs than in pitchers with more varied repertoires, who can afford not to show all their best pitches early in the game.[7] This suggests that the TTOP at least partially reflects the advantage conferred by

Figure 1. Number of Pitchers per Team

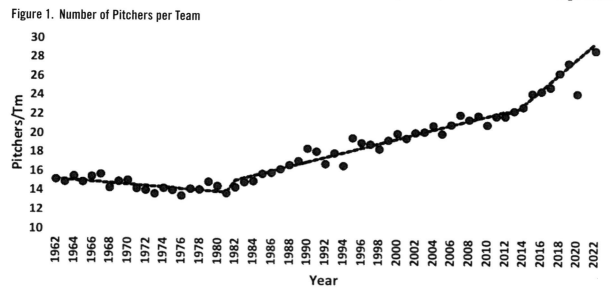

Figure 2. Complete Games (CG) as Percent of All Games

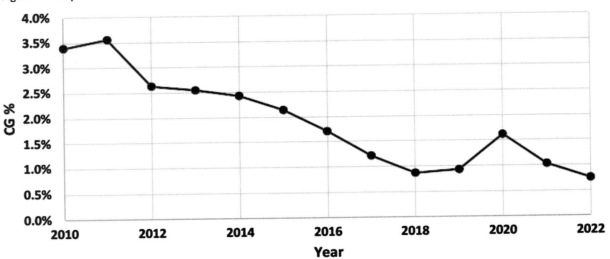

opposing batters' growing familiarity with the pitcher's offerings over the course of a game and not just pitcher fatigue. To avoid paying the TTOP, managers have made it their standard practice to remove a starting pitcher when the batting order turns over for the third time, regardless of pitch count, even if he is throwing a no-hitter. The performance of Hall of Famer Roy Halladay, who completed more than a quarter of his starts (42/162) in 2007–11 seems almost as old-fashioned today as Iron Man Joe McGinnity's 1903 feat of pitching and winning both games of a doubleheader three times in one month seemed in Halladay's time.[8]

Of course, the downside of removing starting pitchers after two turns through the batting order—typically about five innings—is that relief pitchers have to make up the difference. Major league teams have addressed this problem by carrying an eight-man bullpen (including several pitchers with options remaining) and shuttling in fresh relievers as needed from their triple-A affiliates. The implementation of the automatic runner rule in extra innings in 2020, which tends to curtail the number of extra innings, and the use of non-pitchers to pitch in lopsided games have also helped lighten bullpen workloads. Since teams rarely face each other more than four games in a row, there is little chance of overexposure to opposing lineups. However, this all changes in the League Championship Series and World Series, where teams must face each other up to seven times in nine days with a fixed pool of 12–13 pitchers, in which replacements are permitted only for significant injuries, and where there are no automatic baserunners to shorten extra-inning games.

This paper will describe and quantify the progressive degradation in the performance of relief pitchers who make three or more appearances during a best-of-seven postseason series. Specifically, it will test the hypothesis that relief pitchers lose effectiveness over the course of a single postseason series—especially those relief pitchers who are used most frequently and heavily.

METHODOLOGY

This paper will focus on the 27 best-of-seven postseason series (nine World Series and 18 League Championship Series) that took place from 2014 through 2022. I chose to begin with 2014 because it is the season when the concept of the times through the order penalty first gained traction, as evidenced by the sharp upturn in the yearly growth of the number of pitchers per team (Figure 1). While the fixed nature of postseason rosters precludes using number of pitchers per team as a metric, Table 1 compares several more directly relevant measures of changes in the usage of starting pitchers in the nine-year period of interest to the two preceding nine year periods (1996–2004 and 2005-13).[9]

The similarity of the first two time periods suggests that these metrics were relatively stable before 2014. However, the unmistakable differences between the

Table 1. Recent Temporal Trends in Starting Pitcher (SP) Usage in the LCS and WS

| Years | GS | ≤18BF | | ≤20BF | | % of IP |
		All	≤2ER	All	≤2ER	SP
1996–2004 (as % of GS)	312	36 12%	4 1%	54 17%	11 4%	64%
2005–13 (as % of GS)	298	29 10%	6 2%	52 17%	15 5%	63%
1996–2004 (as % of GS)	310	89 29%	53 17%	137 44%	86 28%	54%

most recent time period (2014–22) and the two earlier time periods is consistent with the in-season data. The percentage of innings pitched by starters fell from 63–64 in 1996–13 to 54 in 2014–2022. In 1996–2013, nearly 90% of starters faced at least 18 batters (i.e., two times through the batting order), and 83% faced at least 20 batters. These rates fell sharply to 71% and 56% in 2014–22. Most tellingly, before 2014, it was rare (less than 5%) for a pitcher who had yielded two or fewer runs to be lifted before facing 20 batters and almost unheard of (1–2%) for such a pitcher to be removed before facing 18 batters (barring injury or an early bout of wildness). In 2014–22, however, giving up two or fewer runs did not prevent 17% of starting pitchers from removal after 18 or fewer batters faced, and 28% from removal after 20 or fewer hitters. The data suggest that managers have carried their TTOP-influenced in-season approach to bullpen management into the postseason.

My analysis includes a total of 880 appearances by 244 pitchers who made three or more relief appearances in any of the 27 World Series, American League Championship Series, and National League Championship Series that took place in 2014–22.[10] A relief pitcher who appeared at least three times in more than one such series is considered separately for each series in which he qualified. There were 127 pitchers who made exactly three appearances in a best-of-seven series; 90 who made four appearances; 24 who made five appearances; two who made six appearances; and

one pitcher—Brandon Morrow of the Los Angeles Dodgers in the 2017 World Series—who appeared in all seven games. I have treated six appearances by "openers" as the equivalent of relief appearances, since the managers' intent was to replace them after no more than an inning or two and since all their other appearances in the series came in relief.

My metric of pitcher efficacy, wOBA, is a weighted sum of non-intentional walks (multiplied by 0.69), hit batsmen (0.72), singles (0.89), doubles (1.27), triples (1.62), and home runs (2.10)—i.e., wOB—divided by PA (batters faced minus sacrifice bunts minus intentional walks).[11] The wOBA metric was chosen because of its strong correlation with runs scored, which has made it the metric of choice for previous analyses of times through the order penalty for starting pitchers. Although the precise weights used to calculate wOBA for regular season games vary slightly from season to season and by hitting environment, using season-by-season weights would have added undue complexity to the calculation of wOBA in postseason play without necessarily adding predictive value for runs scored.[12]

The distribution of wOBA for the 880 relief appearances in our database (Figure 3) is skewed and bimodal with the most frequent value being zero (n-303) and a secondary peak at .200–.250 (n = 90).

Therefore, rather than use parametric analytic methods like ANOVA or linear regression, which assume a normal distribution, I used a more robust non-parametric analytic method—the Wilcoxon signed rank

Figure 3. Distribution of wOBA

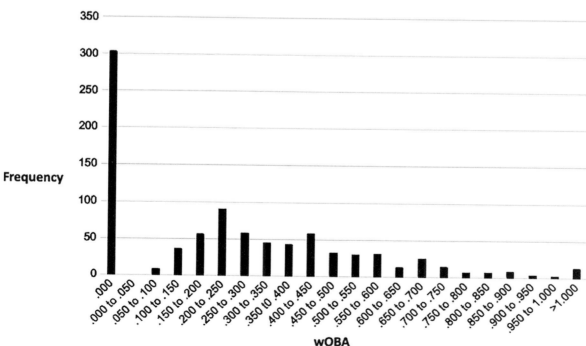

test, which makes no assumptions about the distributions being compared.[13] In this method, the absolute value of non-zero differences in wOBA between each pitcher's first appearance in a postseason series and his subsequent appearances (or groups of appearances) in the same series are ranked, and the sum of ranks (W) is calculated for pitchers who experienced an increase in wOBA after their initial appearance. For large samples like ours, the W statistic can be transformed as follows to a normally distributed Z-score:

$$Z = (W - n*(n+1)/4) \div SQRT(n*(n+1)*(2n+1)/24)$$

where **n** is the number of non-zero wOBA differences. All reported P-values are one-sided, with the null hypothesis being that the wOBA of opposing batters is not greater in a pitcher's subsequent appearances than in his first appearance in a postseason series. Because the ALCS and NLCS cannot begin until the Wild Card and LDS are completed, it is impossible for a pitcher making his first appearance in the LCS or World Series to have faced the same opponent within at least a week.

The 880 individual relief appearances of each of the 244 pitchers in Figure 1 were classified according to the ordinal number of the appearance (first, second, third, fourth, etc.) and (for appearances other than the first in a series) according to their pitching load during the two days before a given appearance (defined as "red" for relievers appearing on consecutive days or facing five or more batters within the two days preceding an appearance) and "green" for all other relief appearances. (The selection of the cutoff between four and five PA is based on the observation that 4.2 PA was the mean for all 880 relief appearances.) Because wOBA are compared only within the same pitcher within the same series, differences in wOBA are not confounded by quality differences among pitchers. Table 2 illustrates the classification process for Aroldis Chapman of the Chicago Cubs in the 2016 World Series.[14]

Overall, Cleveland batters made 30 plate appearances against Chapman in the 2016 Series; there were

no IBB or sacrifice bunts. They collected two walks, one HBP, and five hits, the most damaging being a game-tying two-run home run by Rajai Davis in Game Seven. Chapman's overall wOBA was a solid .271—but that doesn't tell the whole story. His wOBA was less than .165 in his first three appearances, .316 in his fourth appearance, and a whopping .609 in his rocky fifth appearance. The fact that Chapman's Game Six and Seven appearances came on consecutive days and that he had faced 10 batters in Game Five two days before Game Six may have contributed to his subpar performance in Game Seven. Concern about Chapman's workload was expressed by contemporaneous commentators, particularly the aftereffects of his 2⅔-inning save in Game Five, a 3–2 nailbiter that the Cubs had to win to stay alive.

Of course, one pitcher's experience in one postseason series proves little. However, we shall see how this plays out among the 244 pitchers analyzed.

RESULTS

The cohort of 244 relief pitchers who made at least three appearances in a postseason series compiled a respectable .286 composite wOBA (1024.6 wOB in 3574 PA) in their 880 relief appearances. However, their average effectiveness (as measured by the wOBA of opposing batters) clearly declined over the course of a series. In Table 3, the wOBA for the second through the seventh appearance for each pitcher is compared with the wOBA for their initial appearance in the same series.

The severity of the performance decline increases from a .018 wOBA increase in a pitcher's second appearance to a whopping .139 wOBA increase (P = 0.054) for pitchers making their fifth series appearance. The number (3) of pitchers making six or seven appearances is too small to be analyzed. The .059 wOBA increase in the third appearance is highly significant (P = 0.0053) and quantitatively larger than the TTOP for starting pitchers facing a lineup for the

Table 2. Classification of the Five Appearances of Aroldis Chapman in the 2016 World Series

Game	Rest Days	PA_prev	Category	PA	BB-IBB	HBP	1B	2B	3B	HR	wOB	wOBA
2			Initial	5	1	0	0	0	0	0	0.69	.138
3	1	5	Red	3	0	0	0	0	0	0	0.00	.000
5	1	3	Green	10	0	1	1	0	0	0	1.61	1.61
6	1	10	Red	5	1	0	1	0	0	0	1.58	.316
7	0	5	Red	7	0	0	1	1	0	1	4.26	.609
			Initial	5	1	0	0	0	0	0	0.69	1.38
	Category Totals		Green	10	0	1	1	0	0	0	1.61	.161
			Red	15	1	0	2	1	0	1	5.84	.389
	Overall Totals			30	2	1	3	1	0	1	8.14	.271

third time.[15] The substantial wOBA increases for the fourth and the fifth appearances fall short of statistical significance (barely in the latter case) due to their smaller sample sizes. However, when the numbers for the second through seventh appearances are pooled to provide a large (244) sample size, the .297 composite wOBA is .041 higher than the .256 mean wOBA for the first appearance of the same cohort of pitchers—a highly significant difference (P < 0.0001).

But Table 3 does not tell the whole story. The magnitude of the performance decline following a relief pitcher's first appearance in a series depends on the spacing and length of a pitcher's appearances. Specifically, has a pitcher had at least one day of rest since his preceding appearance? If he has had only a single day's rest since his last outing, how many batters did he face in that appearance? In Table 4, the 636 (880-244) non-initial relief appearances are divided into four categories: 1) those coming after no days off, 2) those coming after exactly one day off but in which the reliever faced five or more batters in his most recent appearance, 3) those coming after exactly one day off and in which the reliever faced four or fewer batters in his most recent appearance, and 4) those coming after two or more days off.

In the first row of Table 4, we see that 180 of the 244 relievers made at least one appearance after pitching on the previous day. Opposing batters amassed a .310 wOBA in these appearances, in contrast to the .241 wOBA of these same 180 pitchers in their first ap-

pearance in the series. This .069 wOBA difference was highly significant (P = 0.001). There were also 50 relievers who appeared following exactly one day of rest and who had faced at least five batters in their most recent appearance. Opposing batters lit up these pitchers for a .347 wOBA after compiling only a .216 wOBA against these same 50 pitchers in their first appearance in the series. This .131 wOBA difference was also statistically significant (P = 0.005) despite the relatively small size of this cohort. The wOBA of opposing batters in the cohort of 94 pitchers who made at least one appearance after a single day's rest but had faced four or fewer batters in their most recent appearance and n the cohort of 169 pitchers who made at least one appearance following two or more days of rest did not increase significantly after their first appearance in the series.

Based on the observed contrast between relief appearances made either on consecutive days or one day after facing at least five batters versus relief appearances made after a longer break, I combined the first two rows of Table 4 into a single category called "Red" appearances and combined the next two rows into a single category called "Green" appearances. Opposing batters compiled a .319 wOBA against the 206 pitchers who made at least one Red relief appearance—.076 higher than in their initial appearance of the series (P < 0.0001). By contrast, opposing batters hit for a .279 wOBA against the 227 pitchers who made at least one Green appearance—only .017 higher than in their

Table 3. Table 3: Impact of Appearance Number on wOBA

Appearance Number	No of Relievers	nth Appearance			Initial Appearance			ΔwOBA	Wilcoxon Signed Rank Test	
		PA	wOB	wOBA	PA	wOB	wOBA		Mean Z-Score	P-Value
2	244	943	259.2	.275	984	252.3	.256	.018	0.84	0.22
3	244	1026	323.2	.315	984	252.3	.256	.059	2.55	0.0053
4	117	502	145.3	.290	470	111	.236	.053	1.22	0.11
5	27	119	42.8	.360	104	23.0	.222	.139	1.61	0.054
6	3	9	1.5	.176	11	2.3	.210	−.034		
7	1	1	0	.000	3	0	.000	.000	Insufficient Data	
Any	244	2600	772.2	.297	984	252.3	.256	.041	4.76	<0.0001

Table 4. Impact of Appearance Category on wOBA

Days of Rest	PA within 2 Days	No of Relievers	≥ 2nd Appearance			Initial Appearance			Mean ΔwOBA	Wilcoxon Signed Rank Test	
			PA	wOB	wOBA	PA	wOB	wOBA		Z-Score	P-Value
0	—	180	923	286.3	.310	693	167.0	.241	.069	3.06	0.0011
1	≥5	50	273	94.7	.347	231	49.8	.216	.131	2.57	0.0051
1	0–4	94	484	126.4	.261	337	83.2	.247	.014	0.67	0.24
≥2	All	169	828	228.2	.276	718	206.9	.288	−.013	−0.76	0.78
Red		206	1196	381.0	.319	814	194	.238	.076	3.85	<0.0001
Green		227	1404	391.2	.279	907	237.2	.262	.017	0.78	0.23

initial appearance of the series (P = 0.23). Thus, based on the 244 pitchers in my database, each of whom made three or more appearances against the same team in a best-of-seven postseason series, managers need to heed the flashing red light when considering deploying a relief pitcher on consecutive days or one day after facing five or more batters in their previous outing. However, managers have a green light for deploying relief pitchers under scenarios in which they had at least two days rest or had been used lightly one day earlier.

DISCUSSION

There is little doubt that the conventional wisdom of limiting most starting pitchers to two turns through the order is generally a sound strategy during the regular season, when there are no seven-game series and fresh relievers can be easily shuttled in from AAA. Carrying a 13-man pitching staff and limiting the number of batters a starting pitcher must face not only avoids the TTOP but allows every pitcher to pitch at maximum effort while he is in the game, rather than to hold back to ensure he has something left for the later innings. But this calculus does not hold for postseason series, in which rosters are fixed and the opponent does not change. In the postseason, limiting starting pitchers in this manner inevitably opens the door to overwork and overexposure of relief pitchers.

My analysis cannot distinguish between the effects of overexposure of a relief pitcher who must face the same lineup repeatedly over the course of 4–7 games versus the effect of fatigue on performance. To address this issue, one would have to compare the effect of relievers working on short rest against the same versus differing opponents during the regular season. Josh Kalk in the *Hardball Times* has suggested that fatigue may affect different relief pitchers differently, hurting those who rely on fastballs or sinkers, and neutral for those who rely on sliders.[16] But regardless of whether we are dealing with overexposure, fatigue, or both, relief pitchers' diminished effectiveness in "Red Category" situations is something managers ought to consider in their postseason pitching decisions. Focusing only

on the TTOP of starters in the LCS and WS, when a pitching staff must face the same team up to seven times in nine days without the luxury of streaming in fresh bullpen arms from AAA, is a recipe for trouble. A comparison of two classic winner-take-all World Series games 25 years apart illustrates the intervening sea change in postseason bullpen strategy (Table 5).[17]

Game 7 starters, veteran Twins ace Jack Morris (18–12, 3.43 ERA) and budding Cubs ace Kyle Hendricks (16–8, 2.16 ERA), were each coming off highly successful seasons in 1991 and 2016, respectively, and had pitched well in their preceding World Series starts. Morris had given up 3 ER in 13 IP in Game 1 (a win) and Game 4 (no decision), while Hendricks had been used lightly, having given up no runs in 4.1 IP (no decision) in the Cubs' Game 3 win. Hendricks's short stint in WS Game 3 was atypical; before that, he had logged at least 5 IP in all of his 30 regular season starts and in two of four prior postseason starts in 2016.[18,19] He had logged at least 6 IP in 21 of these previous 34 starts.

Both Morris and Hendricks were inefficient in the early innings of their Game 7 starts, finishing two full turns through the opposing batting order before completing the fifth inning, but had nevertheless entered the fifth inning relatively unscathed. Morris began the fifth inning of a scoreless game by putting Atlanta runners on first and third with one out to bring his wOBA to .307 for the game. But Twins manager Pat Kelly, blissfully unaware of the TTOP, allowed Morris to pitch out of trouble. Morris then proceeded to allow only two more hits in the ensuing 5.2 IP to complete a 1–0, 10-inning shutout. His .127 wOBA in his last two turns through the batting order was .180 less than that during his first 2.1 turns. By contrast, Cubs manager Joe Maddon, acutely aware of the TTOP, lifted Hendricks in favor of veteran ace Jon Lester after he walked Carlos Santana with two outs in the fifth inning, despite the fact that Hendricks was well-rested, enjoyed a 5–1 lead, and had held Cleveland to a meager .244 wOBA up to that point. Lester, who had pitched six innings in Game 5 three days earlier, quickly allowed the inherited runner plus another run

Table 5. Contrasting Game 7 Pitching Strategies in the 1991 and 2016 World Series

Year	Pitcher	IP	Score	BF	PA	BB-IBB	HBP	1B	2B	3B	HR	wOB	wOBA
1991	Morris	4.1	0–0	19	18	1	0	4	1	0	0	5.52	.307
	Morris	5.2	1–0	18	17	0	0	1	1	0	0	2.16	.127
2016	Hendricks	4.2	5–1	19	19	1	0	3	1	0	0	4.63	.244
	Relievers	5.1	3–6	25	25	2	0	5	1	0	1	9.20	.368

NOTE: Batters faced (BF) and plate appearances (PA) are not identical. PA (the denominator for wOBA) does not include intentional walks (IBB) or sacrifice hits (SH).

to score before finishing the inning. The overworked and overexposed Aroldis Chapman (Table 2) then replaced Lester with two outs and a man on first in the eighth inning and promptly blew the Cubs' 6–3 lead before recovering to hold off any further damage through the ninth inning. Carl Edwards (third appearance) and Mike Montgomery (fifth appearance) held Cleveland to one run in the 10th inning after the Cubs had retaken a two-run lead. Overall, the Cubs' bullpen was torched for a .368 wOBA over the final 5.1 IP (.124 worse than Hendricks's .244 wOBA). While things ended happily for both the 1991 Twins and 2016 Cubs, their bullpen strategies could not have differed more starkly.

The point of this illustration is not to praise Kelly or fault Maddon; both managers were merely following the conventional wisdom of their times. In 1991, even the most trigger-happy manager would not have considered removing his ace from a scoreless game in the fifth inning, but Kelly would not have looked so smart if Morris coughed up another hit or two and given Braves starter John Smoltz all the margin he needed to win the game and close out the Series. Similarly, Maddon's Game 7 strategy might have worked better had the Cubs not dug a 1–3 hole in Games 1–4 that left him little choice but to ride Chapman hard in Games 5–6. In general, the strategy of routinely removing an effective starter in the fifth or sixth inning when the batting order turns over for the third time may win some games early by rescuing starters from the TTOP, but it leaves a shortfall of IP that must be covered by overusing a limited pool of relievers later in the series. This analysis strongly suggests that the deleterious effect of using relievers in "Red" situations—as much as .076 in wOBA—substantially outweighs the deleterious effect—approximately a .030 increase in wOBA— of the TTOP on starters. Thus, a manager who rigidly removes his starter after two turns through the batting order, regardless of how well he is pitching, will often find himself in Maddon's predicament with no fresh relievers when the Series is on the line in Game 7—a short-sighted strategy at best. Protecting your starters from the significant but relatively small TTOP at all costs does no good if your best high-leverage relievers become fatigued and/or "old hat" to opposing hitters by the time they are needed in the deciding game.

In short, during the postseason far more than in the regular season, a manager must be mindful not only of the possibility of overextending his starters, but of the even more damaging possibility of overexposing his relievers to opposing batters. A rigid TTOP-based algorithm forbidding starting pitchers from being allowed to face batters a third time, no matter what, is ill-suited to the framework and roster constraints of the postseason. ∎

Acknowledgment
I would like to thank my friend Richard Cohn, PhD, a statistical consultant from Chapel Hill, North Carolina, for guiding my statistical analysis to control for differences among pitchers without assuming normality of the distribution of wOBA changes.

Erratum
In the author's previous contribution to the *Baseball Research Journal*, "Standardized Peak WAR," one table and two figures were omitted. The corrected article is online at https://sabr.org/journal/article/standardized-peak-war-spw-a-fair-standard-for-historical-comparison-of-peak-value.

Notes
1. Pitchers in 1876 also threw underhand from behind a line 45 feet from home plate. "Major League Pitching Year-By-Year Averages," Baseball-Reference, https://www.baseball-reference.com/leagues/majors/pitch.shtml.
2. "Player Pitching Season & Career Stats Finder (1876)," Stathead Baseball, https://stathead.com/baseball/player-pitching-season-finder.cgi?request=1&order_by=p_bfp&year_min=1876&year_max=1876&ccomp%5B1%5D=gt&cval%5B1%5D=1&cstat%5B1%5D=p_bfp.
3. "Major League Pitching Year-By-Year Averages," Baseball Reference.
4. Michael Lewis, *Moneyball: The Art of Winning an Unfair Game* (New York: W. W. Norton & Company, 2004).
5. David W. Smith, "Do Batters Learn During a Game?" Retrosheet, June 7, 1996; Tom M. Tango, Mitchel G. Lichtman, Andrew E. Dolphin, *The Book: Playing the Percentages in Baseball* (Washington: Potomac Books, 2007; Lichtman, "Baseball ProGUESTus: Everything You Always Wanted to Know About the Times Through the Order Penalty," *Baseball Prospectus*, November 5, 2013, https://www.baseballprospectus.com/news/article/22156/baseball-proguestus-everything-you-always-wanted-to-know-about-the-times-through-the-order-penalty/.
6. Piper Slowinski, "wOBA," FanGraphs, February 15, 2010, https://library.fangraphs.com/offense/woba/; Chris Teeter, "Pitcher's Pitch-Type Arsenal and Getting Through the Order," *Beyond the Boxscore*, January 15, 2014, https://www.beyondtheboxscore.com/2014/1/15/5308808/pitchers-pitch-type-arsenal-and-getting-through-the-order.
7. Mitchel G. Lichtman, "TTOP and a Starting Pitcher's Repertoire," *MGL on Baseball*, November 11, 2013, https://mglbaseball.wordpress.com/2013/11/11/ttop-and-a-starting-pitchers-repetoire/; Ethan Moore, "Pitch Quality 3: Times Through The Order," *Prospects 365*, July 8, 2020, https://prospects365.com/2020/07/08/pitch-quality-3-times-through-the-order/; Moore, "Pitch Quality 4: Solving the Times Through the Order Penalty," *Prospects 365*, July 16, 2020, https://prospects365.com/2020/07/16/pitch-quality-4-solving-the-times-through-the-order-penalty/.
8. "Roy Halladay," Baseball Reference, https://www.baseball-reference.com/players/h/hallaro01.shtml; Don Doxsie, "Joe McGinnity," Society for American Baseball Reasearch, https://sabr.org/bioproj/person/Joe-McGinnity/.
9. "Player Pitching Game Stats Finder (1996–2013 Postseason Starters)," Stathead Baseball, https://stathead.com/baseball/player-pitching-game-finder.cgi?request=1&match=player_game&order_by_asc=1&order_by=name_display_csk&year_min=1996&year_max=2022&comp_type=post&team_game_min=1&team_game_max=165&player_game_min=1&player_game_max=9999&is_pitcher=1&role=GS&days_rest_comp=%3D&location=pob&locationMatch=is&min_temperature=0&max_temperature=120&min_wind_speed=0&max_wind_speed=90.

10. "Player Pitching Game Stats Finder (2014–22 Postseason)," *Stathead Baseball*, https://stathead.com/baseball/player-pitching-game-finder.cgi?request=1&match=player_game&order_by_asc=0&order_by=name_display_csk&year_min=2014&year_max=2022&comp_type=post&team_game_min=1&team_game_max=165&player_game_min=1&player_game_max=9999&is_pitcher=1&role=anyGS&days_rest_comp=%3D&location=pob&locationMatch=is&min_temperature=0&max_temperature=120&min_wind_speed=0&max_wind_speed=90.

11. Slowinski, "wOBA."

12. "wOBA and FIP Constants," FanGraphs, https://www.fangraphs.com/guts.aspx?type=cn.

13. Myles Hollander and Douglas A. Wolfe, *Nonparametric Statistical Methods*, 3rd Edition (New York: John Wiley & Sons, 2013), 40–55; "Wilcoxon Signed-Ranks Test for Paired Samples," *Real Statistics Using Excel*, https://real-statistics.com/non-parametric-tests/wilcoxon-signed-ranks-test/.

14. "2016 World Series," Baseball Reference, https://www.baseball-reference.com/postseason/2016_WS.shtml.

15. Lichtman, "Baseball ProGUESTus."

16. Josh Kalk, "Do relief pitchers suffer from pitching back-to-back days?," *Hardball Times*, April 2, 2008, https://tht.fangraphs.com/do-relief-pitchers-suffer-from-pitching-back-to-back-days/.

17. "1991 World Series," Baseball Reference, https://www.baseball-reference.com/postseason/1991_WS.shtml; "2016 World Series," Baseball Reference, https://www.baseball-reference.com/postseason/2016_WS.shtml.

18. "Player Pitching Game Stats Finder (Kyle Hendricks Regular Season Starts)," *Stathead Baseball*, https://stathead.com/baseball/player-pitching-game-finder.cgi?request=1&match=player_game&order_by_asc=0&order_by=p_ip&player_id_hint=Kyle+Hendricks&player_id_select=Kyle+Hendricks&player_id=hendri001kyl&year_min=2016&year_max=2016&comp_type=reg&is_pitcher=1&role=GS&days_rest_comp=%3D&location=pob&locationMatch=is&min_temperature=0&max_temperature=120&min_wind_speed=0&max_wind_speed=90.

19. "Player Pitching Game Stats Finder (Kyle Hendricks 2016 Postseason Starts)," *Stathead Baseball*, https://stathead.com/baseball/player-pitching-game-finder.cgi?request=1&match=player_game&order_by_asc=0&order_by=p_ip&player_id_hint=Kyle+Hendricks&player_id_select=Kyle+Hendricks&player_id=hendri001kyl&year_min=2016&year_max=2016&comp_type=post&team_game_min=1&team_game_max=165&player_game_min=1&player_game_max=9999&is_pitcher=1&role=GS&days_rest_comp=%3D&location=pob&locationMatch=is&min_temperature=0&max_temperature=120&min_wind_speed=0&max_wind_speed=90.

More Relief Pitchers Belong
in the Hall of Fame: Which Ones?

Elaina and John Pakutka

I still think relief pitchers are slighted or faintly patronized in most fans' and writers' consideration. Ask somebody to pick an all-time or all-decade lineup for his favorite team or for one of the leagues and the chances are the list will not include a late inning fireman.

– Roger Angell[1]

Much has changed since 1985, when one of the greatest of baseball writers penned these words. Still, much has stayed the same. A simple Google search reveals the ongoing, prevailing sentiment among baseball writers and analysts that "relief pitchers are failed starters."[2] The implication seems to be that short-inning firemen really aren't that important to team success. True greatness lies elsewhere in baseball.

No reliever has won the Cy Young Award since 2003. Many of the best never make a National Baseball Hall of Fame ballot or are summarily dismissed with less than 5% of the vote on their initial appearance. 2012 National Sportswriter of the Year Joe Posnanski does not commit the sin of exclusion Angell regularly encountered. Posnanski includes relief pitcher Mariano Rivera—and only Mariano Rivera—in *The Baseball 100*, his rich collection of essays on the one hundred greatest baseball players of all-time. (Even the great Rivera, it must be admitted, failed as a starter.)

As demonstrated in Figure 1, the role of the relief pitcher has progressively increased in importance since World War I, when complete games were the norm.[3] Since then, as each quarter century has passed, starters have pitched on average about an inning less per game. In 2019, Cubs President of Baseball Operations Theo Epstein put it bluntly: "More is being asked out of bullpens."[4]

Many fans and analysts do not like this development, especially in its more recent iterations: bullpen games and seventh-inning specialists. In 2019, statistician Nate Silver went so far as to claim, "relief pitchers have broken baseball." His restoration plan called for capping the number of pitchers on an MLB roster at 10.[5] Despite the criticism of the game's evolution, greatness is visible in whatever form the action takes at a given time. In the last five decades, greatness has often taken the form of Roger Angell's "fireman."

In 2017, sabermetric pioneer Bill James tested whether championship teams were more likely to have top-10 closers than top-10 players at other positions. James considered the period 1976 to 2016, when relief pitching assumed its modern form. (Let's agree for now that bullpen games are the post-modern form.) James was shocked to find top-10 closers on 31 World Series champions, significantly more than any other position. According to James's rankings, the average World Series champion had the eighth-best closer in baseball in a given year. No other position averaged better than tenth place. "The proposition that to win a World Championship you need a great closer and that a great closer is more important than a great player at other positions," James concluded, "appears to be true."[7]

Relief pitching presents great challenges: irregular, sometimes daily usage, multiple warmups before getting

Figure 1. Innings Pitched per Start (1901–2022)

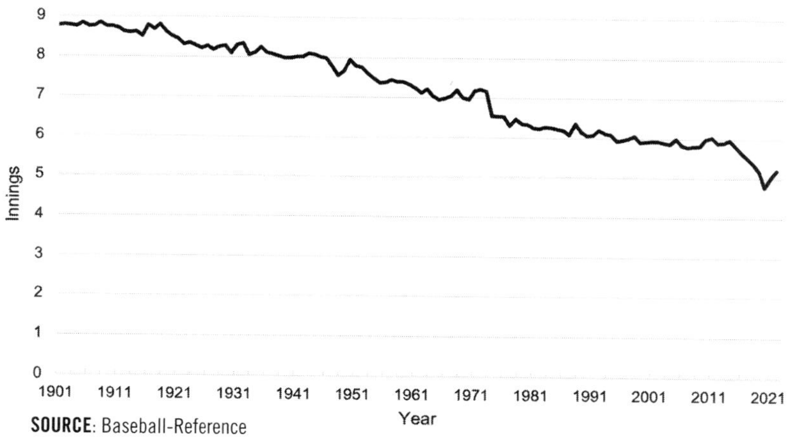

SOURCE: Baseball-Reference

the call (or not), and entrance to the game in high leverage situations. Relievers must bounce back quickly from failure. The psychological command required is probably unparalleled in baseball.[8]

Plaques of only seven relief pitchers grace the walls of the Hall of Fame: Richard Gossage, Hoyt Wilhelm, Rollie Fingers, Bruce Sutter, Lee Smith, Trevor Hoffman, and Rivera. Converted starters Dennis Eckersley and John Smoltz also won induction. Billy Wagner will likely need the full 10 years of eligibility to complete the slow climb to 75%, the voting threshold for admission. One worries about the prospects for Craig Kimbrel, Kenley Jansen, and Aroldis Chapman, the most accomplished relievers of the past decade. Josh Hader and Liam Hendricks have barely started the journey to Cooperstown that so few relievers have completed.

Injuries have derailed many pitching careers that began on Hall of Fame trajectories. The Hall's 10-year service requirement surely disadvantages pitchers. It is well understood that pitchers are more likely than other position players to get injured. The average pitching career is two to three years shorter than the average non-pitching career.[9]

In this article, we argue the best relief pitchers belong in the Hall of Fame and estimate the number of those missing in action. We review the back-of-the-baseball-card relief pitching data and then consider modern advanced analytics to produce our estimate of the best relief pitchers not in the Hall of Fame. In the concluding section, we profile briefly those we consider Hall-worthy.

THE MISSING IN ACTION

Jane Forbes Clark, Chairman of the Board of Directors of The National Baseball Hall of Fame, reminds us each year that the Hall contains the top 1% of major-league players.[10] But that 1% is not evenly distributed across eras or positions. The approximately 20,000 players who have appeared in a major-league game have been almost equally split between pitchers and non-pitchers.[11] Since 2000, pitchers have actually outnumbered hitters by close to a 3:2 ratio.[12] Nonetheless, voters have enshrined 186 non-pitchers and just 84 pitchers.[13] So 1.9% of hitters, but only 0.8% of pitchers have been inducted.

The bias against modern pitchers is much worse than the overall numbers suggest. Figure 2 breaks down the number of pitchers inducted in 30-year increments. The downward trend is actually understated by the graph, as the overall number of players has increased over time due to expansion. With the statistically deserving Roger Clemens and Curt Schilling falling off the ballot this past year, the book on 1970-1999 is mostly complete. Two pitchers of that era remain on the ballot: Andy Pettitte and Billy Wagner. Only one, Wagner, received over 20% of the vote last year.[14]

Why the structural discrimination? After all, as Casey Stengel famously declared, "Good pitching will always stop good hitting and vice-versa."[15] While causality is not established, this drop-off is correlated with the rise of the relief pitcher. What if instead of lamenting the rise of the reliever, we embraced it? Our best guess is that the Hall of Fame is short 10 to 15 pitchers from the 1970-99 period, and many of them are relievers.

BACK OF THE BASEBALL CARD DATA

What do we know about the relief pitchers in Cooperstown? All of them saved more than 150 games and made at least six All-Star games. All but one played at least 17 years and struck out over 1,000 batters. The seven career relievers had ERAs below 3.03, WHIPs below 1.26, and at least 225 saves. (See Table 1.)

Based on that information, we found 20 pitchers from the 1970s onward who met the following criteria: better ERA and WHIP than the worst of our seven Hall of Famers, at least 600 strikeouts, and at least 85 saves.[16] In Table 2, statistics for those 20 pitchers are juxtaposed with those of the Hall of Fame relievers. In this, and all following tables, Hall of Famers are in bold, and active players are italicized.

How about accolades? Sometimes the numbers do not capture the essence of the player, especially in big

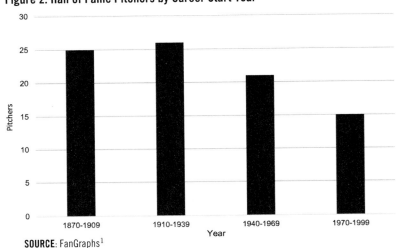

Figure 2. Hall of Fame Pitchers by Career Start Year

SOURCE: FanGraphs[1]

spots. Looking at a range of awards tells us how those around the game viewed the players contemporaneously. We looked at the Cy Young Award voting to see how often a reliever appeared on ballots, how many first-place votes they received in their career, and the total weighted points they compiled.[17] Table 3 (page 116) shows that by these measures, firemen Mike Marshall and Dan Quisenberry stand out for their sustained

Table 1. Hall of Fame Relief Pitchers

Name	Yrs	G	IP	ERA	WHIP	SV	SO	ASG	Role
Mariano Rivera	19	1115	1283.2	2.21	1.00	652	1173	13	Reliever
Trevor Hoffman	18	1035	1089.1	2.87	1.06	601	1133	7	Reliever
Lee Smith	18	1022	1289.1	3.03	1.26	478	1251	7	Reliever
Rollie Fingers	17	944	1701.1	2.90	1.16	341	1299	7	Reliever
Rich Gossage	22	1002	1809.1	3.01	1.23	310	1502	9	Reliever
Bruce Sutter	12	661	1042	2.83	1.14	300	861	6	Reliever
Hoyt Wilhelm	21	1070	2254.1	2.52	1.12	228	1610	8	Reliever
Dennis Eckersley	24	1071	3285.2	3.50	1.16	390	2401	6	Hybrid
John Smoltz	21	723	3473	3.33	1.18	154	3084	8	Hybrid
Average	**19**	**960**	**1914**	**2.91**	**1.15**	**384**	**1590**	**7.9**	
Relievers Only	**18**	**978**	**1495**	**2.77**	**1.14**	**416**	**1261**	**8.1**	

SOURCE: Baseball Reference

Table 2. Hall of Fame Relievers and Comparables

Name	G	IP	SV	ERA	WHIP	SO	K/9
Hoyt Wilhelm	1070	2254.1	227	2.52	1.12	1610	6.4
Rich Gossage	1002	1809.1	310	3.01	1.23	1502	7.5
Rollie Fingers	944	1701.1	341	2.91	1.16	1299	6.9
Lee Smith	1021	1289.1	478	3.03	1.26	1251	8.7
Billy Wagner	853	903	422	2.31	1.00	1196	11.9
Mariano Rivera	1115	1283.2	652	2.21	1.00	1173	8.2
Craig Kimbrel	758	735.1	412	2.37	0.98	1163	14.2
Kenley Jansen	805	804.1	415	2.48	0.95	1149	12.9
Francisco Rodriguez	948	976	437	2.86	1.15	1142	10.5
Trevor Hoffman	1034	1089.1	601	2.87	1.06	1133	9.4
Aroldis Chapman	708	679.1	318	2.48	1.07	1116	14.8
David Robertson	774	786.1	172	2.87	1.15	1028	11.8
Don McMahon	874	1310.2	153	2.96	1.25	1003	6.9
Joe Nathan	787	923.1	377	2.87	1.12	976	9.5
Tom Henke	642	789.2	311	2.67	1.09	861	9.8
Bruce Sutter	661	1042	300	2.83	1.14	861	7.4
Jonathan Papelbon	689	725.2	368	2.44	1.04	808	10.0
John Wetteland	618	765	330	2.93	1.13	804	9.5
Robb Nen	643	715	314	2.98	1.21	793	10.0
Kent Tekulve	1050	1436.2	184	2.85	1.25	779	4.9
Steve Cishek	737	710.2	133	2.98	1.20	743	9.4
Huston Street	668	680	324	2.95	1.07	665	8.8
Edwin Diaz	404	399.1	205	2.93	1.06	657	14.8
Rob Dibble	384	477	89	2.98	1.19	645	12.2
Mark Melancon	732	726.2	262	2.94	1.17	643	8.0
Rafael Soriano	591	636.1	207	2.89	1.08	641	9.1
Josh Hader	331	373	158	2.51	0.92	625	15.1

SOURCE: FanGraphs

performance, with comparable numbers to the seven Hall of Famers.

Two other sets of honors warrant some consideration. The first is All-Star Game selections. Four retired relievers, Billy Wagner, Joe Nathan, Jonathan Papelbon, and Francisco Rodriguez, met the Hall of Fame standard of six selections.[19]

The second is a series of awards instituted specifically for relievers. From 1976 to 2012, the Rolaids Relief Man Award used a rudimentary formula with points for saves, wins, losses, and eventually blown saves to crown the best reliever in each league.[20] Starting in 2014, the Reliever of the Year Award has filled the same role, though it is voted on by a panel of retired relief pitchers. From 2005 to 2013, the Delivery Man of the Year Award went to the best closer in all of Major League Baseball.[21] Eight Hall of Fame relievers won these awards, six of them multiple times. Nine relievers outside of the Hall won multiple times, but Dan Quisenberry again stands out from the pack with

five awards. Table 4 lists all players since 1970 who either won at least two relief awards or who had at least five All-Star selections pitching primarily as a reliever.

We examined a final set of accolades: Most Valuable Player Awards from the All-Star Game, League Championship Series, and World Series.[23] It was rare for a reliever not named Mariano Rivera to win such awards. He won one of each, for a total of three. Hall of Famer Rollie Fingers won the 1974 World Series MVP, and Dennis Eckersley won the ALCS MVP in 1988. Six relievers outside the Hall won these awards: Larry Sherry was the 1959 World Series MVP; Randy Myers and Rob Dibble were co-MVPs of the 1990 NLCS; John Wetteland won the 1996 World Series MVP; Koji Uehara won the 2013 ALCS MVP; and Andrew Miller won the 2016 ALCS MVP.

ADVANCED ANALYTICS

What can modern statistics tell us about the best relievers? These metrics were mostly unavailable to

Table 3. Cy Young Award Voting Performance by Relief Pitchers

Name	Total Points	First Place Votes	Years with Votes
Dan Quisenberry	208	22	5
Trevor Hoffman	170	25	4
Mike Marshall	166	28	5
Dennis Eckersley	164	20	4
Eric Gagné	157	28	3
Rollie Fingers	153	24	4
Mariano Rivera	147	9	6
Bruce Sutter	136	12	5
Craig Kimbrel	112	1	5
Mark Davis	107	19	1
Willie Hernandez	88	12	1
Zack Britton	72	5	1
Lee Smith	65	4	4
Sparky Lyle	59	9	2
Steve Bedrosian	57	9	1
Jose Mesa	54	2	1
Rich Gossage	49	2	5
Al Hrabosky	42	2	2
Fernando Rodney	38	1	1
Francisco Rodriguez	38	0	3
Bobby Thigpen	20	2	1
Robb Nen	20	2	1

SOURCE: Cy Young Pitchers[18]

Table 4. Relief Pitcher Career Honors

Name	Awards	ASG
Mariano Rivera	8	13
Dan Quisenberry	5	3
Craig Kimbrel	4	9
Bruce Sutter	4	6
Rollie Fingers	4	7
Josh Hader	3	5
José Valverde	3	3
Heath Bell	3	3
Lee Smith	3	7
Edwin Díaz	2	2
Liam Hendriks	2	3
Kenley Jansen	2	4
Francisco Rodríguez	2	6
Brad Lidge	2	2
Trevor Hoffman	2	7
Eric Gagné	2	3
Randy Myers	2	4
Dennis Eckersley	2	4
John Franco	2	4
Dave Righetti	2	2
Bill Campbell	2	1
Rich Gossage	1	8
Aroldis Chapman	1	7
Billy Wagner	1	7
Jonathan Papelbon	1	6
Joe Nathan	1	6
Doug Jones	0	5

SOURCES: Baseball Reference, Stathead[22]

twentieth-century sportswriters, but they now enable fairer comparisons within and across different eras of baseball. Many of the metrics control for the role of luck in traditional stats. We will examine four salient advanced metrics: FIP, ERA–, WAR and JAWS.

Fielding Independent Pitching (FIP) is an attempt to take the randomness of team fielding out of the equation when comparing pitchers. FIP considers only at-bats that result in a strikeout, walk, or home run, ignoring all other batted balls. "Think of it as what the pitcher's ERA should be," one ESPN analyst explained, "if the defense behind him turned batted balls into outs at a major-league average rate."[24] FIP rewards those pitchers with bad luck or bad fielding behind them with lower adjusted earned run averages.

Only 22 relief pitchers have thrown at least 450 innings and maintained a FIP under three. Four of the nine Hall of Fame relievers (along with hybrid Dennis Eckersley) meet this standard, with Mariano Rivera the best among them. Four active and one retired relievers boast a better career FIP than Rivera. (See Table 5, page 118.)

We also examined season-by-season FIP from the last five decades. What was most interesting was the short duration of relief success. Few relievers have been able to maintain league FIP dominance for more than a four-year stretch. As Figure 3 indicates, league-leading FIP has been falling over time as strikeout percentages have increased.

In an attempt to quantify career FIP dominance, we used a rudimentary scale that awarded five points for league-leading FIP among qualified relievers, three points for second place, and one point for third. We then summed each reliever's career points and calculated what we call "FIP123." Six Hall of Famers had dominant stretches, as did a handful of relievers outside of Cooperstown.

ERA– (ERA Minus) enables comparisons between pitchers of different eras, since a 3.00 ERA was more impressive in the PED Era than the Deadball Era, to name one example.[25] Each pitcher's ERA is scaled for the scoring environment: 100 is average, 80 is 20% better than average, and 120 is 20% worse.

The data here are perplexing. Mariano Rivera is safely at the top of the list, but other Hall of Famers, though still excellent, do not fare as well. Many of the best ERA– performers failed to impress the voters. Presumably those voters either did not consider ERA– or did not give it much weight. This seems like a significant oversight. (See Table 6, page 118.)

Of all the advanced metrics, Wins Above Replacement (WAR) has probably penetrated furthest into baseball's vernacular. We use FanGraphs data in our analysis. Table 7 (page 119) provides the raw career numbers for relief pitchers. Unsurprisingly, the Hall of Famers mostly lead the race.

We excluded hybrids Eckersley and Smoltz, with career WARs of 61.8 and 79.5, from Table 7, so as not to distort the pure reliever data, but that discrepancy highlights a shortcoming in WAR. As a counting stat, it is positively correlated with number of innings pitched. The best relievers will never compile WAR in line with an average starter, and modern one-inning closers will not approach the WAR of the earlier generation of multi-inning relievers.

WAR is a good way of comparing relief pitchers, but a poor way of comparing relievers to starting pitchers or non-pitchers. Relief pitchers generate about 10% of the total WAR each year, but constitute only 3% of Hall of Famers.[26]

The final advanced analytic metric is probably the most important one: JAWS, the Jaffe WAR Score. Influential sabermetrician Jay Jaffe created the metric in 2004 with the explicit purpose of "measuring a candidate's Hall of Fame worthiness by comparing him to the players at his position who are already enshrined."[27] Reliever JAWS scores, derived from Baseball Reference WAR, will be lower than those of starters, but Jaffe's insight was in creating a measure that encourages comparisons within rather than across positions. Of course, not all will use JAWS this way, leaving relievers at a disadvantage.

The central issue with JAWS for relievers is that prevailing attitudes over time have kept the bar of entry very high. To use it as a standard is to

Figure 3. League Leading FIP Among Qualified Relievers (1970–2022)

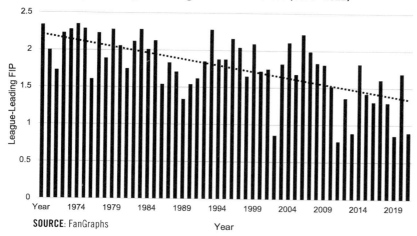

SOURCE: FanGraphs

A two-time All-Star, in 1974 Mike Marshall finished third in the NL MVP voting and became the first reliever ever to win a Cy Young. That season, his 106 games pitched set a record that will almost certainly never be broken. (No other reliever has appeared in more than 94 games in a season.)

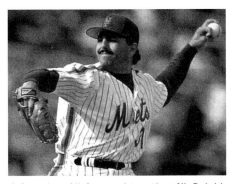

A four-time All-Star and two-time NL Rolaids Relief Man of the Year, John Franco ranked second all-time in saves (424) upon his retirement and still holds the National League record for games pitched (1,119), but was named on only 4.6% of Hall of Fame ballots—missing the 5% threshold required to remain eligible.

Dan Quisenberry won five Rolaids Relief Man Awards, was a three-time All-Star, and a member of the 1985 World Series champion Royals. In 1983, he set single-season records with 45 saves and 35 multi-inning saves—and the multi-inning record still stands. He received 3.8% of the vote in 1996, and failed to gain the necessary 12 votes from the 16-member Expansion Era Committee in 2013.

Table 5. Career Reliever FIP (Minimum 400 IP) and FIP123

Name	G	IP	FIP	Name	FIP123
Aroldis Chapman	722	693	2.34	Rob Dibble	18
Rob Dibble	384	477	2.43	*Aroldis Chapman*	14
Craig Kimbrel	772	749.1	2.45	Al Hrabosky	13
Kenley Jansen	816	813.2	2.50	*Craig Kimbrel*	13
Liam Hendriks	432	468.1	2.55	**Rollie Fingers**	13
Mariano Rivera	1105	1233.2	2.67	Doug Jones	11
Tom Henke	642	789.2	2.72	**Rich Gossage**	11
Billy Wagner	853	903	2.73	Robb Nen	11
Koji Uehara	424	414	2.74	**Trevor Hoffman**	11
Duane Ward	460	664.1	2.75	**Bruce Sutter**	10
Jonathan Papelbon	686	709.2	2.76	Dave Smith	10
Dennis Eckersley	710	807.1	2.77	Hong-Chih Kuo	10
Bob Locker	576	879	2.81	Jay Howell	10
Joe Nathan	758	761	2.85	Eric Gagne	9
Robb Nen	639	697	2.88	*Kenley Jansen*	9
Rollie Fingers	899	1553.1	2.88	Tom Henke	9
Lee Smith	1015	1252.1	2.93	Billy Wagner	8
Don Mossi	273	459.1	2.93	**Dennis Eckersley**	8
Bruce Sutter	661	1042	2.94	Joe Sambito	8
Sean Doolittle	463	450.2	2.95	Jonathan Papelbon	7
Andrew Miller	546	504	2.95	**Mariano Rivera**	7
Steve Hamilton	421	663	2.96	Brad Lidge	6
David Robertson	784	796.1	2.99	Duane Ward	6
Larry Andersen	698	990.2	3.00	*Liam Hendriks*	6

SOURCE: FanGraphs

Table 6. Career Reliever ERA– (Minimum 400 IP)

Name	IP	ERA	ERA–
Mariano Rivera	1233.2	2.06	45.8
Billy Wagner	903	2.31	54.0
Koji Uehara	414	2.43	57.4
Craig Kimbrel	749.1	2.40	58.2
Jonathan Papelbon	709.2	2.45	58.5
Joe Nathan	761	2.50	58.8
John Wetteland	683	2.62	59.7
Mike Adams	407.1	2.41	60.0
Darren O'Day	609	2.59	60.6
Aroldis Chapman	693	2.49	60.9
Kenley Jansen	813.2	2.51	63.8
Tom Henke	789.2	2.67	63.9
Raisel Iglesias	471.2	2.79	64.0
Scott Downs	504	2.68	64.0
Rafael Soriano	594	2.73	66.8
Derek Lowe	417.2	3.15	67.2
Blake Treinen	467	2.85	67.5
Brad Ziegler	717.1	2.75	67.8
Hoyt Wilhelm	1872.1	2.49	68.0
Keith Foulke	749.1	3.15	68.4
Francisco Rodríguez	976	2.86	68.6
Dennis Eckersley	807.1	2.85	69.0
Mark Eichhorn	847.2	2.89	69.1
Ellis Kinder	610.2	2.80	69.3
Troy Percival	707.2	3.18	69.3
Pat Neshek	488	2.82	69.4
David Robertson	796.1	2.90	69.6
Dan Quisenberry	1043.1	2.77	69.6
Andrew Miller	504	2.95	69.8

SOURCE: FanGraphs

Table 7. Relief Pitching Only Career WAR

Name	IP	WAR
Mariano Rivera	1233.2	38.6
Rich Gossage	1578	28.8
Trevor Hoffman	1089.1	25.9
Rollie Fingers	1553.1	25.9
Lee Smith	1252.1	25.8
Billy Wagner	903	24
Kenley Jansen	804.1	23.4
Aroldis Chapman	680.1	21.8
Doug Jones	1097.1	21.8
Craig Kimbrel	736.1	21.2
Tom Henke	789.2	20.6
Dennis Eckersley	807.1	20.4
Joe Nathan	761	19.5
Hoyt Wilhelm	1840.2	19.4
Lindy McDaniel	1793	19.3
Jonathan Papelbon	709.2	19.2
Bruce Sutter	1042	19.2
Robb Nen	697	17.9
Dan Plesac	1003	16.3
Francisco Rodriguez	976	16.3
John Franco	1245.2	16.1
Tom Gordon	847.1	15.5
David Robertson	785.1	15.5
Joakim Soria	762	15.5
John Wetteland	683	15.3

SOURCE: FanGraphs

Table 8. Relief Pitcher Career JAWS

Rank	Name	R-JAWS	JAWS
1	**Mariano Rivera**	48.8	42.5
2	**Dennis Eckersley**	39.6	49.9
3	**Hoyt Wilhelm**	34.5	36.7
	Average Hall of Fame Reliever	29.7	32.5
4	**Rich Gossage**	29.5	36.4
5	**Trevor Hoffman**	27.2	23.7
6	Billy Wagner	24.9	23.7
7	Joe Nathan	24.4	24.2
8	Firpo Marberry	24.3	28.9
9	Tom Gordon	23.6	29.1
10	Jonathan Papelbon	21.7	21.4
11	Ellis Kinder	21.5	26.7
12	*Craig Kimbrel*	21.1	21.2
13	Francisco Rodríguez	21.1	20.9
14	**Lee Smith**	21	24.8
15	*Kenley Jansen*	20.9	18.3
16	Stu Miller	20.3	25.2
17	Tom Henke	19.4	20.2
18	Dan Quisenberry	19.3	23.6
19	**Rollie Fingers**	19	22.2
20	Tug McGraw	18.8	20.9
21	Bobby Shantz	18.4	29.7
22	*David Robertson*	18.2	17.7
23	John Hiller	18.1	28.4
24	**Bruce Sutter**	18.1	24.2
25	*Aroldis Chapman*	17.9	17.9

SOURCE: Baseball-Reference

accept the overly restrictive barriers that have kept out many of the best relievers. Table 8 shows JAWS as well as R-JAWS, a refined measure that attempts to account for the problem of comparing relievers to hybrid relievers.

Using the current 29.7 R-JAWS average as the standard keeps out not only some of the top historical candidates, but also could block the last decade's best: Kimbrel, Jansen and Chapman. We would argue that a better application of R-JAWS would be to use the lower end Hall of Famer performance—the 18-21 range of Sutter, Fingers, and Smith—as the bar to clear. This would still weigh against the vast majority of relief pitching candidates to the HOF, but would lead to enshrinement of some deserving candidates.

THE TERRIFIC TEN

There is no straightforward formula for synthesizing the comprehensive data. Any relief pitcher who made the lists above had a stellar major league career. How might

we judge who belongs in the Hall? Recall the Hall of Fame's selection criteria: "Voting shall be based upon the player's record, playing ability, integrity, sportsmanship, character, and contributions to the team(s) on which the player played."[28] Before our attempt to apply the criteria and find the top ten relief pitchers not (yet) in Cooperstown, we'd like to mention two groups:

Not Yet Retired but Already Worthy of Consideration: Aroldis Chapman, Kenley Jansen, Craig Kimbrel, and David Robertson.

Historical Honorable Mention: Steve Bedrosian, Francisco Cordero, Mark Davis, Eric Gagné, Tom Gordon, Willie Hernandez, John Hiller, Al Hrabosky, Sparky Lyle, Firpo Marberry, Tug McGraw, Don McMahon, Stu Miller, Randy Myers, Robb Nen, Troy Percival, Dan Plesac, Dick Radatz, Jeff Reardon, B.J. Ryan, Bobby Shantz, Rafael Soriano, Huston Street, Kent Tekulve, Duane Ward, and John Wetteland.

We'll now count down the most deserving relievers:

10. John Franco ("Johnny B Good")

Franco was a four-time All-Star and two-time NL Rolaids Relief Man of the Year. His 424 saves ranked second all-time upon his retirement, and are still the record for a left-handed pitcher. Only 5'10" and 170 pounds, Franco's 1,119 games pitched are third in major-league history and first in the NL. He had a career ERA of 2.89, and 1.88 ERA in 15 postseason appearances. His 16.1 fWAR as a reliever rank twenty-first all-time.[29] Franco won the Lou Gehrig Memorial Award in 2001 for his work in support of the first responders at the World Trade Center site. "He helped us get through a very difficult time," said NYC Fire Commissioner Sal Cassano.[30] In 2011, Franco was named on 4.6% of Hall of Fame ballots, just below the 5% threshold required to remain eligible.

9. Doug Jones ("The Sultan of Slow")

Jones was a five-time All-Star whose 303 saves ranked second all-time when he retired. Although his fastball topped out in the mid-80s, his 21.8 fWAR as a reliever rank ninth all-time. Released by the Brewers at age 27, he paid his own way to spring training with Cleveland, where he developed a devastating changeup that saved his career.[31] Jones died of COVID-19 complications at the age of 64 in 2021.[32] He received only 0.4% of the vote in 2006.

8. Rob Dibble ("The Nasty Boy")

Dibble was a two-time All-Star who won the 1990 NLCS MVP en route to a World Series championship with the Reds. Injuries and the 1994 strike limited his playing career to seven years, but his dominance over that period was Hall-worthy. Dibble had a career ERA of 2.98 and WHIP of 1.19. Among retired relievers with at least 450 innings pitched, he is the all-time leader in FIP at 2.43. Dibble's 12.17 strikeouts per nine innings, more than any reliever in Cooperstown, came at a time well before strikeout rates across the league exploded. At 213, his K%+ is second-highest among all pitchers with at least 200 innings pitched. As a setup man in 1989, Dibble didn't receive a single vote for the NL Cy Young despite a better WHIP, FIP, fWAR, and strikeout rate than winner Mark Davis, who led the league with 44 saves. Dibble's 1990 numbers were even better and included 29 saves, but he still earned no Cy Young votes. Dibble established the prototype for the shutdown set-up man role. His short but stellar career is an argument against the Hall's 10-year career length requirement. Dibble continues his work in baseball as a Connecticut ESPN radio host and youth coach.

7. Jonathan Papelbon ("The Strangler")[33]

Papelbon was a six-time All-Star and played on the 2007 World Series champion Red Sox. He ranks tenth all-time with 21.7 R-JAWS, and eleventh with 368 saves. Papelbon set a postseason record with 26 consecutive scoreless innings to start his career.[34] He danced the Irish Jig at Fenway after the Red Sox clinched the AL East title in 2007, earning forever the enmity of Yankees fans.[35] A hotheaded competitor, Papelbon earned multiple suspensions, including one for a dugout fight with Bryce Harper and another for throwing at the head of Manny Machado.[36] He received only 1.3% of the vote in 2022.

6. Tom Henke ("The Terminator")

Henke was a two-time All-Star, winner of the 1995 NL Rolaids Relief Man Award, and was on the 1992 World Series champion Blue Jays. When he retired, his 311 saves ranked fifth all-time. His 861 career strikeouts match Bruce Sutter, but his 2.67 ERA and 1.09 WHIP are better. He ranks seventeenth all-time with 19.4 R-JAWS. Since retirement, he has hosted an annual golf tournament to raise money for The Special Learning Center, a school for handicapped children.[37] Henke received only 1.2% of the vote in 2001. Asked whether Henke deserved induction, Tony La Russa declared, "Absolutely. Tom had everything you want in a Hall of Famer."[38]

5. Joe Nathan ("Stand Up and Shout")

A six-time All-Star, Nathan won the AL Rolaids Relief Man Award in 2009. His 377 saves ranked eighth when he retired. Among pitchers with at least 100 saves, his 89.1% save percentage is the third-highest of all-time. Among relievers, his 19.5 fWAR rank thirteenth all-time, and his 24.4 R-JAWS rank seventh. By his own admission "not a good high school athlete," Nathan didn't throw a single pitch in high school or college at Division III Stony Brook, where he played shortstop and was a two-time Academic All-American.[39] He finished with only 4.3% of the vote. "This is above and beyond what I dreamt about," Nathan said in response, "My dreams were, 'I'd love to play in the big leagues someday.' To be on this ballot is an honor in itself. That's baseball heaven."[40]

4. Mike Marshall ("Iron Mike")

A two-time All-Star, in 1974 Marshall finished third in the NL MVP voting and became the first reliever ever to win a Cy Young. That season, his 106 games pitched set a record that will almost certainly never be broken. No other pitcher has ever appeared in more than 94 games. Marshall relied on an elusive screwball to lead his league in saves three times, and is one of five relievers to receive Cy Young votes in five or more seasons. Marshall earned a Ph.D. in Exercise Physiology from Michigan State in 1978, then led the AL in saves in 1979. At his Florida pitching academy, Marshall pioneered innovative training methods that have since become widespread, such as weighted balls, video, and focus on spin. Marshall received 1.5% of the vote in 1987. He died in 2021 at the age of 78. "He lived long enough to see some of his most foundational ideas," ESPN's Jeff Passan reported, "co-opted by major league organizations and spread to the masses."[41]

3. Dan Quisenberry ("Quis")
Despite going undrafted, Quisenberry won five Rolaids Relief Man Awards, second only to Mariano Rivera. A three-time All-Star and member of the 1985 World Series champion Royals, Quisenberry is one of five relievers who received Cy Young votes in five or more seasons. His 19.3 R-JAWS ranks eighteenth. In 1983, Quisenberry set single-season records with 45 saves and 35 multi-inning saves. The multi-inning record still stands.[42] A submariner lacking high-end velocity but possessing pinpoint control, Quisenberry relied on a devastating sinker. "The pressures on him are so tough—you have no idea, because he doesn't let it show," teammate Paul Splittorff said in 1984. "His job is the toughest on the roster, because this club is going to sink or swim with him."[43] Known for his wit, when accepting the 1982 Rolaids Award, Quisenberry said, "I want to thank all the pitchers who couldn't go nine innings and manager Dick Howser who wouldn't let them go."[44] Quisenberry died from brain cancer, as had Howser, in 1998 at the age of 45. He received 3.8% of the vote in 1996, and failed to gain the necessary 12 votes from the 16-member Expansion Era Committee in 2013.

2. Francisco Rodriguez ("K-Rod")
Rodriguez was a six-time All-Star and played for the 2002 World Series champion Angels. He won the Rolaids Relief Man Award twice, and earned Cy Young votes in three seasons. His 62 saves in 2008 are still an MLB record. Among relievers, he ranks fourth with 437 saves, tenth with 1,142 strikeouts, twentieth with 16.3 fWAR, and twelfth with 21.1 R-JAWS. As a rookie and the youngest pitcher in the American League, Rodriguez tied a record with five postseason wins in 2002.[45] Two off-the-field domestic

incidents—one of which resulted in a guilty plea—will dissuade some voters.[46] After receiving 10.8% of the vote in 2022, Rodriguez will appear on the ballot again in 2023.

1. Billy Wagner ("Billy the Kid")
A seven-time All-Star, Wagner was named the NL Rolaids Relief Man in 1999. Among relievers with at least 300 innings pitched, his 54 ERA− is second all-time, his 190 K%+ is fourth, and his 1.00 WHIP is tenth. The 5'10" southpaw boasts 422 saves, 1,196 strikeouts, 24 fWAR, and 24.9 R-JAWS ranking sixth among relievers in all four categories. In his sophomore season at Division III Ferrum College, Wagner set an NCAA record by averaging 19.1 strikeouts per nine innings.[47] Wagner's charity, Second Chance Learning Center, provides at-risk youths with counseling and other assistance.[48] In 2022, his eighth year on the ballot, he received votes from 68.1% of the voters, up 17% from 2021.

CONCLUSION
Today, the average team uses over four pitchers per game, up from 2.5 in the 1970s.[49] Only one of those pitchers is a starter. (See Figure 4.) According to FanGraphs, 10,236 players have pitched in the American and National Leagues. Of those players, 54.2% pitched more innings as a reliever, and 63.2% made more appearances as a reliever. 34.3% of them pitched in relief without ever starting a game, but only 4.6%, just 495 pitchers, started without ever entering a game in relief. 4,402 pitchers are credited with at least one save, and 2,447 are listed as qualified relievers.[50]

Figure 4. Pitchers Per Team Game (1900–2022)

SOURCE: FanGraphs

Were the "best 1%" standard applied to this subset of relief pitchers, 20 to 30 of them would be in the Hall of Fame. Only nine have won induction. The standard for admission has been set extremely high for those excelling in this crucial role. In 1985, Roger Angell reminded his readers of the "clear evidence that relief men—the best of them, at least—are among the most highly rewarded and most sought after stars of contemporary baseball."[51] With the ever-expanding dominion of the relief pitcher, his argument seems even more salient today.

It is up to the Era Committees to induct more of history's best relief pitchers into their ranks. The news for those eligible today and in the future seems promising. Billy Wagner's election seems likely in the next year or two. Francisco Rodriguez cleared the 5% bar in his initial vote, unlike earlier superb relief pitchers. These developments suggest that future Cooperstown-worthy closers will receive warmer welcomes from the Baseball Writers Association of America.[52] ■

Notes

1. Roger Angell, "Quis," *The New Yorker*, September 30, 1985: 41–72.
2. Matt Snyder, "Why Billy Wagner's Hall of Fame case will show how voters judge relievers moving forward," CBSSports.com, January 26, 2021, https://www.cbssports.com/mlb/news/why-billy-wagners-hall-of-fame-case-will-show-how-voters-judge-relievers-moving-forward/, accessed January 26, 2021. See also Rick Weiner, "10 Best 'Failed' Starters in MLB History," Bleacher Report, May 25, 2013, https://bleacherreport.com/articles/1650473-10-best-failed-starters-in-mlb-history, accessed July 28, 2022.
3. Emma Baccellieri, "Why Shorter Starts for Pitchers Shouldn't Be Surprising in 2020," *Sports Illustrated*, August 18, 2020, https://www.si.com/mlb/2020/08/18/shorter-starts-pitchers-trend, accessed May 31, 2022.
4. Alden Gonzalez, "Why relief pitchers have been so hard to figure out," ESPN.com, June 17, 2019, https://www.espn.com/mlb/story/_/id/26989473/why-relief-pitchers-hard-figure-out.
5. Nate Silver, "Relievers Have Broken Baseball. We Have A Plan to Fix It," FiveThirtyEight, February 25, 2019, https://fivethirtyeight.com/features/relievers-have-broken-baseball-we-have-a-plan-to-fix-it/, accessed May 31, 2022.
6. FanGraphs, https://www.fangraphs.com/leaders/major-league?pos=all&lg=al&lg=nl&qual=y&type=8&month=0&ind=0&team=0%2Css&startdate=&enddate=&stats=sta&season1=1900&season=2022&sortcol=0&sortdir=asc&pagenum=1, accessed August 28, 2023.
7. Bill James, "The All Important Closer," February 3, 2017, https://www.billjamesonline.com/the_all_important_closer/.
8. An illustration of a reliever who mastered anxiety: As a teenager, Mariano Rivera helped his father aboard an aging fishboat in shark-infested waters. He saw an uncle die in a horrific shipboard accident. More than once, the young Rivera feared for his life as his father tinkered with failing pumps and engines and the boat, weighed down by the day's catch, took on water. "I wonder if I am going to have to swim for my life," Rivera recounted. "I wonder how many of us—or if any of us—will make it." We suspect facing down even the best hitters did not provoke comparable anxiety. Mariano Rivera with Wayne Coffey, *The Closer, My Story* (New York: Little Brown and Company, 2014), 22–30.
9. Robert Arthur, "Attrition by Position: How Long Do Players at Each Position Last?" Baseball Prospectus, March 13, 2014, https://www.baseballprospectus.com/news/article/23041/attrition-by-position-how-long-do-playersat-each-position-last/.
10. John and Elaina attended the 2022 Hall of Fame Induction Ceremony, 2022 Baseball Hall of Fame Induction Ceremony transcript, July 24, 2022, https://collection.baseballhall.org/objects/21660/2022-baseball-hall-of-fame-induction-ceremony-transcript?ctx=3edd374352a89ee351d3edb0f5d903521b22b77d&idx=0, accessed July 25, 2022.
11. The Hall of Fame puts the number at over 23,000.
12. Jordan Shusterman, "MLB is Closing in on its 20,000th Player, and We're Counting Them Down," FOX Sports, April 28, 2021, https://www.foxsports.com/stories/mlb/20000-players-countdown-major-league-debuts.
13. "Hall of Famers by Position," National Baseball Hall of Fame, https://baseballhall.org/discover-more/stories/hall-of-famer-facts/hall-of-famers-by-position, accessed June 1, 2022.
14. Baseball Hall of Fame Vote Tracker, http://www.bbhoftracker.com/, accessed June 8, 2022.
15. Casey Stengel Quotes, Baseball Almanac, https://www.baseball-almanac.com/quotes/quosteng.shtml, accessed August 16, 2022.
16. Holds and blown saves were not tracked until late in the period and could not be included in the analysis. To ensure we did not exclude dominant setup men, we used a low bar for saves.
17. MLB Cy Young Award Winners, Baseball Reference, https://www.baseball-reference.com/awards/cya.shtml, accessed July 12, 2022.
18. Cy Young Pitchers, https://cyyoungpitchers.com/voting-history/, accessed August 7, 2023.
19. Most Seasons on All-Star Roster, Baseball Reference, https://www.baseball-reference.com/leaders/leaders_most_asgame.shtml, accessed July 12, 2022.
20. MLB Mariano Rivera, Trevor Hoffman, & Rolaids Relief Award Winners, Baseball-Reference, https://www.baseball-reference.com/awards/reliever.shtml, accessed September 11, 2023.
21. MLB Delivery Man of the Year Award Winners, Baseball Reference, https://www.baseball-reference.com/awards/delivery.shtml, accessed September 11, 2023.
22. Stathead, 2023. https://stathead.com/tiny/HrHS5, accessed September 11, 2023.
23. MLB Awards, ESPN.com, https://www.espn.com/mlb/history/awards/_/id/62, accessed July 12, 2022.
24. MLB stat definition: What is FIP?, ESPN.com, February 17, 2011, https://www.espn.com/mlb/blog/statsinfo/post/_/id/62051/mlb-stat-definition-what-is-fip, accessed July 10, 2022.
25. Bryan Grosnick, "ERA+ Vs. ERA-," Beyond the Box Score, September 14, 2012, https://www.beyondtheboxscore.com/2012/9/14/3332194/era-plus-vs-era-minus.
26. FanGraphs, https://www.fangraphs.com/leaders.aspx?pos=all&stats=bat&lg=all&qual=y&type=8&season=2021&month=0&season1=2021&ind=0&team=0&rost=0&age=0&filter=&players=0&startdate=&enddate=, accessed July 16, 2022.
27. Jay Jaffe, *The Cooperstown Casebook* (New York: Thomas Dunne Books, St. Martin's Press, 2017), 23. Three-time National Sportswriter of the Year Peter Gammons keeps Jaffe's seminal tome The Cooperstown Casebook on his "essentials desk right through the end of December when (his) ballot is mailed." See also Michael Silverman, "Controversial Candidates Still Get the Nod," *The Boston Globe*, January 10, 2023, accessed August 5, 2023: https://apps.bostonglobe.com/sports/graphics/2023/01/baseball-hall-of-fame-voting-2023/.
28. Hall of Fame Election Requirements, BBWAA.com, https://bbwaa.com/hof-elec-req/, accessed August 5, 2023.
29. FanGraphs, https://www.fangraphs.com/leaders/major-league?pos=all&lg=all&type=8&season=2023&month=0&season1=1871&ind=0&team=0&rost=0&players=0&stats=rel&qual=0, accessed July 21, 2022.
30. Rory Costello, "John Franco," SABR.org, https://sabr.org/bioproj/person/john-franco/, accessed July 21, 2022.
31. Richard Riis, "Doug Jones," SABR.org, February 11, 2022, https://sabr.org/bioproj/person/doug-jones/, accessed July 21, 2022.

32. Dan Lyons, "Five-Time MLB All-Star Doug Jones Has Died," SI.com, November 22, 2021, https://www.si.com/mlb/2021/11/22/doug-jones-cleveland-baseball-death-cause-covid-19-astros-phillies, accessed July 21, 2022.

33. The Boston Strangler or the DC Strangler? We like Boston, but take your pick. Grey Papke, "Jayson Werth has Funny New Nickname for Papelbon," June 14, 2016, https://www.yardbarker.com/mlb/articles/jayson_werth_has_funny_new_nickname_for_papelbon/s1_127_21101593, accessed July 21, 2022.

34. Jay Jaffe, "JAWS and the 2022 Hall of Fame Ballot: Jonathan Papelbon," FanGraphs, January 20, 2022, https://blogs.fangraphs.com/jaws-and-the-2022-hall-of-fame-ballot-jonathan-papelbon/, accessed July 21, 2022.

35. Gordon Edes, "Sox Clinch First Division Title in 12 Years," The Boston Globe, September 29, 2007, http://archive.boston.com/sports/baseball/redsox/articles/2007/09/29/sox_clinch_first_division_title_in_12_years/ (Accessed July 21, 2022). See also Jack Curry, "Save the Last Dance for the Red Sox' Closer," The New York Times, October 28, 2007, https://www.nytimes.com/2007/10/28/sports/baseball/28papelbon.html, accessed July 21, 2022.

36. Gabe Lacques, "Jonathan Papelbon Suspended Seven Games for Obscene Gesture," USA Today, https://www.usatoday.com/story/sports/mlb/2014/09/15/jonathan-papelbon-suspended-seven-games-obscene-gesture/15697537/, accessed July 21, 2022.

37. Eric Vickrey, "Tom Henke," SABR.org, https://sabr.org/bioproj/person/tom-henke/, accessed September 11, 2023.

38. Graham Womack, "Tom Henke's Early Retirement Might've Cost Him the Hall of Fame," The Sporting News, June 30, 2017, https://www.sportingnews.com/mlb/news/tom-henke-blue-jays-cardinals-rangers-stats-saves-best-closers-mlb-history-hall-of-fame/1dvq9xt8g8gnb1v18pq9t7omq4, accessed July 21, 2022.

39. David Bilmes, "Joe Nathan," SABR.org, https://sabr.org/bioproj/person/joe-nathan/, accessed July 21, 2022.

40. David Bilmes, "Joe Nathan," SABR.org, https://sabr.org/bioproj/person/joe-nathan/, accessed July 21, 2022.

41. Jeff Passan, "Why Pitching as We Know it Today Wouldn't Exist Without Mike Marshall," ESPN.com, June 2, 2021, https://www.espn.com/mlb/story/_/id/31553574/why-pitching-know-today-exist-mike-marshall, accessed July 19, 2022.

42. Joe Posnanski, "Dan Quisenberry for the Hall of Fame," NBC Sports, November 5, 2013, https://mlb.nbcsports.com/2013/11/05/dan-quisenberry-for-the-hall-of-fame/, accessed July 30, 2022.

43. Roger Angell, "Quis," The New Yorker, September 30, 1985: 41–72.

44. "Dan Quisenberry Quotes," Baseball Almanac, https://www.baseball-almanac.com/quotes/quoquis.shtml, accessed July 20, 2022.

45. Tyler Kepner, "Giants Find Fault with Perfect Reliever," The New York Times, October 24, 2002, https://www.nytimes.com/2002/10/24/sports/baseball/giants-find-fault-with-perfect-reliever.html, accessed July 20, 2022.

46. "Francisco Rodriguez arrested in Sept.," ESPN.com, October 13, 2012, https://www.espn.com/mlb/story/_/id/8497593/, accessed September 11, 2023.

47. Jake Mintz, "Billy Wagner Went from Div. III to MLB with 'Magic' Fastball," FOX Sports, January 19, 2022, https://www.foxsports.com/stories/mlb/billy-wagner-went-from-div-iii-to-mlb-with-magic-fastball, accessed July 19, 2022.

48. Leslie Heaphy, "Billy Wagner," SABR.org, March 15, 2021, https://sabr.org/bioproj/person/billy-wagner/, accessed July 19, 2022.

49. Kerry Miller, "The Newest Trend Taking over MLB in 2022 and Beyond," Bleacher Report, April 27, 2022, Accessed August 7, 2023: https://bleacherreport.com/articles/2955675-the-newest-trend-taking-over-mlb-in-2022-and-beyond, accessed August 7, 2023. See also Nate Silver, "Relievers Have Broken Baseball. We Have A Plan to Fix It," FiveThirtyEight, February 25, 2019, https://fivethirtyeight.com/features/relievers-have-broken-baseball-we-have-a-plan-to-fix-it/, accessed May 31, 2022.

50. FanGraphs, https://www.fangraphs.com/leaders/major-league?pos=all&stats=pit&lg=al%2Cnl&qual=y&type=8&season=2023&month=0&season1=1871&ind=0&team=0&rost=0&players=0, accessed September 10, 2023.

51. Roger Angell, "Quis," The New Yorker, September 30, 1985: 41–72.

52. 2023 Hall of Fame Voting, Baseball Reference, https://www.baseball-reference.com/awards/hof_2023.shtml, accessed August 5, 2023.

Baseball's 4-Dimensional Players

George W. Towers

Defining baseball's best all-around players begins with Branch Rickey. The maverick executive instrumental in integrating baseball, Rickey was also a pioneering sabermetrician. He invented the category "five-tool players" for the rare talents who excelled at hitting for average, hitting for power, running, fielding, and throwing.[1] Since Rickey tagged Willie Mays and Mickey Mantle as the archetypal all-around players, many others have compiled their own lists. Sportswriters mix their informed perceptions of players' ability with accomplishment of career milestones.[2] Scouts and Statcasters narrow the focus to ability alone. Scouting grades lend themselves to rankings and Statcast supplements the sifting of athletic gifting with high-tech precision.[3] And armchair sabermetricians like me can rely upon data from FanGraphs and Baseball Reference.[4]

Instead of Rickey's five tools, I analyze four dimensions of performance. With historical quantification of the separate tools of catching and throwing unavailable, I condense fielding, catching, and throwing into player defense.[5] Following the foundational sabermetric insight that getting on base matters more than hitting for average, I rate players by their on-base percentages (OBP) rather than their batting averages. Therefore, my final four are getting on base, hitting for power, speed, and defense. Finally, I identify 4-Dimensional (4D) Seasons, which reflect above average performance in each area. This approach rewards longevity and durability by recognizing the players who posted the most 4D Seasons while celebrating their best seasons. With respect to Rickey and Jackie Robinson for redressing the wrong of segregated baseball, my study covers only the post-integration era.

DEFINING THE 4 DIMENSIONS
The following four criteria are the 4 Dimensions:

1. Getting on Base. I use On-Base Plus (OBP +) to gauge getting on base. "Plus" statistics like OBP + standardize rates for comparison between and within seasons by expressing them as the percentage of the league average

score adjusted for park and league effects. Therefore, my criterion for an above average season of getting on base is an OBP + score over 100.

2. Hitting for Power. I use Isolated Power Plus (ISO +), which, by calculating slugging without singles, separates the power hitters from the singles hitters. Above average power displays are distinguished by ISO + scores over 100.

3. Speed. Meeting either of two criteria qualifies as above average speed. Seasons that meet the first criterion score above average on both FanGraphs' Base Running (BsR) and the FanGraphs version of Bill James' Speed Score (Spd). BsR converts base-running events into runs above or below average.[6] Like the Plus statistics, BsR is calibrated to annual league averages, with league average BsR set to zero. Spd is based on stolen base percentage, frequency of stolen base attempts, triples, and runs. This metric is scored on a 0 to 10 scale with an average of 4.5. The second criterion supplements these equations with their fundamental variable, stolen bases. I consider ten or more stolen bases to be indicative of above average speed regardless of the metrics.[7]

4. Defense. I use FanGraphs' Fielding Runs Above Average (Fielding) and Defensive Runs Above Average (Def) to measure defense. Def adjusts Fielding to account for the relative importance of each position.[8] By using both, players at all positions receive consideration. Fielding gives good defenders at the hitters' positions a chance; Def gives credit for capable play at the key defensive positions. I consider positive scores on either measure to be indicative of above average defense.

Additionally, while I am unwilling to abandon defensive metrics and agree with Rickey that "There is nothing on earth anybody can do with fielding," I have added Gold Glove awards as a qualitative qualification.[9] This is a significant concession, as 145 (14%) of the 1,037 Gold Glove winners who met my plate appearance threshold had negative Fielding *and* Def scores. While voters might occasionally extrapolate a great bat or a great reputation into an undeserved "Fool's-Gold Glove," I won't assume that one out of every seven Gold Gloves went to below-average fielders.[10] Therefore, these 145 statistically challenged Gold Glove seasons count as above average.

My method defines a 4D Season as one that meets each of these four criteria while making at least 400 plate appearances.[11] Even though a 4D Season only requires a player to be above average in each dimension, merely above-average seasons are not likely to be 4D Seasons. FanGraphs lists 12,306 seasons with at least 154 games played. In these full seasons, players averaged 2.5 fWAR. There were 5,637 (46%) seasons with above-average fWAR, but only 1,037 (8%) 4D Seasons.[12]

THE GREATEST 4D PLAYERS
Qualifying stats and statements dispensed with, the results are ready to be revealed. The record holder with 14 4D Seasons is, fittingly, an original five-tool icon, Willie Mays. Table 1 shows that Mays' protégé, Barry Bonds, comes in second with 12, and Hall of Famers Hank Aaron, Jeff Bagwell, Ken Griffey Jr., Joe Morgan, and Larry Walker are tied for third with 10 4D Seasons.[13] Frank Robinson is next with nine, followed by seven players who have achieved eight elite seasons: Carlos Beltran, Mookie Betts, Bobby Bonds, George Brett, Rickey Henderson, Mike Schmidt, and Chase Utley. While 491 other players have had at least one shining season, these top 15 soak up the spotlight by combining for 13% of all 4D Seasons.

Seven players have recorded seven 4D Seasons: Mike Cameron, Roberto Clemente, Bryce Harper, Al Kaline, Minnie Miñoso, Alex Rodriguez, and Andy Van Slyke. Eight players have six: Bobby Abreu, Cesar Cedeno, Barry Larkin, Tony Oliva, Jackie Robinson, Scott Rolen, Ryne Sandberg, and Alan Trammell. Together, the 30 players named in these two paragraphs posted 22% of all 4D Seasons. Their dominance reinforces a truism of baseball's talent distribution: the outliers are more valuable by orders of magnitude.

Since 19 of the top 30 players are outfielders, constructing teams of the players with the most 4D Seasons at each position highlights a few more complete ballplayers.[14] For example, this data expedition captures the leading specimens of a rare breed, the 4D catchers Ivan Rodriguez and Carlton Fisk. First basemen, who earn their keep for what they do at bat, are also underrepresented. Paul Goldschmidt, the 2022 NL MVP, backs up Bagwell at first. Shortstop is a likely spot to find 4D players. Only one 4D Season short of A-Rod's seven, Alan Trammell noses out Barry Larkin

Table 1. Most 4D Seasons, 1947–2022

Player	4D Seasons	First 4D Season	Last 4D Season	Longest 4D Streak
Willie Mays	14	1954	1971	11, 1954–64
Barry Bonds	12	1988	2000	11, 1988–98
Hank Aaron	10	1955	1968	5, 1964–68
Joe Morgan	10	1971	1983	7, 1971–77
Ken Griffey, Jr.	10	1989	1999	6, 1989–94
Larry Walker	10	1991	2003	5, 1991–95
Jeff Bagwell	10	1992	2003	8, 1992–99
Frank Robinson	9	1956	1969	5, 1960–64
Bobby Bonds	8	1969	1979	4, 1976–79
Mike Schmidt	8	1974	1982	5, 1974–78
George Brett	8	1975	1985	6, 1975–80
Rickey Henderson	8	1981	1992	4, 1984–87
Carlos Beltran	8	2001	2012	4, 2001–04
Chase Utley	8	2005	2013	7, 2005–11
Mookie Betts	8	2015	2022	8, 2015–22

for the second team based on a higher average fWAR. Active players Francisco Lindor and Trevor Story are on their heels with five 4D Seasons at shortstop.

4D FIRST TEAM
CF – Willie Mays (14 4D Seasons, average fWAR of 4D Seasons = 8.3)
LF – Barry Bonds (12, 8.2)
RF – Hank Aaron (10, 7.4)
2B – Joe Morgan (10, 7.1)
1B – Jeff Bagwell (10, 6.1)
3B – Mike Schmidt (8, 8.0)
SS – Alex Rodriguez (7, 7.3)
 C – Ivan Rodriguez (5, 5.8)

4D SECOND TEAM
CF – Ken Griffey, Jr. (10, 6.5)
RF – Larry Walker (10, 5.2)
LF – Frank Robinson (9, 6.3)
3B – George Brett (8, 7.0)
2B – Chase Utley (8, 6.4)
SS – Alan Trammell (6, 6.0)
1B – Paul Goldschmidt (5, 5.7)
 C – Carlton Fisk (4, 5.1)

CONVENING WITH CONVENTIONAL WISDOM
Table 2 compares my leaderboard with four lists of the greatest five-tool players in baseball history, supporting their consensus that Willie Mays is the greatest all-around player of all time. The unanimity of appreciation in these lists extends to Hank Aaron, Barry Bonds, and Ken Griffey Jr. Beyond that, comparison invites us to reconsider some under the radar all-around players

and others whose toolsy reputations may have stretched a little too far.

First, only two players made a five-tool list without posting a 4D Season: Ichiro Suzuki and Bo Jackson. A perennial Gold Glover who excelled at getting on first and stealing second, Ichiro did not hit for power.[15] In 2005, when he hit a career-high 15 homers, his ISO+ was 84. In the three seasons preceding his catastrophic 1991 football injury, Bo Jackson's superhuman plays made him a baseball legend.[16] His defensive finesse and on-base percentage would have surely improved had his career continued.

Second, I've assembled an All Under the Radar Team of the players with the most 4D Seasons at each position who were left off all four five-tool lists. The most notable name missing is Joe Morgan. Evidently, as Mike Petriello titled his excellent eulogy, "Morgan was better than you remember."[17] It's not a coincidence that first baseman Jeff Bagwell is the only other member of the All Under the Radar Team with double-digit 4D Seasons. The logic for leaving first and second basemen out of the five-tool player conversation is compelling: if a player had a strong arm, he would be positioned where it would make a bigger difference. In the case of first basemen, this argument extends to speed as well. Indeed, not a single first baseman makes any of the four historical lists.[18] With reference to Bagwell, Jeff Peterson considers him the first baseman closest to being a five-tool player but disqualified by his lack of arm strength.[19] Since I subsume throwing within my defense criteria, we can accept the apparently incompatible positions that Bagwell is tied for third in 4D Seasons and not a five-tool player.

ALL UNDER THE RADAR TEAM
2B – Joe Morgan (10 4D Seasons, average
  fWAR of 4D Seasons = 7.1)
1B – Jeff Bagwell (10, 6.1)
CF – Carlos Beltran (8, 6.0)
RF – Bobby Bonds (8, 4.9)
LF – Minnie Miñoso (7, 5.1)
SS – Alan Trammell (6, 6.0)
3B – Eddie Mathews (4, 7.0)
C – Ivan Rodriguez (5, 5.8)

SUPER SEASONS
In keeping with my seasonal emphasis, I searched for Super Seasons amongst the 4D Seasons. In a Super Season, the given player is above-average in each statistic compared to all 4D Seasons. Therefore, the Super Season on-base criterion is an OBP+ of 112; the power threshold is an ISO+ of 136; the baseline for speed is a BsR score of 1.4, a Spd score of 5.7, and 17 stolen bases.[20] The cutoff for defense is a Fielding score above 5 and a Def score over 3 or a Gold Glove.

Of the 1,104 4D Seasons, only 43 (4%) are Super Seasons. Table 3 lists them chronologically. The list reinforces the greatness of Mays and Barry Bonds. With six Super Seasons each, together they own 28% of the total. Indeed, Mays was the only player to post a Super Season from the start of the post-integration era until 1973.

Six others appear twice on the Super Season list: Mookie Betts, Eric Davis, Carlos Gonzalez, Rickey Henderson, Dave Parker, and Larry Walker. Betts, Henderson, and Walker are among the leaders in 4D Seasons. Henderson and Walker are Hall of Famers, and Betts is well on his way to joining them. Both Parker and Davis dominated the National League with back-to-back Super Seasons. Parker was a tall, graceful outfielder who fit "The Natural" mold. Tragically, cocaine truncated his career trajectory.[21] He

Table 2. Comparison of Ranking of 4D Players with Rankings of 5-Tool Players

Player	Author Date		Sbalcio 2011	James* 2018	Langford 2021	Shefchick 2022
Total Players Listed			5	44	20	10
Post-1947 Players Listed			5	34	14	9
	4D Rank	4D Seasons	5T Rank	5T List	5T Rank	5T Rank
Willie Mays	1st	14	1st	Listed	1st	1st
Barry Bonds	2nd	12	2nd	Listed	7th	2nd
Hank Aaron	3rd	10	4th	Listed	10th	5th
Jeff Bagwell	3rd	10	–	–	–	–
Ken Griffey Jr.	3rd	10	5th	Listed	2nd	3rd
Joe Morgan	3rd	10	–	–	–	–
Larry Walker	3rd	10	–	Listed	–	–
Frank Robinson	8th	9	–	Listed	–	–
Carlos Beltran	9th	8	–	–	–	–
Mookie Betts	9th	8	**	–	–	–
Bobby Bonds	9th	8	–	–	–	–
George Brett	9th	8	–	Listed	–	–
Rickey Henderson	9th	8	–	–	18th	–
Mike Schmidt	9th	8	–	–	14th	–
Chas Utley	9th	8	–	–	–	–

* James's list is unranked.
** Betts's career postdates Sbalcio's list.

Table 3. Super Seasons

Player	Year	AS	MVP	GG	SS	OBP	HR	SB	4Ds
Willie Mays	1955	Yes	4th	NA	NA	—	MLB	—	14
Willie Mays	1956	Yes	17th	NA	NA	—	—	MLB	14
Willie Mays	1958	Yes	2nd	CF	NA	—	—	MLB	14
Willie Mays	1959	Yes	6th	CF	NA	—	—	NL	14
Willie Mays	1962	Yes	2nd	OF	NA	—	MLB	—	14
Willie Mays	1964	Yes	6th	OF	NA	—	NL	—	14
Bobby Bonds	1973	Yes	3rd	OF	NA	—	—	—	8
Cesar Cedeno	1973	Yes	11th	OF	NA	—	—	—	6
Joe Morgan	1973	Yes	4th	2B	NA	—	—	—	10
Joe Morgan	1976	Yes	WIN	2B	NA	MLB	—	—	10
Dave Parker	1978	No	WIN	OF	NA	—	—	—	3
Dave Parker	1979	Yes	10th	OF	NA	—	—	—	3
Dale Murphy	1983	Yes	WIN	OF	OF	—	—	—	5
Rickey Henderson	1985	Yes	3rd	—	OF	—	—	AL	8
Eric Davis	1987	Yes	9th	OF	OF	—	—	—	3
Eric Davis	1988	No	13th	OF	—	—	—	—	3
Barry Bonds	1990	Yes	WIN	OF	OF	—	—	—	12
Rickey Henderson	1990	Yes	WIN	—	OF	MLB	—	AL	8
Barry Bonds	1991	No	2nd	OF	OF	NL	—	—	12
Barry Bonds	1992	Yes	WIN	OF	OF	MLB	—	—	12
Barry Bonds	1995	Yes	12th	—	—	NL	—	—	12
Larry Walker	1995	No	7th	—	—	—	—	—	10
Reggie Sanders	1995	Yes	6th	—	—	—	—	—	3
Barry Bonds	1996	Yes	5th	OF	OF	—	—	—	12
Barry Larkin	1996	Yes	12th	SS	SS	—	—	—	6
Ellis Burks	1996	Yes	3rd	—	OF	—	—	—	2
Barry Bonds	1997	Yes	5th	OF	OF	—	—	—	12
Larry Walker	1997	Yes	WIN	OF	OF	NL	NL	—	10
Carl Everett	1999	No	17th	—	—	—	—	—	3
Bobby Abreu	2000	No	No votes	—	—	—	—	—	6
Cliff Floyd	2001	Yes	22nd	—	—	—	—	—	2
Alex Rodriguez	2003	Yes	WIN	SS	SS	—	MLB	—	7
Carlos Beltran	2006	Yes	4th	OF	OF	—	—	—	8
Ben Zobrist	2009	Yes	8th	—	—	—	—	—	3
Chase Utley	2009	Yes	8th	—	2B	—	—	—	8
Carlos Gonzalez	2010	No	3rd	OF	OF	—	—	—	5
Jacoby Ellsbury	2011	Yes	2nd	CF	OF	—	—	—	1
Matt Kemp	2011	Yes	2nd	CF	OF	—	NL	—	2
Mike Trout	2012	Yes	2nd	—	OF	—	—	MLB	4
Carlos Gonzalez	2013	Yes	No votes	LF	—	—	—	—	5
Mookie Betts	2018	Yes	WIN	RF	OF	—	—	—	8
Mookie Betts	2020	MLB*	2nd	RF	OF	—	—	—	8
Jose Ramirez	2021	Yes	6th	—	—	—	—	—	5

AS = All-Star Selection

MVP = Place in MVP voting. Competition with pitchers for the MVP award was reduced in 1956 with the introduction of the Cy Young Award and again in 1967 when Cy Young Awards were given in each league.

GG = Gold Glove. The award was established in 1957 with one for each position across MLB. Gold Gloves were awarded in each league beginning in 1958.

SS = Silver Slugger. Beginning in 1980, the award was given to the best hitter at each position in each league.

OBP, HR, SB = Led league or MLB in category.

4Ds = Career 4D seasons.

*While there wasn't an All-Star Game in 2020, Betts was named to the All-MLB 1st Team. Since the 1st and 2nd All-MLB teams were established in 2019, Betts' 2020 is the only Super Season to be so recognized.

went from averaging almost seven fWAR from 1977 to 1979 to less than one fWAR over the next four years. Much like Jackson, Davis's exceptional athleticism inspired hyperbole: he was the "perfect baseball player."[22] But also like Bo, Davis came to know injuries that prematurely ended his prime years. Gonzalez's two Super Seasons are less dominant. To be sure, CarGo established himself as a power-speed star with four consecutive 20–20 seasons from 2010 to 2013. However, in the Super Seasons that bookended his peak, he barely reached the OBP + threshold, and relied on Gold Gloves because his defensive metrics would not have qualified.

Another player whose superiority was brief but spectacular is Jacoby Ellsbury. Ellsbury is the only player whose sole 4D Season, 2011, was also a Super Season. He led MLB in fWAR, became the first Red Sox to join the 30–30 club, won a Gold Glove, and a Silver Slugger, and made the American League All-Star team. As Boston sportswriter John Tomase put it, "He was Mookie before Mookie."[23] But these were all one-time accomplishments for Ellsbury, whose career was plagued by injury before and after his Super Season.

The most decorated Super Season is Alex Rodriguez's 2003 campaign. Like Murphy in 1983, Barry Bonds in 1990 and 1992, Walker in 1997, and Betts in 2018, A-Rod won an MVP, a Gold Glove and a Silver Slugger in 2003. His was, however, the only Super Season to receive the Hank Aaron Award, given to the best hitter in each league.[24] The most fWAR among Super Seasons is 10.5, a level reached by Mays in 1962 and Betts in 2018.

The least respected Super Season is Bobby Abreu's 2000 campaign. It is the only Super Season that wears a Golden Sombrero. That is, Abreu's Super Season struck out four times: he didn't make the All-Star game, get any MVP votes, win a Gold Glove Award, or win a Silver Slugger Award. The Rodney Dangerfield treatment isn't limited to his Super Season, as his long career of excellent all-around play has also gone underappreciated by Hall of Fame voters.[25]

4D ERAS

Based on this inventory of the greatest 4D players since integration, I've divided the 1947–2022 period into 10 eras, each defined by the dominance of its namesake.

THE ROBINSON ERA, 1947–53

Fittingly, the first era is named for Jackie Robinson. During those seven seasons, he was the NL Rookie of the Year in 1947, the MVP in 1949, the league-leader in steals in both of those years, and the league-leader in OBP in 1952. His consistency was equally impressive. He earned MVP votes every year and met the 4D criteria in each of his era's last six seasons. During his era, Robinson's six 4D Seasons were nearly one-sixth of the 38 recorded. Given his dominance on the field and his prominence in not only baseball but American history, it is surprising that Robinson does not appear on any of the four historical lists of five-tool players. As discussed above, this is probably due in part to the lack of arm strength associated with second basemen. Specific to Robinson, power might also be an

Table 4. 4D Eras

4D Era	Dates	Years	4D	AS	MLB	MVP	GG	SS	Aaron	Super	OBP	HR	SB
Robinson	1947–53	7	6	4	NA	7(1)	NA	NA	NA	0	1(1)	0	2(1)
Mays	1954–64	11	11	11	NA	11(1)	8	NA	NA	6	0	3(2)	4(3)
Yastrzemski	1965–70	6	4	6	NA	6(1)	4	NA	NA	0	4(2)	1(1)	0
Morgan	1971–77	7	7	6	NA	5(2)	5	NA	NA	2	4(2)	0	0
Schmidt	1978–83	6	4	5	NA	5(2)	6	4	NA	0	3(2)	3(3)	0
Henderson	1984–87	4	4	4	NA	1(0)	0	1	NA	1	0	0	3(0)
Bonds	1988–98	11	11	8	NA	9(3)	8	7	NA	6	4(1)	1(1)	0
Rodriguez	1999–2004	6	4	5	NA	6(1)	2	5	3	1	0	3(2)	0
Utley	2005–14	10	8	6	NA	5(0)	0	4	0	1	0	0	0
Betts	2015–22	8	8	6	2(1)	7(1)	6	5	0	1	0	0	0

4D = 4D Seasons during era

AS = All-Star Selections. All-Star Selections were not made in 2020.

MLB = 1st Team (2nd Team) All-MLB Team selections. All-MLB Teams were established in 2019.

MVP = Years receiving MVP votes (MVP Awards).

GG = Gold Glove Awards. See key to Table 3.

SS = Silver Slugger Awards. See key to Table 3.

Aaron = Hank Aaron Awards. Beginning in 1999, the award was given to the best hitter in each league.

Super = Super Seasons

OBP, HR, SB = Years leading league (years leading MLB).

issue. While his ISO + score was at least 113 during his era, he never hit more than 19 home runs. On the other hand, his 19 were good enough for 11th in the NL in 1952, and he placed in the top 10 in slugging in 1949, 1951, and 1952. In the Robinson Era, Enos Slaughter trailed him with four 4D Seasons followed by Duke Snider and Earl Torgeson with three. With 55 fWAR, Stan Musial was the only player to generate more fWAR than Robinson's 48. Unlike Snider and Torgeson, Jackie's fellow rookies in 1947, Cardinals Musial and Slaughter were established 4D stars whose careers were bifurcated by integration. Musial achieved three 4D Seasons in his four full pre-integration seasons, and Slaughter in achieved two in his six pre-integration seasons.

THE MAYS ERA, 1954–64

Rickey was right: Willie Mays set the standard for all-around excellence. During the Mays Era of 1954–64, he rated a 4D Season and an All-Star selection every year. Reviewing his performance dimension by dimension, his defense defined the Gold Glove Award. He won one in the award's inaugural year, 1957, and annually thereafter for the next 12 seasons. He was a premier power hitter by any measure, leading the majors in slugging in 1954 and homers in 1963. His average ISO + of 197 was nearly double the MLB mean. Same goes for speed: he led the majors in steals three times and triples twice during these 11 years. He got on base at a .392 clip during his era, broke .400 four times and placed in the NL's top 10 every year. Even with elite metrics in all four dimensions, Mays' six Super Seasons are a startling stat. To elaborate on a previous observation, his half-dozen were the only Super Seasons among the 3,164 individual full-time seasons between 1947 and 1972.

Respecting Rickey, discussion of Mays' peer group begins with Mantle. To be sure, Mantle was a 4D contemporary, recording his five career 4D Seasons between 1956 and 1961. Mantle was not, however, Mays' leading 4D rival. Instead, Frank Robinson split the difference between Mays and Mantle with eight 4D Seasons in the Mays Era. Beginning with his first full season in 1956, Frank went on a 4D tear over the rest of the Mays Era, only missing the 4D list in 1959 due to defensive metrics. Three other stars squeezed between Robinson and Mantle on the Mays Era 4D leaderboard. First, Minnie Miñoso matched Mays with a string of five 4D Seasons from 1954 to 1958. Miñoso bounced back for his final 4D Season in 1960. Like Robinson and Mantle, when Miñoso missed a 4D Season it was due to defense. Al Kaline and Hank Aaron

tied Miñoso with six 4D Seasons between 1954 and 1964. Both became full-time players in 1954, and they mirrored each other's strengths of hitting and defense. During the Mays Era, they stitched together four-season 4D stretches, Kaline from 1956 to 1959 and Aaron from 1959 to 1962.

THE YASTRZEMSKI ERA, 1965–70

Mays was too tough of an act to follow, and no one came close to dominating the late 1960s as he had the preceding 11 years. Instead, there were four comparably accomplished 4D stars between 1965 and 1970: Hank Aaron, Roberto Clemente, Tony Oliva, and Carl Yastrzemski. Oliva led the way with five 4D Seasons, the others followed with four. However, Yaz emerges as the era's emblematic 4D figure based on both peak and sustained performance. He began his run of four 4D Seasons with his historic triple crown in 1967. Not only did Yaz post the highest single season fWAR of his era (11.1 in 1967), he also had the most fWAR overall (45) and in sub-totaled 4D Seasons (35). Indeed, each of Yaz's top three 4D Seasons, 1967 (11.1 fWAR), 1968 (9.3), and 1970 (8.9) were better than Aaron's best season (7.6, 1965), Clemente's (7.7, 1967), and Oliva's (5.8, 1966). Yaz's 4D Seasons were recognized with annual All-Star selections and MVP votes, an MVP Award, and three Gold Gloves. In his historic season of 1967, he was the best hitter in baseball by far, leading MLB in home runs, slugging, total bases, OBP, and times on base. He followed it up by leading the majors in OBP in 1968, hitting 40 homers in both 1969 and '70, and leading the AL in OBP in 1970. Speed was his short suit, but he added base stealing to his repertoire in mid-career, cracking double digits in 1967 and increasing his annual total through his career high of 23 in 1970.

The Yastrzemski Era is also defined by the competition. Aaron and Clemente, of course, are remembered as superstars whose heroic legacies transcend sport. Oliva, on the other hand, played an underrated 4D game alongside the face of the Twins' franchise, six-time AL home run champ and 1969 MVP Harmon Killebrew. A perennial All-Star and MVP candidate, Oliva has lived to see his overdue HOF induction.[26]

THE MORGAN ERA, 1971–77

Naming the next era is a no-brainer. A review of Joe Morgan's all-around game supports Petriello's case that "[Morgan was] likely the single greatest position player of the 1970s, the best player on what might have been baseball's best team."[27] Every season of the 1971–77 Morgan Era was a 4D Season for him, and

1973 and 1976 were Super Seasons. Along the way, he picked up back-to-back MVPs and World Series championships in 1975 and 1976. His outspoken criticism of statistical analysis cost him sabermetricians' admiration as an announcer, but appreciation for Morgan as a player has been enhanced by sabermetricians' success in demonstrating the value of OBP. From 1972 through 1977, he walked at least 111 times a year and never posted an OBP below .406. Consequently, he led the NL in OBP in four of those seasons and the majors in two. Morgan complemented getting on base with baserunning, and, in this same time frame, he set the live-ball era record with six consecutive seasons with 40 stolen bases and a .400 OBP.[28] That he also dominated on defense was recognized with annual Gold Glove Awards from 1973 to 1977.

The careers of a dozen other Hall of Famers spanned the Morgan Era, but none were among Joe's closest 4D competitors.[29] Instead, my 4D database retrieves a trio of less famous, yet familiar names to Baby Boomer baseball fans: Bobby Bonds, Cesar Cedeño, and Bobby Grich. Bonds's combination of power and speed was historic. His family has presided over the 30–30 Club since 1975, when Bobby became the first player to record three 30–30 seasons. He would finish with five, a record matched only by his son Barry. Less well-known but even more impressive is his dominance of Bill James's "Power-Speed" index, which merges home runs with stolen bases. Bonds's nine Power-Speed league titles, five of which came during the Morgan Era, are an MLB record. Bonds was also a top defender, earning Gold Gloves in 1971, 1973, and 1974.

Swift center fielder Cesar Cedeño and standout second baseman Bobby Grich were 4D contemporaries. They both debuted in 1970 and last played in 1986, posting the only 4D Seasons of their careers in concurrent streaks during the Morgan Era. Cedeño's six 4D Seasons were from 1972 through 1977, Grich's five from 1972 through 1976. In their shared prime, they were regular All-Stars, MVP candidates, and Gold Glovers. In each category, Cedeño stayed one step ahead, with five Gold Gloves to Grich's four, four All-Star Games to Grich's three, and four seasons with MVP votes to Grich's three.

THE SCHMIDT ERA, 1978–83

The next six seasons were cornered by two of history's greatest third basemen, Mike Schmidt and George Brett. During this stretch, they each posted four 4D Seasons and earned MVP votes five times. Schmidt's dominance in three dimensions, defense, power, and on base percentage, earns him top billing. In his 4D

Seasons of 1978, 1980, 1981, and 1982, he won four Gold Gloves, three Silver Sluggers, and two MVPs, and led the majors in homers twice and OBP twice. The fourth criterion, speed, held Schmidt back from tying Mays and Bonds with 11 straight 4D Seasons. Beginning with his breakout 1974 season, he missed a 4D 1979 by one stolen base. While he kept on winning Gold Gloves, leading the league in homers, and sustaining his elite OBP through 1984, he slowed down for good in 1983. Brett started his own run of 4D Seasons a year after Schmidt, with six in a row from 1975 through his historic flirtation with .400 in 1980. Brett won the AL MVP that year and led the majors not only in batting average, but also in OBP and slugging percentage.

Of the other two players with four 4D Seasons between 1978 and 1983, one fits James's bill as a five-tool star, but the other may be a surprise. The 4D Andre Dawson was a young power-speed center fielder leading the great Expos teams of the Schmidt Era. In his run of 4D Seasons from 1980 to 1983, he earned MVP votes and a Gold Glove every year. He was also a three-time member of the 20–20 club. Less obvious is the 4D game of Keith Hernandez. Unlike the Hawk, however, Hernandez is not remembered for home runs or stolen bases. Indeed, he cleared the ISO+ bar by hitting doubles, most notably an MLB-best 48 in his co-MVP 1979 season, and never had a 4D Season of more than 14 stolen bases. Instead, he is "widely regarded as the best defensive first baseman in MLB history," and was in the NL's top three in OBP every year from 1979 through 1984, leading the league in 1980 at .408.[30]

THE HENDERSON ERA, 1984–87

In the mid-1980s calm before Barry Bonds stormed MLB's 4D landscape in 1988, a one-of-a-kind superstar walked alone on his way to four consecutive 4D Seasons. Rickey Henderson was in his prime from 1984 to 1987, averaging 68 stolen bases, 21 home runs and a .397 OBP. In his 1985 Super Season, his SB/HR/OBP slash line was 80/24/.419, and he led the majors by amassing 9.7 fWAR.

During the Henderson Era, Dale Murphy, Alan Trammell, and Andy Van Slyke trailed Rickey with three 4D Seasons each. Murphy's six-season peak from 1982 to 1987 included five 4D Seasons, one Super Season, and two MVPs, home run titles, and NL RBI crowns. Foreshowing the path of fellow Atlanta center fielder Andruw Jones (whose offensive career happens to be the most similar to Murphy's in MLB history according to Baseball Reference), Murphy's lofty performance plateau does not yet sufficiently overshadow its abrupt terminus to gain his election to the Hall of Fame. Conversely, Hall of Famer Alan Trammell never won an MVP or led the league in a triple crown stat, but did sustain a level of excellence that extended before and after his mid-1980s peak. He made the All-Star team and/or received MVP votes eight times from 1980 to 1990, and qualified for his sixth and final 4D Season in 1993 at age 35. Finally, Van Slyke offers a segue to the Bonds Era. Before joining Bonds in Pittsburgh in 1987, Van Slyke was an underutilized all-around talent in St. Louis, coming off back-to-back 4D Seasons while platooning in the outfield and at first base. As the Pirates' full-time center fielder, Van Slyke's slick play resulted in five 4D Seasons supporting Pittsburgh's ascendance to divisional dominance from 1987 to 1992.

THE BONDS ERA, 1988–98

Bonds's 4D greatness preceded his steroid use. The Steroid Era, however, began during this time and the intersection between steroids and my 4D criteria merits discussion.[31] Steroids were and are widely seen to be responsible for the era's inflated batting statistics, home runs in particular.[32] The criteria I used to measure getting on base and hitting for power, OBP+ and ISO+ respectively, are relative measures that are normalized seasonally. I do not consider raw home run totals. Accordingly, the share of full-time seasons that were above average in these dimensions was consistent before, during, and after the 1980s, 1990s, and 2000s.[33]

Returning to Barry Bonds, my 4D analysis is a statement of the obvious: he and Mays are the greatest all-around players in baseball history. But with memories of Bonds's 11 straight 4D Seasons from 1988 to 1998 clouded by his alleged subsequent PED use and colored by his off-the-field issues, his across-the-board highlights bear recounting. During the Bonds Era, Barry was a power-speed phenom, leading the league in Power/Speed six times and finishing in the top 10 the other five years. He averaged 34 homers and 34 steals, posting the second of only four 40–40 seasons in baseball history in 1996 and matching his dad's record of five 30–30 seasons. On defense, his speed helped garner eight Gold Gloves in the 1990s. Years before opposing managers shamelessly escorted him to the three highest single season walk totals in history, he first set the NL single season record in 1996 with 151 bases on balls. Between 1988 and 1998, his OBP was .423 and he led the league four times. These years saw Bonds win his first three MVPs and rack up 91 fWAR, 27 more than anyone else.

The Bonds Era was a golden age of 4D stars, featuring four of the seven players who have totaled 10 or more 4D Seasons. Besides Bonds, Ken Griffey Jr., Larry Walker, and Jeff Bagwell played their best baseball between 1988 and 1998. If not for Bonds, the '90s would be the Griffey Era. Second in fWAR with 64 in the Bonds Era, Griffey recorded a 4D Season as a 19-year-old rookie in 1989 and repeated the feat in every year of the 1990s except 1995. In that year, a broken left wrist suffered while making an iconic catch prevented him from reaching the plate appearance threshold. A dominant hitter and defender, Griffey was an annual Gold Glover, seven-time Silver Slugger, and four-time AL home run champ in the '90s.

While 1990s fans debated whether Griffey or Bonds was the best player in baseball, Walker and Bagwell weren't far behind.[34] Walker's 4D game was sustained—beginning in 1991 he went 4D in eight of the next nine years—and superlative—he posted Super Seasons in 1995 and 1997. As noted above, Walker's MVP year of 1997 is among the greatest all-time all-around seasons. He fired on all four cylinders, leading the league in OBP, home runs, and slugging while stealing 33 bases and winning the third of his seven Gold Gloves. Bagwell, previously presented as the prime example of underappreciated all-around first basemen, started an eight-year streak of 4D Seasons in 1992. During that streak he won an MVP and led MLB position players in fWAR twice. In the 4D categories, his highlights include two 40-30 seasons, three NL times-on-base titles, and a Gold Glove.

THE RODRIGUEZ ERA, 1999–2004

Just as the Mays Era gave way to a six-year interregnum featuring competing cases for 4D dominance, so did the Bonds Era. Between 1999 and 2004, Mike Cameron led the way with a fistful of 4D Seasons. He was followed by a foursome with four: Bobby Abreu, Carlos Beltran, Alex Rodriguez, and Scott Rolen. I've designated it the Rodriguez Era based on A-Rod's peak performances in 2000 and 2003. These were the only two 4D Seasons above 9.0 fWAR between 1999 and 2004, giving A-Rod a substantial overall fWAR lead.[35] 2003 was A-Rod's Super Season, an MVP year in which he led MLB with 47 homers, stole 17 bases, got on base nearly 40 percent of the time, and won a Gold Glove.

A-Rod's 4D contemporaries are an intriguing group of relatively unsung stars. As Van Slyke is remembered as Bonds's understudy, our memories of Mike Cameron are merged with Griffey. The central player in Cincinnati's trade package for Griffey prior to the 2000 season, Cameron replaced The Kid as Seattle's center fielder, flipping the script on the apparent "steal of the century."[36] He went four-for-four in 4D Seasons in his 2000–03 stint in Seattle, contributing mightily to the four winningest seasons in franchise history, including the 2001 team that tied the all-time record with 116 wins.

Abreu and Beltran achieved comparable Power/Speed performances during the Rodriguez Era. Abreu averaged 24 home runs and 31 stolen bases, Beltran 24 and 32. Abreu was among the NL's top 10 in Power/Speed in all six seasons, Beltran in five. Abreu joined the 30–30 club in 2001, Beltran in 2004. Their complementary strengths diverged, however. Abreu was an on-base machine, drawing over 100 walks and finishing in the NL's top eight in times-on-base annually in the Rodriguez Era. Beltran built a reputation as one of the top defensive center fielders in baseball history, founded upon his three times leading the AL in assists and buttressed by his three Gold Gloves.[37] Defense was newly-elected Hall of Famer Scott Rolen's strongest suit. He was the NL's Gold Glove third baseman in five of the six years of the Rodriguez Era, with the metrics to back it up. In these six seasons, he led NL third basemen in range factor three times, defensive runs above average twice, and assists twice. Rolen was also a great hitter, averaging 28 homers with a slash line of .287/.377/.533 in the Rodriguez Era.

THE UTLEY ERA, 2005–14

Chase Utley is the ultimate under-appreciated all-around player. Even though he achieved eight 4D Seasons, he isn't on anyone's list of five-tool players. Even though he led the majors in total fWAR between 2005 and 2014 and finished in the NL's top three annually from 2005 to 2009, he never even received the most MVP votes on his own team. Even though he led NL second basemen in defensive runs saved in 2005, 2008, 2009, and 2010, he never won a Gold Glove. Utley was also among the best on the bases and at the plate: he was in the NL's top 10 in stolen base percentage three times (going a perfect 23 for 23 in 2009 and 14 for 14 in 2011), OBP three times, slugging twice, and homers once.

In his era, no one came close to Utley's eight 4D Seasons. Alex Rios trails him with five, followed by a pack of All-Stars with four, including Carlos Beltran, Carlos Gonzalez, Alex Gordon, Matt Holliday, Andrew McCutcheon, Grady Sizemore, and David Wright. Beltran and Rios stand out for their timing. Beltran's run of eight 4D Seasons is bisected by the dividing line between the A-Rod and Utley Eras. Conversely, Rios's lesser career happened to bookend the Utley Era by one year on either side. Rios's speed made him a perennial threat on the bases and gave him elite range in right field. At the plate, however, his free-swinging approach resulted in a marginal OBP and a hit-and-miss 4D record.

THE BETTS ERA, 2015–PRESENT

Mookie Betts is the first player to achieve a 4D season in each of his first eight full seasons, surpassing Utley's seven. A six-time Gold Glover and five-time Silver Slugger with five top-10 finishes in stolen bases, Betts' all-around game is flawless. He has earned MVP votes in seven seasons and All-Star selections in six. His 2018 Super Season saw him join the 30-30 club, lead the majors in batting average and slugging percentage, and earn the AL MVP.

Four players follow Betts with five 4D Seasons in the last eight years: Bryce Harper, Francisco Lindor, José Ramírez, and Trevor Story. Harper is first among them, having begun his career with 4D Seasons in 2012 and 2013, and joining Betts as the only players to go 4D in each of the last four years. With a career slash line of .280/.390/.523, Harper has never had a subpar year at the plate. Instead, defense and/or speed have kept him off the 4D list in three of his 10 full seasons. Lindor is Harper's reverse image: since he came up in 2015, speed and defense have been his strengths. His three 4D misses are due to his OBP dipping below average in 2021 and power outages in 2016 and 2020. Lindor's 2017–19 run of 4D Seasons was matched by the emergence of his Cleveland teammate Ramírez. Since 2017, Ramírez has only once missed a top six finish in the AL MVP vote, and only once missed a 4D Season (in 2020, due to defense). Coming up in 2016, Trevor Story posted five 4D Seasons in his six-year Colorado career, peaking with a 2018–20 slash line of .292/.355/.554.

Three other active players have had four career 4D Seasons: Manny Machado, Starling Marte, and Mike Trout. That Trout only has four begs explanation. After all, his name is synonymous with all-around excellence and he held the unofficial title of best player in the game for a decade.[38] The answer is singular: defense.[39] Trout's historic peak from 2012 to 2019 would have been a run of eight straight 4D Seasons if not for his defense metrics.[40] Finally, while I've strictly adhered to my rules to this point, I must make an exception for the most exceptional player on the planet, Shohei Ohtani.[41] While he has met all four dimensions for position players only in 2021, his other-dimensional pitching made him a 5D phenomenon that year and a 4D star ever since.

The 16 players who turned in 4D Seasons last year made my 2022 4D Team.[42] Led by Aaron Judge, who won the AL MVP and broke the AL record with 62 home runs, the team features established 4D stars Betts, Harper, Lindor, and Ramirez. Among the other 4D veterans, J.T. Realmuto stands out for assembling three consecutive 4D Seasons as a catcher, a level of durable excellence demonstrated only by Ivan Rodriguez. In addition to Judge, breakout star Andrés Giménez and NL Rookie of the Year Michael Harris II were 4D first-timers.

2022 4D FIRST TEAM

C – J.T. Realmuto (3 4D Seasons, 6.5 fWAR in 2022)
1B – Freddie Freeman (3, 7.1)
2B – Jose Altuve (2, 6.6)
SS – Francisco Lindor (5, 6.8)
3B – Jose Ramirez (5, 6.2)
OF – Aaron Judge (1, 11.4)
OF – Mookie Betts (8, 6.6)
OF – Michael Harris (1, 4.8)
DH/P – Shohei Ohtani (2, 9.4)

RESERVES

2B – Andrés Giménez (1, 6.1)
SS – Dansby Swanson (2, 6.4)
OF – Kyle Tucker (2, 4.7)
OF – Randy Arozarena (2, 2.7)
OF – Bryce Harper (7, 2.4)
UT – Trea Turner (3, 6.3)
UT – Bo Bichette (2, 4.5)

SUMMARY AND NEXT STEPS

By shifting the focus from five tools to four dimensions, and from entire careers to single seasons, my approach to identifying baseball's all-around players is at once more restrictive and more inclusive than others. For example, the gifted Byron Buxton is on Jake Mintz's short list of five-tool players, but with the realization of his immense potential postponed by injury, Buxton has never had a 4D Season.[43] Conversely, my method brings to light the overlooked all-around games of greats like Jackie Robinson, Joe Morgan, and Jeff Bagwell.

The next steps in this research project are to mine the other 15 combinations of the four dimensions. That is, from the four types of 3D players who excel in three dimensions but fall short in one to the rare zero-D guys who managed to stay on the field without a redeeming performance in any area. In between are the four 1D profiles and the six types of 2D players. I look forward to tunneling into these data and unearthing nuggets along the way. ∎

Acknowledgments

The author thanks two anonymous reviewers and the editors for their helpful comments. Thanks also to Arthur Towers and the members of the Richard Hayden Memorial RBI League for their love of the game.

Notes

1. Branch Rickey, *The American Diamond* (New York: Simon and Schuster, 1965).
2. Bill James, "Five Tool Players," Bill James Online, September 23, 2018, accessed February 26, 2023: https://www.billjamesonline.com/five_tool_players.
   • Herm Krabbenhoft, "Honus Wagner: Baseball's Prototypical Five-Tooler?," in *The National Pastime: Steel City Stories*, ed. Cecilia M. Tan (Phoenix: Society for American Baseball Research, 2018). Accessed February 26, 2023: https://sabr.org/journal/article/honus-wagnerbaseballs-prototypical-five-tooler/.
   • Richard Langford, "Top 20 Best 5-Tool Players in Baseball History," Bleacher Report, January 16, 2021: https://bleacherreport.com/articles/574665-top-25-best-5-tool-players-inbaseball-history.
   • Randy Newsom, "How Many Five-Tool Players Are There in MLB?," *The Sporting News*, December 31, 2014, accessed February 26, 2023: https://www.sportingnews.com/us/mlb/news/how-many-five-tool-players-are-there-in-the-mlb/.
   • Chris Sbalcio, "Ranking the 5 Best 5-Tool Players in MLB History," Bleacher Report, September 20, 2011, accessed February 26, 2023: https://bleacherreport.com/articles/853734-ranking-the-5-best-5-tool-players-in-mlb-history.
   • Thomas Shefchik, "The Top Ten Five-Tool Players in MLB History," Fueled by Sports, March 1, 2022, accessed February 26, 2023: https://www.fueledbysports.com/top-ten-five-toolplayers-mlb-history/.
3. Jake Mintz, "Mike Trout, Mookie Betts, Julio Rodríguez: Grading MLB's Five-Tool Players," FOX Sports, June 29, 2022, accessed February 26, 2023: https://www.foxsports.com/stories/mlb/trout-betts-rodriguez-the-definition-of-mlbs-five-tool-players.
   • David Adler, "Hot Stove Standouts: 5 Tools, 5 Free Agents," MLB.com, November 28, 2022. https://www.mlb.com/news/mlb-free-agents-best-tools-2022-23.
   • Anonymous, "5-tool Standout Statcast Players," MLB.com, 2022. Accessed February 26, 2023: https://www.mlb.com/stories/5-tool-statcast-standout-players.
4. Baseball-Refernce.com.
5. For a similar approach, see Newson, "How Many Five-Tool Players Are There in MLB?"
6. Neil Weinberg, "BsR," FanGraphs, September 14, 2014, accessed February 26, 2023: https://library.fangraphs.com/offense/bsr/
7. I prorated the stolen base threshold for seasons of less than 154 games as follows: 1995: 9 SB, 1981 and '94: 7 SB, 2020: 5 SB.
8. Neil Weinberg, "Def," FanGraphs, September 4, 2014, accessed February 26, 2023: https://library.fangraphs.com/defense/def/.
9. Branch Rickey, "Goodby to Some Old Baseball Ideas," *Life*, August 2, 1954, accessed August 26, 2023: https://books.google.com/books?id=9FMEAAAAMBAJ&lpg=PP1&pg=PA78#v=onepage&q&f=false.
10. Randy S. Robbins, "Thurman Munson's 22 Errors Deserved a Fool's-Gold Glove," Bleacher Report, June 28, 2014, accessed February 26, 2023: https://bleacherreport.com/articles/2112676-thurman-munsons-22-errors-deserved-a-fools-gold-glove.
11. I defined seasons of at least 400 plate appearances as full-time. Rather than the 502 plate appearances required to qualify for league leadership in rate statistics, I chose 400 so that catchers would be better represented. I prorated the 400 PA threshold downward for the shortened seasons of 1981 (250 PA), 1994 (250 PA), 1995 (350 PA), and 2020 (150 PA).
12. The annual number of 4D Seasons ranged from 3 in 1947 to 24 in 1976, 1998, and 1999.

13. Listing Bonds as one of baseball's best is sure to generate debate due to his alleged steroid use. But, Bonds's all-time great 4D game wasn't steroid-fueled. As documented by Mark Fainaru-Wada and Lance Williams in *Game of Shadows: Barry Bonds, BALCO, and the Steroids Scandal that Rocked Professional Sports* (New York: Avery, 2007), Bonds began using steroids in 1998. Before steroids, Bonds was a 4D player who posted 10 straight 4D Seasons from 1988 to 1997. Moreover, as described below in the "Super Seasons" section, all six of Bonds's best 4D Seasons came prior to 1998. With steroids and age, Bonds's speed and defense declined. He put up only two 4D years, 1998 and 2000, in his last 10 seasons.

14. To break ties between players with the same number of 4D Seasons, I referred to the average fWAR of their 4D Seasons.

15. Ichiro Suzuki led the AL in singles every year from 2001 to 2010.

16. Jeff Pearlman, *The Last Folk Hero: The Life and Myth of Bo Jackson* (Boston: Mariner Books, 2022).

17. Mike Petriello, "Morgan Was Even Better Than You Remember," MLB.com, October 12, 2020, accessed February 26, 2023: https://www.mlb.com/news/joe-morgan-was-an-even-better-player-than-you-remember.

18. Roberto Alomar, Craig Biggio, and Larry Doby are on James's list, the only appearances of post-integration second basemen on the four lists. Each had multiple 4D Seasons: Alomar five, Biggio three, and Doby two.

19. Jeff Peterson, "Have There Been Any Great MLB First Basemen That You Consider as Being 5-Tool Players?: Comment," Quora, no date, accessed February 26, 2023: https://www.quora.com/Have-there-been-any-great-MLB-first-basemen-that-you-consider-as-being-5-tool-players.

20. The median stolen base total among 4D Seasons in 154-game years was 16, 60% above the 4D threshold. Therefore, I increased this threshold by 60% for the short seasons. The stolen base thresholds are 12 in 1981 and 1994, 15 in 1995, and nine in 2020.

21. Michael Goodwin, "Parker Admits to Cocaine Use," *The New York Times*, September 12, 1985, accessed February 26, 2023: https://www.nytimes.com/1985/09/12/sports/parker-admits-to-cocaine-use.html.

22. Jeremy Lehrmann, *Baseball's Most Baffling MVP Ballots* (Jefferson, NC: McFarland & Company, 2016).

23. John Tomase, "Yankees Cut Jacoby Ellsbury Proving Sometimes Stars Don't Come Back to Haunt You," NBC Sports, November 21, 2019. Accessed February 26, 2023: https://www.nbcsports.com/boston/red-sox/yankees-cut-jacoby-ellsbury-proving-sometimes-stars-dont-come-back-haunt-you.

24. The Hank Aaron Award was established in 1999, which compromises comparison with pre-1999 award totals.

25. Brian Murphy, "Here's Why Bobby Abreu Has HOF Credentials," MLB.com, December 27, 2022, accessed February 26, 2023: https://www.mlb.com/news/bobby-abreu-hall-of-fame-case. Bill James included Abreu in his list of five-tool players.

26. Like Yaz, all three made the All-Star team and received MVP votes every year from 1965 to '70, except for Clemente in 1968. Clemente, however, was the only one to win an MVP. While an MVP season, Clemente's 1966 did not meet the speed criteria to be a 4D Season.

27. Petriello, "Morgan Was Even Better Than You Remember."

28. In the pre-1920 dead-ball era, Billy Hamilton set the all-time record with 10 from 1889 to 1898. Honus Wagner is second with six from 1903 to 1908.

29. The 12 Hall of Famers whose careers included the years 1971 through 1977 are Johnny Bench, Lou Brock, Rod Carew, Carlton Fisk, Reggie Jackson, Willie McCovey, Tony Perez, Brooks Robinson, Ted Simmons, Willie Stargell, Joe Torre, and Carl Yastrzemski.

30. Ryan Finkelstein, "JB Hall of Fame Cases: Keith Hernandez," *Just Baseball*, January 13, 2022, accessed February 26, 2023: https://www.justbaseball.com/mlb/jb-hall-of-fame-cases-keith-hernandez.

31. Anonymous, "The Steroids Era," ESPN.com, December 5, 2012, Accessed August 26, 2023: https://www.espn.com/mlb/topics/_/page/the-steroids-era.

32. Recent research has raised doubts about the extent of the increase in offensive stats due to steroids. See Ben Lindbergh, "How Much of a Role Did Steroids Play in the Steroid Era?," Bleacher Report, September 28, 2018, accessed August 26, 2023: https://www.theringer.com/mlb/2018/9/28/17913536/mark-mcgwire-sammy-sosa-steroid-era-home-run-chase.

33. Percentage of full-time seasons above average, on-base dimension: 1970s: 58%, 1980s: 56%, 1990s: 56%, 2000s: 57%, 2010s: 58%. Percentage of full-time seasons above average, power dimension: 1970s: 53%, 1980s: 55%, 1990s: 54%, 2000s: 54%, 2010s: 56%.

34. Mike Anderson, "MLB's Greatest Everyday Players of the 1990s: Nos. 25-1," Bleacher Report, September 30, 2010, accessed February 26, 2023: https://bleacherreport.com/articles/476761-mlbs-100-greatest-everyday-players-of-the-1990s-nos-25-1. Anderson ranks Griffey first, Bonds second, Bagwell fourth, and Walker sixth.

35. In their 4D Seasons between 1999 and 2004, Rodriguez compiled 30 fWAR, Cameron 25, Abreu 24, Beltran 24, and Rolen 21.

36. Manny Randhawa, "It Was Billed as an All-Time Heist: The Real Story of Griffey to the Reds," MLB.com, February 10, 2023, accessed February 26, 2023: https://www.mlb.com/news/ken-griffey-jr-reds-trade-in-2000; Dave Cameron, "Revisiting a Blockbuster That Was Actually a Heist," FanGraphs, February 4, 2014, accessed February 26, 2023: https://blogs.fangraphs.com/revisiting-a-blockbuster-that-was-actually-a-heist/.

37. Michael W. Hamilton, "Best Ever Defensive Center Fielders: Unblurring History," Bleacher Report, March 19, 2009, accessed February 26, 2023: https://bleacherreport.com/articles/141703-best-ever-defensive-center-fielders-unblurring-history; Matt Varvaro, "Mets Hall of Fame Case: Carlos Beltran," SBNation: Amazin' Avenue, December 24, 2015 February 26, 2023: https://www.amazinavenue.com/2015/12/24/10242344/new-york-mets-carlos-beltran-hall-fame. Hamilton ranks Beltran eighth overall and Varvaro reports that Beltran recorded the 15th most total zone runs as a center fielder.

38. Mintz, "Mike Trout, Mookie Betts, Julio Rodríguez." Manny Randhawa, "Top 100 Players Right Now: No. 1 Revealed," MLB.com, February 23, 2023, accessed August 26, 2023: https://www.mlb.com/news/mlb-network-top-100-right-now-for-2023.

39. It is perhaps surprising that Trout never won a Gold Glove award. For discussion, see Vincent Page, "Will Mike Trout Ever Win a Gold Glove Award?," HaloHangout, November 4, 2019, accessed: August 29, 2023: https://halohangout.com/2019/11/04/will-mike-trout-ever-win-gold-glove-award/.

40. Craig Edwards, "Mike Trout and the Greatest Decades of All Time," Fangraphs, May 1, 2020, accessed August 26, 2023: https://blogs.fangraphs.com/mike-trout-and-the-greatest-decades-of-all-time/; Jay Jaffe, "We've Reached Peak Mike Trout, Again," Fangraphs, August 16, 2019, accessed August 26, 2023: https://blogs.fangraphs.com/weve-reached-peak-mike-trout-again/.

41. Randhawa, "Top 100 Players Right Now."

42. First teamers based on 2022 fWAR.

43. Mintz, "Mike Trout, Mookie Betts, Julio Rodríguez."

134

Contributors

RON BACKER is an attorney from Pittsburgh who has written five books on film, his most recent being *Baseball Goes to the Movies*, published in 2017 by Applause Theatre & Cinema Books. He has also lectured on sports and the movies for Osher programs at local universities. Feedback is welcome at: rbacker332@aol.com.

CHRISTOPHER D. CHAVIS's love affair with the Boston Red Sox began as an undergraduate at Dartmouth College, where his frequent trips to Fenway Park instilled in him a love of the Olde Towne Team that spawned a deep interest in baseball history. A nonprofit executive by day and amateur baseball historian by night, he can usually be found reading a book or watching a documentary about the Sox. He lives in Los Angeles, with his wife and two cats, Teddy and Yaz.

DR. WILLIAM "RON" COBB, PhD is a retired Engineer and Management Consultant who spends his time researching and writing history—mostly baseball and the Civil War. He has nine books to his credit. Ron served on the Board of Advisors of the Ty Cobb Museum from 2004–14, rejoined in 2018, and continues to serve in this position. Ron authored the breakthrough SABR *National Pastime* article in 2010 that first exposed Al Stump's forgeries and fake Ty Cobb memorabilia enterprise.

STEPHEN DAME is a teacher of Humanities at Royal St. George's College in Toronto. He is a member of the Hanlan's Point Chapter of SABR and has presented various research papers at the annual Canadian Baseball History Conference since 2017.

STEPHEN D. DERTINGER, PhD is Director of Research at Litron Laboratories, Rochester, New York. Stephen's day job has taught him the importance of synthesizing multifactorial data into visuals that can be readily-interpreted by a broad range of audiences. Stephen looks forward to fielding questions and receiving suggestions about his research at sderting@rochester.rr.com.

WOODY ECKARD, PhD is Professor of Economics Emeritus at the University of Colorado-Denver Business School. His academic publishing record includes several papers on sports economics. More recently he has published in the *BRJ*, *The National Pastime*, and *Nineteenth Century Notes*. He and his wife Jacky live in Evergreen, Colorado, with their two dogs Petey and Violet. He is a Rockies fan, both the baseball team and the mountains, and a SABR member for over 20 years.

DAVID J. GORDON, MD, PhD is a retired medical scientist and longtime Cubs fan, who joined SABR in 2016. Since 2016, he has authored six *BRJ* papers and a book called *Baseball Generations* (published by Summer Game Books). He has a keen interest in baseball history and in metrics to assess career value across historic eras.

PAUL HENSLER received his Master's Degree in History from Trinity College in Hartford, Connecticut, and has been a SABR member for over thirty years. The author of five books, Paul has contributed to numerous SABR publications as well as articles and book reviews for *NINE: A Journal of Baseball History and Culture*. He has presented at the SABR national convention and the NINE Spring Training Conference, as well as many times at the Cooperstown Symposium on Baseball and American Culture.

DOUGLAS JORDAN is a professor emeritus at Sonoma State University in Northern California. He has been a regular contributor to the *BRJ* since 2014. He runs marathons and plays chess when he is not watching or writing about baseball. You can contact him at jordand@sonoma.edu.

FRANCIS KINLAW has been a member of SABR since 1983. He resides in Greensboro, North Carolina, and has contributed numerous articles to the *BRJ*, *The National Pastime*, *Turnstyle*, and several other SABR publications. In the years before automatic runners became deciding factors in major-league baseball, he spent hundreds of hours watching or listening to broadcasts of long extra-inning games.

HERM KRABBENHOFT, a SABR member since 1981, is a retired research chemist. His numerous baseball research accomplishments include: (a) Restoring the 1912 NL Triple Crown to Heinie Zimmerman; (b) Establishing, in collaboration with Keith Carlson, David Newman, and Dixie Tourangeau, the accurate Major League record for most runs scored in a single season by an individual player—Billy Hamilton, 196 runs for Philadelphia in 1894; (c) Determining the longest consecutive games on base safely streak in Major League history—84 games by Ted Williams in 1949; (d) Creating, in collaboration with Jim Smith and Steve Boren, the definitive SBK Triple Play Database. Herm is the author of *Leadoff Batters* published by McFarland in 2001. Krabbenhoft has been the recipient of three SABR Baseball Research Awards (1992, 1996, 2013).

DAVE C. OGDEN, PhD is professor emeritus in the School of Communication at the University of Nebraska at Omaha. His research focuses on baseball and culture, with specific emphasis on the relationship between African American communities and baseball. He has presented his research at the Cooperstown Symposium on Baseball and American Culture, NINE Spring Training Conference, and other conferences. His work can be found in the *BRJ*, *Journal of Leisure Research*, *Journal of Black Studies*, *Journal of Sport Behavior*, and *Great Plains Research Journal*. He has edited three volumes on sports and reputation. He also co-authored the book *Call to the Hall*.

ELAINA PAKUTKA, a Red Sox fan, is a ninth grade student at Hopkins School in New Haven, Connecticut. She is a sportswriter for *The Razor*, the school's student newspaper. Her dad, **JOHN PAKUTKA**, a Yankee fan, is a health management and policy consultant. He is the co-author of *Getting Away with Murder: Prescription Drug Coverage in America* (American Affairs, Winter 2018) and *Social Insurance: America's Neglected Heritage and Contested Future* (Sage/Congressional Quarterly, 2013). See sixthreats.com for a book summary and John's blog. John and Elaina can be reached at jpakutka@thecrescentgroup.com.

BARRY SPARKS, a York, Pennsylvania, freelance writer, has been writing about baseball for more than 50 years. His first article appeared in the July 1970 issue of *Baseball Digest*. He is the author of four books, including *The Search for the Next Mickey Mantle: From Tom Tresh to Bryce Harper* (Sunbury Press, 2022).

GEORGE W. TOWERS is a geography professor at a branch campus of Indiana University. Having spent his formative years in Providence, Rhode Island, he is a longtime Red Sox fan.

ANALYTICS CONFERENCE
MARCH 8-10, 2024
PHOENIX, AZ

THE SABR ANALYTICS CONFERENCE RETURNS TO THE
BEUS CENTER FOR LAW AND SOCIETY ON ARIZONA STATE UNIVERSITY'S
DOWNTOWN PHOENIX CAMPUS AS MLB SPRING TRAINING HITS FULL SWING.

FOR MORE INFORMATION VISIT SABR.ORG/ANALYTICS.

AUGUST 7-11, 2024
MINNEAPOLIS, MN

SAVE THE DATE!

SABR WILL BE HEADING TO THE TWIN CITIES FOR OUR
52ND ANNUAL CONVENTION AT THE HYATT REGENCY MINNEAPOLIS HOTEL.

FOR MORE INFORMATION VISIT SABR.ORG/CONVENTION.